MARKEDNESS

SUNY Series in Linguistics

Mark Aronoff, Editor

MARKEDNESS

THE EVALUATIVE SUPERSTRUCTURE OF LANGUAGE

EDWIN L. BATTISTELLA

STATE UNIVERSITY OF NEW YORK PRESS

Published by
State University of New York Press, Albany

For information, address the State University of New York Press,
State University Plaza, Albany, NY 12246

Library of Congress Cataloging-in-Publication Data

Battistella, Edwin L.
    Markedness : the evaluative superstructure of language / Edwin L.
Battistella.
        p.   cm.—(SUNY series in linguistics)
    Includes bibliographical references.
    ISBN 0-7914-0369-6.—ISBN 0-7914-0370-X (pbk.)
    1. Markedness (Linguistics)   2. English language—Markedness.
I. Title.   II. Series.
P299.M35B38   1990
410—dc20

10 9 8 7 6 5 4 3 2 1

Contents

Preface   ix
Permissions   xi
Acknowledgments   xiii

1. Prolegomenon to a Theory of Markedness   1

Markedness
Roman Jakobson: *Linguista sum: linguistici nihil a me alienum puto*
The Mystery of the Word: Opposition and Feature
The System of Language: Duality of Patterning and
    Hierarchization of Structure

2. On Markedness   23

Toward a Theory of Markedness
Markedness and Markedness Values
Semantic Markedness: Nonequivalence of Signifieds
Formal Marking and Distribution
Syncretization
Prototypes and Best Examples
Summary: Diagnostics of the Breadth of Meaning
Phonological Markedness
The Phonological Features and Markedness
    Reversals in Phonology
Markedness Reversals in Semantics
Syntactic Markedness
A Theory of Markedness

3. Markedness Principles and the Values
      of Grammatical Categories   69

Introduction: The Alignment of Units and Contexts
Case Oppositions
Nominative and Objective Cases
The Genitive
Elliptical Contexts

Zero-Objective and Zero-Nominative Pronouns
Reflexive versus Personal Pronouns
Singular and Plural in the Pronominal System:
   The Markedness of Singular Pronouns
Person, Gender, and Animacy
Summary: Values, Assimilation, and Form-Content Alignment
The Verbal Categories: An Introduction
Form Categories of the Verb
Semantics of the Verbal Categories
Finite Indicative Verbs
Verbal Aspect
The Progressive
Mood Distinctions
Finiteness and Voice
Word Order
The Complementarity of Form and Content
Summary: Determining Values and Finding Principles

4.   Phonology, Morphology, and Morphophonemics   117

The Markedness Values of Phonological Features
Markedness Values of the English Consonants
The Markedness Assignments of Vowels and Glides
Marked and Unmarked Features in English Syllable
   Onsets and Codas
Sound-Meaning Diagrammatization in Morphology
   and Morphophonemics
Universality Revisited
Concluding Remarks on Markedness Patterns

5.   Markedness and Language Change   151

Markedness in Theories of Language Change
Laws of Synchrony and Diachrony
Syntactic Naturalness as Complexity
Phonotactic Change as Unmarking
The Tendency Not to Accumulate Marks
Markedness Diagrams as a Goal of Change
The Shifting of Second Person Pronoun Forms
The Direction of Change

6.   Retrospective and Prospectus   183

A Look Back
Wider Horizons

Right and Left in Symbol Classification
The Greeks
The Kaguru
The Nyoro
Markedness Assimilation in Symbol Classification
Inversions
A Few Final Examples

Notes   201
Bibliography   235
Name Index   257
Subject Index   261

Preface

The principle of markedness is a central part of structuralist theories of language and of the linguistics-based approaches to literature, semiotics, art, and culture that derive from these theories. Though there has been much interest in markedness over the last half century, something has remained lacking in our understanding of this concept. Different approaches to markedness (and there are many) define the markedness relation in different ways, apply the concept to different domains of inquiry, and integrate it into different theoretical approaches. The purpose of this book is to introduce and examine the concept of markedness and its applications in linguistics, drawing parallels and distinctions between various themes and approaches where such parallels and distinctions emerge.

I begin with the origins of markedness in the theories of the Prague School of linguistics and proceed forward to its present-day incarnations. Among the approaches considered are the universalist perspective of Joseph Greenberg and the biological view reflected in some of Roman Jakobson's work and in the Universal Grammar framework of Noam Chomsky. A major focus is also on the role of markedness as part of a language-particular semiotic analysis that explicates patterns of relations among different levels of linguistic structure. This focus reflects both the Prague School origins of markedness and Jakobson's concern with diagrammatic relations in language. The study of markedness that unfolds in this book concentrates on markedness relations from the reference point of English grammar and sound structure. As a result, this study complements much previous work on markedness, which has been oriented largely to markedness as a universal (often a phonological universal) or to the study of semantic markedness relations in the grammatical categories of various Slavic languages.

Besides providing a complementary outlook, the orientation of this book toward English has the goal of making the book accessible to nonlinguists as well as linguists. While professional linguists are one primary audience of this book, they are not intended to be its only audience. The book is also intended for a more general academic audience of critics and critical theorists, rhetoricians, philosophers, logicians, semioticians, and others who might have an interest in the asymmetry of language. My hope is that the extensive treatment of English data that illustrate the theory of markedness will make it accessible to many scholars who may have found previous treatments exotic or opaque.

I should add a few notes on the typographical conventions in this book. In order to maintain as much as possible a sense of the chronology of ideas, I have indicated the original publication date in citations to material that has been reprinted or translated. The form of such references is as follows: (date of reference [date of original work]). For quoted material, I have excised references and footnotes that are of only marginal interest, and in some cases, I have also corrected obvious printer's errors in the original. To the best of my judgment, this has in no case distorted a quote. Also, where there is more than one citation to a single author for a given year, I cite one of the works by the date alone (e.g., 1990) and other works with suffixed letters (1990a, 1990b). Finally, I follow the usual convention of using italics for orthographic citations, slashes for broad phonemic transcriptions, and brackets for more detailed phonetic transcriptions.

Permissions

I gratefully acknowledge the permission of the following:

The Roman Jakobson Trust for permission to cite material from *Russian and Slavic Grammar Studies 1931–1981* by Roman Jakobson (Berlin, Mouton de Gruyter, 1984) and *Fundamentals of Language* by Roman Jakobson and Morris Halle (The Hague, Mouton, 2nd revised edition, 1971).

University of Chicago Press for permission to cite material from *Right and Left: Essays on Dual Symbolic Classification* edited by Rodney Needham (Chicago, University of Chicago Press, 1973).

Mouton de Gruyter for permission to cite material from *Language Universals* by Joseph Greenberg (The Hague, Mouton, 1966).

Karoma Publishers, Inc. for permission to cite material from *Morphological Naturalness* by Willi Mayerthaler (Ann Arbor, Karoma Publishers, 1988).

Elsevier Science Publishers for permission to reprint material from "Markedness Isomorphism as a Goal of Language Change" (*Lingua* 65.4, 1985, 327–42).

University of Missouri for permission to reprint material from "Markedness Isomorphism and the Auxiliary *Do*," published in *To Honor Roman Jakobson: Papers from the 1984 Mid-America Linguistics Conference* (Columbia, Mo., University of Missouri, 1985, 159–68).

The SECOL Review for permission to reprint material from "Marked and Unmarked Pronouns" (*The SECOL Review* 1986, 66–77).

The Linguistic Society of America and Michael Shapiro for permission to cite material from "Explorations in Markedness" (*Language* 48,2, 1972, 343–64).

Acknowledgments

In the course of writing this book I received assistance—intellectual, financial and technical—from a number of individuals and institutions. I want to acknowledge that indebtedness here.

My English Department colleagues Ada Long, Alan Perlis, and Jane Bellamy read rough drafts of chapters 1 through 3 and encouraged me to continue this project. I am also grateful to Rosalie Robertson, my editor at SUNY Press, and to Mark Aronoff, the linguistics series editor, for their comments and assistance. Also, Michael Shapiro, Henning Andersen, Linda Waugh, and Geoff Nathan all took time from their own teaching and research to provide me with very helpful comments and suggestions on the final draft. And for service above and beyond the call of duty, I am overwhelmingly grateful to Catherine Chvany and Margaret Winters for their many pages of observations and suggestions, which have improved the finished product in ways too numerous to mention.

I owe a double debt of gratitude to the National Endowment for the Humanities for their financial support. A fellowship from their Summer Seminars for College Teachers program allowed me to attend Michael Shapiro's 1984 seminar on Peirce and Jakobson, where the idea for this book first took root. A later NEH Fellowship for Independent Study permitted me to complete the research and writing of this book at a sane pace. Given the realities of the professoring business today, this project would not have been possible without the support of the NEH.

I also want to thank some former teachers who have influenced my thinking about markedness: William Derbyshire, with whom I first studied undergraduate linguistics at Rutgers College; Bob Fiengo, Terry Langendoen, Sam Levin, and Bob Vago, my teachers at the City University of New York; and Michael Shapiro, who directed the summer seminar on "Semiotic Perspectives on Linguistics and Verbal Art" at Princeton University in 1984. (It is from Shapiro's work that I have taken the subtitle of this book.)

For technical support, I am particularly grateful to Dean Anthony Barnard of the Graduate School of the University of Alabama at Birmingham for providing financial support for preparation of the final manuscript, to Tinker Dunbar, of the University of Alabama at Birmingham's Sterne Library, for tracking down all those out-of-the-way books and articles

I found myself needing, and to Lisa Buckingham, for her help in the preparation of diagrams for the manuscript.

I also want to thank my friends in the Computational and Theoretical Linguistics Group at the Thomas J. Watson Research Center in Yorktown Heights, N.Y. for providing me with a pleasant, stimulating, and entertaining environment during the first part of 1989, when I had completed the manuscript and was ready to work on something other than markedness.

Finally and above all, I want to thank Maureen Battistella for her help and her good example over the years and for her tolerance while I was writing this book.

Prolegomenon to a Theory of Markedness

Markedness

One of the hallmarks of human language is the existence of polar oppositions among the signs of any linguistic system. Such polarities are manifest at the level of individual lexical concepts, where we find antonymous ideas, such as beauty and ugliness, trust and betrayal, truth and falsity. Polar oppositions are also evident at the levels of grammatical structure: grammatical oppositions include singular and plural, positive and negative, active and passive, present and past, masculine and feminine. And at the phonological level it has been found that the speech sounds of any language, once thought to be the minimal linguistic signs, are more accurately viewed as composed of more minimal distinctive feature oppositions—such as nasal or oral, and vocalic and consonantal—which comprise the phonological quanta that make up speech sounds.

The principle of markedness developed in the last half century attempts to give organization to the polarities that constitute language. Conceived in the Prague School linguistic theories of Roman Jakobson and Nikolai Trubetzkoy, the notion of markedness posits that the terms of polar oppositions at any level of language are not mere opposites, but rather that they show an evaluative nonequivalence that is imposed on all oppositions.

This evaluative superstructure imposed by the linguistic code takes the form of an implicit hierarchization of polar terms such that one term of an opposition is simpler and more general than its opposite. In technical parlance, the term *markedness* refers to the relationship between the two poles of an opposition; the terms *marked* and *unmarked* refer to the evaluation of the poles; the simpler, more general pole is the unmarked term of the opposition while the more complex and focused pole is the marked term.

The earliest illustration of the division of semantic oppositions into marked and unmarked poles concerns the opposition between masculine and feminine forms in the Russian word for 'donkey':

[When the unmarked category] in a particular context does in fact announce the absence of A [the relevant feature], this merely reflects one of the applications of [the unmarked]. . . . The Russian word *oslíca* 'she-ass' indicates the female sex of the animal, whereas the general meaning of the word *ošël* 'donkey' contains no indication of the sex of the animal in question. If I say *ošël*, I make no decision as to whether I have to do with a male or a female donkey, but if I am asked *eto oslíca?* 'Is it a she-ass?' and I answer *net, ošël* 'no, a donkey', then in this case the masculine gender is indicated—the word is used in a restricted sense. [Jakobson 1984:1–2]

At the semantic level of language, markedness is probably most easily understood as a relation between a very specific linguistic sign (the marked term) and a sign that is unspecified for the grammatical or conceptual feature in question. In this sense, marked and unmarked elements are not strictly opposite. A marked term asserts the presence of a particular feature, and an unmarked term negates that assertion. Oppositions between the presence and absence of a feature—between A and not A—are referred to as privative oppositions. Note that privative oppositions are not the only type of oppositions to which markedness is relevant: the concept may also be applied to oppositions in which the terms of a polarity assert the presence of contrary features rather than the presence or absence of a single feature. Such equipollent oppositions are not of the form A versus not A (e.g., singular vs. nonsingular), but rather are characterized as oppositions of A versus B, where A = not B and B = not A (e.g., singular vs. plural). However, since the concept of markedness has its origins in the study of privative oppositions, and since its development has been closely associated with them, privative oppositions provide the best starting point for our investigations.

The unmarked element thus has two interpretations: it has a general interpretation in which the nonsignalization of the marked feature indicates the irrelevance of the poles of the opposition; and it has a specific interpretation in which the nonsignalization of the marked feature indicates the signalization of the opposite.[1] The double use of the unmarked term both to signal the logical opposite of the marked feature and to deny the assertion of the marked feature reflects a natural economy: two poles of a particular feature may define three values.

If we look more broadly at lexical oppositions, it is apparent that markedness is not only an economical concept but also quite a pervasive one. Consider pairs of words that refer to opposite physical qualities. In instances where we wish to refer to a general quality itself rather than to one of the opposed values of the property, it is often the case that one member of a word pair is used to signal the general property as well as signaling one particular value of it. This is the unmarked pole, again understood as the pole of an opposition that can refer to the enveloping and subsuming general concept.

The oppositions between *old* and *young* or between *short* and *tall* provide a nice illustration. When we wish to ask about height or age in a general unspecified way, we use the (a) sentences below:

(1)   a. How old are you?
        b. How young are you?

(2)   a. How tall are you?
        b. How short are you?

The (a) examples imply nothing specific about the age or height of the addressee. The (b) examples, on the other hand, imply that the addressee is in fact young or short, and would not normally be considered simple paraphrases for the questions *What is your age?* and *What is your height?* The unmarked concepts *old* and *tall* can be used to refer to specific values that are opposite to *young* and *short* (respectively), or they can be used to refer to the general properties *age* and *height*.

Semantic markedness is not merely a lexical phenomenon. Though the abstract character of grammatical oppositions makes them more difficult to analyze, it is not hard to find grammatical oppositions in which one term signals some grammatical feature and the opposed term indicates both the nonsignalization of the feature and its opposite.

A frequently cited grammatical example is the opposition between the past and the present tenses. The past tense is marked with respect to the present. The past tense specifically signals past time whereas the present tense is unspecified with respect to time, enveloping past time, present time, and future time. The past tense marks past time; the present is unmarked, and its actual time reference depends on context or on other semantic properties of the verbs in question. Consider the following examples:

(3)   a. I am stepping through the door.
           I see your point.

        b. I wear sneakers.
           Spiders have eight legs.
           One and one is two.
           I don't understand poetry.

        c. I leave for the continent next week.
           I arrive home Sunday.

    d. He shoots and misses!
       So then I say to him, "Shut up!"

The present tense examples in (a) indicate events happening at the moment of speech. The examples in (b) indicate habitual or general actions or states whose assertion is independent of time. The (c) examples use the present tense to indicate (near) future time. And the (d) examples use the present to indicate past time. The present tense, it is easy to see, is the general enveloping and subsuming tense, as opposed to the more restricted and focused past tense.

Another interesting grammatical example is the opposition between singular and plural number. Here again, one of the terms of the opposition has the ability to envelop both numbers. The unmarked number for nouns is the singular, as we see from the examples below. Singular nouns may be unspecified with respect to number and may refer to either singular or plural entities, as in:

(4)   The *beaver* builds dams.
       When I came to, I saw that *everyone* was staring at me and I smiled up at them.
       The *team* is putting on their uniforms.
       Both Ford and Carter were *president* during difficult times.

The principle of structure expressed by the concept of markedness is that, whenever we have an opposition between two things, one of those things—the unmarked one—will be more broadly defined. The marked/unmarked relation is sometimes compared to the relation between figure and ground or between abnormal and normal.[2] Since the unmarked or unspecified term of an opposition carries less information, it appears as the ground against which the marked term appears as a figure; the unmarked is a conceptual default value that is assumed unless the marked term is specifically indicated or chosen. Of course, the notions figure/ground and abnormal/normal are relative ones; what is the figure and what is the ground depends on the construal of a situation. Like the figure/ground relation, markedness too has a contingent, contextually determined aspect. Markedness relations are not fixed, but rather depend on the language-internal evaluation of the terms of an opposition. Aert Kuipers summarizes the contingent nature of markedness:

if we write in black on a white background the black 'stands out' and is 'marked'. That of which there is less, that which is less usual, will be experienced as 'marked'. If we normally read roman type, italics are marked. In a text printed in italics, a word in roman type will stand out. [1975:43]

While there is more to the markedness relation than mere frequency of occurrence, Kuipers's remark highlights the contingent nature of markedness and its parallel with the notion of figure and ground. The parallel with figure and ground also suggests that markedness may be a useful concept for describing the organization of society, culture, and the arts. One cultural phenomenon which might, for example, be viewed in terms of markedness is the opposition between casual and formal dress. The unmarked style of dress for everyday affairs (the ground) is casual dress. To adopt a formal style of dress for everyday affairs—to go to the supermarket in a tuxedo or to teach a class in an evening gown, for example—would be unusual behavior (the marked case) that would cause one to be singled out against the background of unmarked casualness. And conversely it would be unusual to go to a prom or wedding in casual dress. As we shall see, context may have the effect of reversing markedness relations.

It is telling that the potential for the application of markedness to cultural and literary studies had already been noted by Roman Jakobson in the 1930s. In a letter to Nikolai Trubetzkoy, Jakobson remarks:

. . . your thought about correlation as a constant mutual connection between a marked and unmarked type is one of your most remarkable and fruitful ideas. It seems to me that it has a significance not only for linguistics but also for ethnology and the history of culture, and that such historico-cultural correlations as life~death, liberty~nonliberty, sin~virtue, holidays~working days, etc., are always confined to relations a~non-a, and that it is important to find out for any epoch, group, nation, etc., what the marked element is. For instance, Majakovskij viewed life as a marked element realizable only when motivated; for him not death but life required a motivation. . . . I'm convinced that many ethnographic phenomena, ideologies, etc. which at first glance seem to be identical, often differ only in the fact that what for one system is a marked term may be evaluated by the other precisely as the absence of a mark. [Trubetzkoy 1975:162ff.]

Since its introduction in the Prague School of linguistics in the 1920s and 1930s, markedness has found application in linguistic, cultural, and literary studies. But despite the interest shown by linguists, anthropologists, and critics, markedness has so far resisted a satisfying treatment, and no clearly defined theory of markedness has emerged.[3] This situation is in part due to the fact that the original Praguean notion of markedness has been extended and applied in various ways, not all of them mutually consistent. It is also in part due to the desire of analysts to view markedness as a universal property of sign systems, to see it as applying to all oppositions. This broad-based view of markedness is implicit in Jakobson's early work, as we see from the quote above. In fact, in his 1939 article dealing with the zero sign (1984:151–60), Jakobson pointed to the importance of the concept of the zero interpretation (unmarkedness) for the analysis of declensional paradigms, semantics, word order, stylistic variation, and sound structure. Markedness as a language universal was later taken up by Joseph Greenberg in his book *Language Universals* (1966); there Greenberg developed the idea of markedness as a global property of language structure and attempted to summarize and isolate common features of marked and unmarked categories in phonology, grammar, and the lexicon.

The evident desire to understand markedness as a property of all levels of language leads, however, to a tension between ways of defining the concept. On the one hand, the definition of markedness applicable to phonology, grammar, and the lexicon must be sufficiently protean to encompass the diversity of these sign systems, yet it must also be specific enough for there to be an objective and empirical dimension to markedness values. A number of criteria and correlations have been proposed in the last half century for determining the markedness relations of opposed signs. Part of my task in this book will be to define the core linguistic criteria that enable markedness relations to be determined between phonological, grammatical, and lexical signs.

But exploring the criteria for determining markedness values is only part of the task. We must also come to grips with the question of how markedness functions in language. Jakobson's work, for example, shows a deep interest in markedness as an organizing principle for language-particular patterns and as a framework for establishing language universals. However, this distinction between language-dependent markedness relations and language-independent markedness relations cleaves markedness into two research agendas, one in which markedness is a relation between oppositions within a language and another in which it is a property of a language system (i.e., in which markedness is a relation between a particular language and a theory of universals).

Both of these approaches derive ultimately from the original Prague School conception of markedness, which emphasized substantive typology and semiotic function alike. In post-Prague School developments of markedness, however, the language-particular focus is more closely associated with the semiotic approach of Jakobson's later work, while the universalist perspective is most closely associated with the approaches taken by such linguists as Noam Chomsky, Morris Halle, and Joseph Greenberg.[4]

Rather than attempting to treat both of these approaches to markedness comprehensively, I will look primarily at markedness relations from a language-particular perspective. This choice is grounded in my desire to illustrate the basic concepts of markedness by using relatively familiar English data rather than unfamiliar data from a number of different languages. While this choice gives me the opportunity to develop the Praguean view of markedness in a consistent and accessible fashion, one consequence is that the discussion is tilted in favor of the language-particular variety of markedness. I will raise the issue of universals at various points, where it becomes relevant, but I shall not attempt to develop a theory of universally marked and unmarked categories or systematically relate the English markedness assignments to universal ones.

One application of markedness to the organization of sign systems that I will focus on in some detail is the principle of markedness assimilation.[5] This principle suggests that marked elements tend to occur in marked contexts while unmarked elements occur in unmarked contexts. It involves the claim that there is an iconic diagrammatization between linguistic elements and the contexts in which they occur. Related to this principle is the thesis that language exhibits congruence between the markedness of meanings (signifieds) and the markedness of expressions (signifiers). Markedness assimilation, understood broadly as the diagramming of values by values, provides a semiotic organization to the facts of language according to which units and contexts and expressions and meanings are patterned together in a single superstructure. This organizational superstructure supplements and interacts with the rules of grammar and usage and provides a patterning of value, a hermeneutic, which gives linguistic sign systems a sense of order and which provides an overall direction for structure and change.

This book, then, aims to redeem and extend the theory of markedness in two ways. First, it will try to clarify the status of markedness, defending the view that the more broadly defined nature of the unmarked can be determined by considering a core of conceptual and distributional properties. Second, this book examines how markedness provides a functional rationale for some of the patterns of language.

To achieve the goals of this book we first need to gain a better understanding of the theoretical context and genesis of markedness theory. The origin of the theory of markedness lies in the Prague School of linguistics of the 1920s and 1930s, and in the phonological studies of Nikolai Trubetzkoy and Roman Jakobson. The concept was further elaborated and extended into the domains of grammar and semantics in grammatical studies of Russian and other Slavic languages written by Jakobson during his long career. Since his is the name most associated with markedness, and since his view of the concept is closely connected with other aspects of his linguistic theories, I lay the groundwork for our investigations by first discussing Roman Jakobson and his contributions to linguistics.

Roman Jakobson: *Linguista sum: linguistici nihil a me alienum puto.*[6]

Few modern scholars have enjoyed as wide-ranging and productive a career as Roman Jakobson. Although he was by training a linguist and Slavist and although language remained the locus of his many interests, Jakobson was no narrow specialist in grammar and phonology. The breadth of his interests, which included literature, information theory, folklore, art, film and poetry, neurology and aphasia, history, and semiotic theory, was such that one biographer referred to him as a polyhistor.

Born in Moscow in 1896, Jakobson's first intellectual interests were in poetry, particularly the Futurist poetry of Vladimir Mayakovsky and Velimir Khlebnikov, and it was in the formalist avant-garde climate of early-twentieth-century Russia that he first became interested in language and especially in the phonological aspect of poetry. After receiving a master's degree from Moscow University in 1918 and serving for a time as a research associate in Russian language and literature, Jakobson emigrated to Prague in 1920. In the rich intellectual community of postwar Prague, which benefited both from the Czech cultural Renaissance in the nineteenth century and from the presence of a large émigré intellectual community, Jakobson became a major linguistic and literary theoretician, and, in 1926, a cofounder of the Prague Linguistic Circle, which inspired what has since become known as Prague School linguistics.[7]

Jakobson spent the next twenty years in Czechoslovakia. His early work, which showed the influences of Saussure, Baudouin de Courtenay, and the linguists of the Moscow School, broke away from Neogrammarian traditions of phonetic description and historical analysis to consider how language functions to serve cultural needs. This approach was first evident in Jakobson's study of sound structure. The interesting question for Jakobson was, How are phonic properties used by the speakers of language to determine meaning? The answer that Jakobson pursued, following Saussure, was that the crucial property of a speech sound is not its particular physical makeup, but rather the fact that the speakers of languages use sound differences to signal meaning distinctions. The important properties of, for example, English vowels are the phonic properties that permit us to distinguish *i, e, a* (etc.) so as to recognize that *bid, bed, bad* (etc.) are different words. It was this study of the properties of sound that are used to distinguish meaning that led to the theories of phonological and semantic oppositions and distinctive and conceptual features.

Jakobson's phonological studies, carried out together with Nikolai Trubetzkoy, another Russian émigré living in Vienna,[8] focused on the functional speech sounds, or phonemes, of languages and on the sound relations that characterized phonemic systems. They studied in particular the correlations and symmetries among the phonemes of sound systems—correlations and symmetries that made it evident that sound systems were made up of sets of relations that intersected to determine the phonemic system of a language. In later work these relations became defined as binary distinctive features.

At first the systematization of the phonemic systems into distinctive features was only carried out for vowel sounds. In 1926, however, the Czech poet Jaroslav Durych interested Jakobson in the possibility of a comparable systematization of consonants, and by 1938 Jakobson had succeeded in working out a small number of oppositions that he believed could characterize the sound systems of all languages.

During his productive years in Prague, Jakobson also studied the question of grammatical categories. In his work on the Russian verb and on the case system of Russian nouns, Jakobson extended the principles of his phonology to the analysis of grammatical categories, developing a set of oppositions that could classify verbal and nominal categories. This work also saw the first application of the concept of markedness to grammar and to the lexicon as a means of expressing the indeterminacy of one term of an opposition versus the specificity of the other term.

World War II interrupted Jakobson's career and started him on the journey that would bring him to Harvard and the Massachusetts Institute of Technology. When Hitler invaded Czechoslovakia in 1939, Jakobson fled first to Denmark, then to Norway, and finally to Sweden. Drawing on the wealth of medical literature in Sweden, Jakobson turned his attention to the status of phonological oppositions as universals and their role in childhood language acquisition and in language loss due to aphasia. In his monograph *Child Language, Aphasia, and Phonological Universals* (1968 [1941]), he proposed a mirror-image relationship, mediated by a hierarchy of phonological oppositions, between aphasic loss of oppositions and their order of acquisition in child language. Positing a hierarchy of phonological oppositions based on the implicational laws of phonemic typology, Jakobson argued that "the phonological acquisition of the child and the sound disturbances of the aphasic are based on the same laws of solidarity as the phonological inventory and the phonological history of all the languages of the world." (1968:92 [1941]).

Moving to New York in 1941, Jakobson taught at the École Libre des Hautes Études from 1942 to 1946 and at Columbia University from 1946 to 1949. At the École Libre, Jakobson and Claude Lévi-Strauss met one another, and, according to Lévi-Strauss, Jakobson's demonstration of how a small system of binary oppositions could organize a larger system of phonemes provided the impetus for his own investigation of kinship systems and of mythology.[9]

Jakobson taught at Harvard University from 1949 until he retired in 1967. He also served as Institute Professor at M.I.T. from 1957 until retiring in 1970 (although he continued to work there until his death in 1982). During this period of his career, Jakobson returned to and elaborated his phonological studies, incorporating into them developments in acoustics, articulatory phonetics, and information theory. He pursued and extended his grammatical studies of Russian and other Slavic languages, perhaps most importantly in his article "Shifters, Verbal Categories and the Russian Verb" (1984 [1957]). He applied his linguistic theories to questions of communication theory, elaborating the different functions that a message may have and developing a view of poetic language as one of six basic functions of language (its expressive function). He also laid the groundwork for a theory of literary language by proposing that poetic language was a projection of metaphor onto metonymy. Jakobson's program for literary theory, which draws on his identification of metonymy with contiguity and of metaphor with similarity (Jakobson and Halle 1971:69–96 [1956]), was summarized in his 1960 article "Linguistics and Poetics," in which he asserted that "the poetic function [of language] projects the principle of equivalence from the axis of selection onto the axis of combination." Jakobson also returned to the folklore and epic studies of his youth, particularly to the twelfth-century Russian epic *The Lay of the Host of Igor.* And, drawing on the semiotic theories of the nineteenth-century American philosopher Charles Sanders Peirce, he searched for the discovery of an abstract underlying iconism between linguistic form and linguistic meaning, for a diagrammatic relationship between expression and content that could serve as "the essence of language."

Jakobson was indeed, in C. H. van Schooneveld's words (1978:1), a polyhistor. One of the reasons he was able to turn his formidable intellectual energies to so many interests was that he had a coherent foundation in his own linguistic theories that enabled him to draw parallels and find connections between the structural principles of language and those of other phenomena. Thus the way to begin this inquiry into the structural principle of markedness is with an overview of Jakobson's theory of language.

The Mystery of the Word: Opposition and Feature

The point of departure for Jakobsonian and Prague School theories of language can be summed up as "the mystery of the idea embodied in phonic matter, the mystery of the word, of the linguistic symbol, the Logos" (1978:2). Saussurean structuralism showed that linguistic signs consist of two parts: sound and meaning, or, in other terminology, a material signifier and an intelligible signified. In the Prague School tradition, study focused not just on the phonetic material of the sign and its historical development but on the relation between sound and meaning. The motivation for the Prague School's focus on the sound-meaning relation can be simply stated: since sounds function as the material vehicle for meaning, we must ask how they perform this function—that is, what property of speech sounds enables them to serve as signifiers?

The fundamental property that enables sounds to serve as vehicles of meaning is the fact that sounds are opposed to one another in the structure of a language. These oppositions are language-particular differentiations of sound that allow the individual sounds of any language to differentiate larger units such as morphemes and words. The individual sound values opposed to one another in a particular language we call phonemes of that language. Consider, for example, the English words *beat* and *bit*. Knowing the sound system of English, we recognize the [i] sound of *beat* and the [I] sound of *bit* as different phonemes because we know that *beat* and *bit* are different words—that is, we recognize that the difference between [i] and [I] functions in English to signal a potential meaning difference. In French, on the other hand, these two sounds do not have a differentiating function; for the French, [i] and [I] do not serve to differentiate otherwise identical words. In English [i] and [I] are opposed to one another; in French they are not.[10]

The phonemes of a language represent a set of oppositions in the sense that replacing any phoneme by another destroys the linguistic meaning of a word containing that phoneme. However, there is more to this set of oppositions than the mere fact that its members are opposed to one another. Actually, the phonemes of a language may be more accurately said to represent a system of oppositions. Phonemic oppositions exhibit a definite structure, pattern, and symmetry in that a limited number of phonic relations intersect to classify the opposed phonemes of a language. It is the implementation of the concept of opposition as a theory of features classifying the phonemes of languages that is the linchpin of Roman Jakobson's phonological and grammatical theories.

Jakobson's feature and markedness theories are the outgrowth of the ideas and work of Jakobson and Nikolai Trubetzkoy, both of whom were influenced by the Russian linguists Ščerba, Fortunatov, and Baudouin de Courtenay. The distinctive features first developed as part of Prague School phonology grew out of the discovery of regularities and correspondences within sound systems and among them. The notion of opposition itself was, of course, pioneered by Saussure. What distinguishes the contribution of Jakobson (and Trubetzkoy) is the interpretation of opposition in terms of smaller units of phonological structure than phonemes: distinctive features. To understand the reduction of oppositions to features, we need to consider the character of phonological oppositions in slightly more detail. As a concrete example, consider the vowel system of Turkish, discussed by Jakobson (1978:79ff.). Turkish has eight vowel phonemes:

(5)   Turkish Vowel System

                    a.   o   a   ö   e
                    b.   u   y   ü   i

Although each phoneme is opposed to every other phoneme in the system (yielding a total of twenty-eight oppositions among phonemes), a much more economical analysis of the system results from decomposing phonemes into oppositions between the presence and absence of certain phonological properties. Any phonological property—such as nasality, voicing, vocalicness, or backness—automatically defines two values: presence of the property and absence of the property.[11] The oppositions among phonemes may be characterized in terms of a set of phonological properties that define minimal oppositions. The Turkish vowel system can be reduced to oppositions between height vs. nonheight (of the tongue constriction), backness vs. nonbackness (of tongue constriction), and roundedness vs. unroundedness (of the lips). These three phonological parameters, each an opposition between the presence of some property and its absence, define the phoneme set shown above. The vowels of row (b) are distinguished from the respective vowels on row (a) by relative height. The vowels *o, u, a,* and *y* are respectively opposed to the vowels *ö, ü, e, i* by the presence of backness versus its absence (nonbackness). And *u, o, ü,* and *ö* are opposed to *i, e, y,* and *a* by the presence of roundedness versus its absence. At least one feature value distinguishes each phoneme from every other phoneme.

The distinctions between phonemes, which enable them to serve as carriers of meaning differences, may thus be viewed in terms of the oppositions defined by more minimal distinctive features. In any language a small number of distinctive features can characterize a much larger number of phonemes and an even larger number of oppositions between phonemes.

A phoneme is itself understood as a bundle of distinctive feature values, and the difference between two phonemes may be understood in terms of their different distinctive feature values. Distinctive features are thus autonomous properties or qualities that bundle together to create the sound units of language. Jakobson's investigation of the relation between sound and meaning sought, in his metaphor, to identify "the quanta of language, i.e., . . . the smallest phonic elements bearing signifying value" (1978: 24). Distinctive features, understood as the smallest set of sound properties that define the oppositions between phonemes, are the quanta of language.

(6)   Distinctive Feature Analysis of the Turkish Vowels

o	a	ö	e
nonhigh	nonhigh	nonhigh	nonhigh
back	back	nonback	nonback
rounded	unrounded	rounded	unrounded

u	y	ü	i
high	high	high	high
back	back	nonback	nonback
rounded	unrounded	rounded	unrounded

One important result of the analysis of phoneme systems into features was that sound systems were now analyzed as systems of relations rather than as inventories of phonemes. This is the essence of structuralism: a linguistic or cultural system is a system of relations between features that define structured inventories of material signifiers. The system is not made up of the signifiers themselves, but rather is made up of the relations that define the system. Emphasizing the centrality of relations over signifiers, Jakobson approvingly quotes from the cubist painter Georges Braque, who asserted, "I do not believe in things, I believe only in their relationship," (1962:632).

As an illustration of the importance of relations in understanding the structure of language in its phonological aspect, consider the four-vowel system below, which occurs in such languages as Cayapa (Lass 1984:141):

(7)   Four-Vowel System

                    i   u
                    e   o

The same features that define the phonemes of the Turkish eight-vowel system discussed above are needed to describe the phonic properties of this four-vowel system, but their relationships are different. Since there are fewer phonemes, fewer features are needed to distinguish oppositions among phonemes. Some features will be functionally redundant: they will contribute to the phonetic description of the phonemes, but will be superfluous as far as the task of differentiating phonemes is concerned. Here, for example, *i* and *e* differ from *u* and *o* in being nonback as opposed to back; *e* and *o* differ from *i* and *u* in being nonhigh as opposed to high. The distinguishing characteristics of the phonemes of this system can be given as:

(8)   Feature Analysis of Four-Vowel System

            i   e   u   o

        high   nonhigh   high   nonhigh
        nonback   nonback   back   back

The feature of roundedness is redundant to this system since it is not needed to differentiate between any two phonemes. Its phonetic contribution can be stated by a redundancy rule such as "in this system, all back phonemes are also round and all nonback phonemes are unrounded." What is important is that even though the phonemes of this system may be phonetically identical with those of Turkish, they are phonologically very different. Consider the *i* of this system versus the *i* of Turkish, for example. The features distinguishing *i* here are that it is high and nonback; the features distinguishing *i* in Turkish are that it is high, nonback, and unrounded. The two *i*'s therefore differ in the function of the features that define them, even though they might be pronounced identically. Phonological difference thus depends on the functions of the features within the full phonological system, not just on the physical nature of the elements.[12]

Returning to the nature of oppositions, we may now raise the question of binarism. It is rather easy to find oppositions in language that appear to resist analysis as the presence of a feature versus its absence. In fact, Trubetzkoy's and Jakobson's approaches to phonological oppositions differed on precisely this point.[13] Trubetzkoy proposed that oppositions between phonemes could be classified in several ways simultaneously. Oppositions could be isolated or proportional. They could also be bilateral or multilateral.[14] And most importantly, they could be classified according to their logical character, that is, according to whether they were privative, equipollent, or gradual. Trubetzkoy defined equipollent oppositions as those in which the phonemes in question were logically equivalent. Gradual oppositions were ones in which opposed phonemes contained various degrees of the same property. And privative oppositions were those "in which one member is characterized by the presence, the other by the absence, of a mark" (Trubetzkoy 1969:75 [1939]). For Trubetzkoy, markedness only applied to oppositions whose logical character was privative. Jakobson, however, argued, and maintained throughout his life, that all oppositions were both binary and privative. Gradual and equipollent oppositions, Jakobson maintained, could better be analyzed as the product of a more fundamental and abstract binarism, and he showed that analysis of oppositions into underlying binary relations often reveals inherent symmetries and parallelisms in a system.

We can illustrate the reduction of gradual oppositions to binary ones with a further phonological example. Consider the consonant system of French, of which Jakobson (1978) gives a partial analysis as illustration of the classificatory function of distinctive features. Putting aside the liquid consonants, the consonant system of French can be classified phonetically as below:

(9)   French Consonant System

	bilabial	labiovelar	apical	alveolar	alveopalatal	prepalatal	velar
a.	m		n			ŋ̬	
b.	p/b		t/d				k/g
c.		f/v		s/z	š/ž		

The paired consonants k/g, t/d, and p/b differ only in terms of vocal cord vibration (the feature voiced vs. unvoiced); the nasal consonants of row (a) may be distinguished from the consonants in rows (b) and (c) by nasalization (vs. its absence); and rows (b) and (c) may be distinguished from one another by presence of complete closure of the articulators versus the lack of such complete closure (the feature abrupt vs. nonabrupt). The three articulatory positions on each row, which represent a gradual opposition among seven articulatory positions, can be analyzed as a product of only two further oppositions. We can distinguish the phonemes in rows (a), (b), and (c) from one another—n, ŋ̬, and m; k/g, t/d, and p/b; and s/z, š/ž, and f/v—by treating each articulatory position as defined by a pair of features. Although the articulatory positions of the sounds in the rows are phonetically different, the relative symmetry of the three rows allows us to differentiate all nine positions with two features. Jakobson points out that ŋ̬, k/g, and š/ž are all centrifugal consonants (articulated toward the rear of the mouth) as opposed to the other consonants.[15] Among the noncentrifugal consonants, *m, p/b,* and *f/v* may be distinguished (respectively) from *n, t/d,* and *s/z* by the opposition grave versus nongrave (acute). The analysis accomplishes two things: the three-way opposition is reduced to a pair of binary oppositions, and the binary analysis reveals the proportional nature of the system. As Jakobson says, "The consonant system of French can be seen to be perfectly coherent and symmetrical as soon as the classification of its constituent elements is based on inherent [i.e., featural] criteria," (1978:94).

Jakobson extended this approach into semantics as well, adopting the privative binary opposition as the principal taxonomic tool for grammatical and (to a lesser degree) lexical analysis. While in Trubetzkoy's phonology, the phonemes of a language were all in mutual opposition, Jakobson took the term *opposition* to mean the privative opposition between the presence of a property and its absence.[16] He makes this explicit in the following quote in which he intrinsically links the notions of opposition and markedness: "every single constituent of any linguistic system is built on an opposition of two logical contradictories: the presence of an attribute ("markedness") in contraposition to its absence ("unmarkedness")," (1972:76).

The binarism thesis raises certain questions and possible objections, of course. First, it must be recognized that not all linguistic relations are binary oppositions. The fact that there are many words that have no particular opposite is not a problem for binarism, however. Similarly, that there exist pairs of words not related by a binary opposition (e.g., the words *automobile* and *senator*) is of no great consequence. The point is not that all contrasts can be reduced to binary oppositions, but rather that the oppositions that do exist are binary ones.

A second, more serious, issue is whether oppositions should all be treated as privative or not. Granting a general tendency to classify experience dichotomously, the possibility remains that some oppositions might be more naturally treated as equipollent—as an opposition between two opposite but positive features A and B rather than as an opposition between A and not A. To take just one obvious example, consider the opposition between male and female. Though this opposition shows the asymmetry characteristic of markedness, it is not apparent whether the best analysis is in terms of equipollent contraries male and female or privative complementaries female and nonfemale.

A final point concerns the existence of apparent nonbinary oppositions. It is clear that such oppositions exist, although some cases can be analyzed as oppositions between a set of binary distinctions—as in the phonemic example given above. Still, examples remain that resist decomposition into binary features. As Lyons (1977:287–90) points out, it is hard to imagine the following sets as products of binary oppositions:

(10)   a. {Sunday, Monday, . . . , Saturday}

b. {January, February, . . . , December}

c. {rose, peony, tulip, delphinium, etc.}

d. {field marshall, general, . . . , corporal, private}

e. {spring, summer, autumn, winter}

f. {one, two, . . . }

These are, however, as Lyons notes, specialized taxonomies with per-haps a more rigid serial or cyclical structure than that of everyday vocabu-lary. Such examples clearly attenuate the usual binarism of linguistic relations, but they do not invalidate it as a general principle of classifi-cation.

In the chapters that follow, I will adopt Jakobson's view of opposition as my working hypothesis. This concept is well grounded by lexical and grammatical examples, and it provides a consistent and minimal classifica-tory scheme for oppositions of all types (not just linguistic, as we shall see, but stylistic and cultural as well). In addition, binary classification may prove revealing even in cases of serial or cyclic oppositions. Consider again the opposition among the days of the week. It may turn out that our ordi-nary conceptualization of this cycle is more binary than we think. Suppose we view the week as divided first into a workweek and a weekend, with the workweek subdivided into a beginning, a middle, and an end. A binary classification of this scheme might appear as follows:

(11)

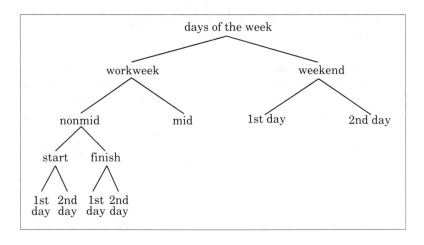

While not part of the dictionary definition of the days of the week, such a binary classification is fairly close to our ordinary way of thinking about this cyclic opposition.

Phonological analysis and the concepts of feature and binary opposition have been necessary starting points for an understanding of Prague School structuralism and Jakobsonian linguistics. These theories, of course, are not restricted to the domain of phonology, but extend into the areas of grammar and meaning. Phonological ideas, however, are what provided the base for extension of the notions of opposition and feature into these domains. Just as phonemes are made up of bundles of simultaneous distinctive features, lexical items and inflectional categories have come to be viewed as made up of conceptual or semantic features representing basic meaning relations.

The concepts of opposition and feature are central tenets of Jakobson's thought. The theory of markedness builds on the notions of feature and opposition, and I will devote the next chapter to it. Before moving on, however, let us touch briefly on another important aspect of Jakobson's linguistic thought: hierarchization.

The System of Language: Duality of Patterning and Hierarchization of Structure

The concepts of opposition and feature are key aspects of Jakobson's linguistic thought, and to understand these ideas more fully it will be helpful to consider the context in which they were developed—the total conception of language within which they fit. This section, therefore, introduces two further concepts of Jakobsonian linguistics: the duality of patterning reflected in the division of language into systems of forms and systems of meanings, and the hierarchization of language manifest at all levels of structure, including, as we will see, the level of feature opposition.

Jakobson's linguistic views may be best categorized as a variety of structuralism:

> Any set of phenomena examined by contemporary science is treated not as a mechanical agglomeration but as a structured whole, and the basic task is to reveal the inner, whether static or developmental, laws of this system. What appears to be the focus of scientific preoccupation is no longer the outer stimulus, but the internal premises of the development; now the mechanical conception of processes yields to the question of their functions. [Jakobson 1973:11]

While Jakobson's theory of language is quite complex, we may profitably focus on several salient aspects. Language is a hierarchically organized system of signs structured both by general principles of sign systems and by specific principles of linguistic sign systems. The primary division-within language falls between phonology and semantics, the latter encompassing both grammatical and lexical analysis. Grammatical categories are those, like tense and number, that are obligatory to a particular language; lexical categories are those that must be selected (as we select the lexical item *scarlet* as opposed to *red*).

Phonology and semantics comprise a duality of patterning in the sense that language is a system of material signifiers linked to a separate system of conceptual signifieds, a system of forms linked to a system of meanings. The signifiers are units of linguistic form—distinctive features, phonemes, morphemes, words, phrases, and utterances. The signifieds are the corresponding units of meaning. Each of these systems is defined by a set of features. Features thus create networks of signifiers or signifieds by encoding oppositions. The focus of study on the plane of signifiers is with features of linguistic expression, while the focus of study at the level of signifieds is on features of meaning. We will have occasion to return to this distinction when we discuss the question of the correlations of semantic markedness with formal marking.

The next point to be made about Jakobson's theory of language is its espousal of the idea that language is a fully hierarchical system—a system of parts and wholes consisting of constituents whose nature is determined by their relationship to one another and to the whole system of relationships.

(12)

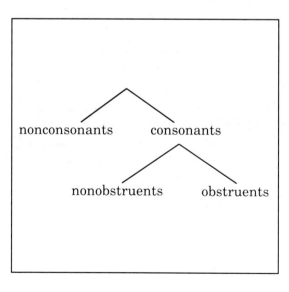

Particularly worth emphasizing is the hierarchical nature of features. Features are ranked in a hierarchy of implication and evaluation in which certain features are superordinate to and are implied by other subordinate features.

The hierarchical nature of lexical and grammatical categories is well established. In lexical analysis, hierarchy is revealed in part through taxonomies of concepts (as in the heuristic taxonomy implied in the organization of a thesaurus or in the formalized meaning postulates or redundancy rules of linguistic semantics). And in traditional grammar, hierarchy is implied by the fact that words and grammatical constructions are listed in dictionaries and handbooks under a main or citation form: one form is taken to be basic, and the others are treated as derived forms.

In more explicitly technical terms, feature hierarchy is a ranking of oppositions often represented graphically as superordinate versus subordinate position in a tree diagram. The analytic point modeled by such trees is that subordinate features subdivide the classes that are defined by the superordinate features. Thus, for example, the class of consonants is subdivided into obstruents (true consonants) and sonorants (nasals and liquids). The features defining the classes obstruent and sonorant, shown in (12) above, are subordinate to the feature defining consonants.

Similarly, pronouns in English are inflected for morphological case, so the case features are subordinate to the feature defining pronouns. The subdivision of features is sometimes only partial; an opposition may be subdivided in both poles by a subordinate correlation or only subdivided in one pole. An example of the first type is the subdivision of nouns and pronouns into singular and plural, shown in (13):

(13)

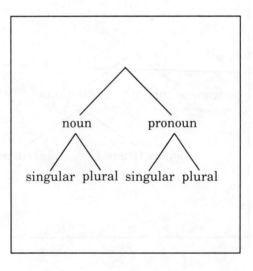

Both nouns and pronouns have singular and plural forms, so the subdivision is symmetrical. The asymmetrical subdivision of a category is illustrated by case declension. In English, pronouns have distinct nominative and objective forms while nouns do not:

(14)

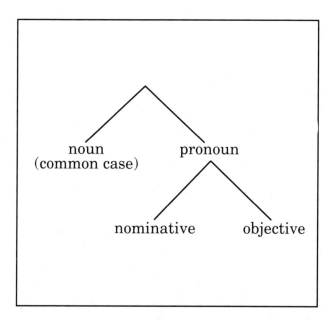

The hierarchial organization of concepts is a well-known principle of structure. But in addition to superordination or subordination of features, hierarchy also characterizes the relation between the terms of an opposition. Hierarchy is reflected in the dominance of more general terms over less general, and we can view markedness as a hierarchization of opposites.[17] The concepts of markedness, opposition, and hierarchy are thus intrinsically linked. Opposition imposes a symmetry or equivalence upon language: within a minimal paradigm two signs are defined by the presence versus the absence of a property. Hierarchy is an evaluative component that organizes related categories. Markedness is the projection of hierarchy onto the equivalence implied by opposition, extending the nonequivalence principle of a ranked taxonomy to the minimal oppositions that make up the quanta of language.[18]

The preceding discussion has not, of course, been a detailed and complete picture of Jakobson's theories of language.[19] It is rather a synopsis of central aspects of them—the dichotomy between signifier and signified, the antinomies between phonology and semantics and between grammatical and lexical meaning, and the notions of opposition, feature, and hierarchy, which will play roles in the explication of the central theme of this work: the concept of markedness.

2

On Markedness

Toward a Theory of Markedness

We customarily evaluate theories according to several criteria. How well do the predictions of the theory stand up under empirical verification? To what extent do the basic constructs of the theory simplify and unify the data they model? Is the theory internally consistent and well defined? Does it suggest appealing new lines of investigation?

The precis above suggests some questions for a discussion of markedness. Exactly what sort of relation is markedness? What does it mean to be a marked or unmarked element? How are the values marked and unmarked determined empirically? What predictions does the theory of markedness make about the behavior of marked and unmarked elements? Do markedness values tend to be constant across languages? Or are they essentially language-particular? Are markedness values consistent and general within a language, or are they sometimes reversed according to local context? Do markedness values change over time?

The task of this chapter is to provide tentative answers to those questions, in order to lay the groundwork for a more in-depth exploration of some of these questions in later chapters.

Three main aspects of a theory of markedness will emerge in this chapter. The problem I will turn to first, and which will occupy much of this chapter, is that of how markedness values are determined. Focusing on the structure and use of linguistic categories, I will look at various criteria and diagnostics that can be used to evaluate oppositions in an attempt to come up with reliable heuristics for ascertaining markedness. Though some of these criteria are problematic, I will argue that there is a ranked set of diagnostics suitable for assigning markedness values in semantics and in phonology.

Closely tied to the problem of determining markedness values is the relation of markedness to universals. One appealing facet of markedness is its applicability cross-linguistically, as a key to general properties of language. In some instances universal tendencies of evaluation are found. Singular number in nouns, for example, seems to be universally unmarked with respect to the plural and dual; present tense is usually unmarked with respect to past. However, the universality of markedness values is only partial, and the idea of markedness as a completely a priori system is attenuated by the fact that a feature value may receive different markedness assignments in different languages. Hence a second major aspect of markedness to be discussed in this chapter concerns the language-particular status of markedness values. While cross-linguistic tendencies do ground some values in universals of language and universalities of culture, values are not fully fixed by the inherent properties of language and culture. What is broadly defined and unmarked in one language (or one dialect or historical period) may be narrowly defined in another. Thus, for example, in Russian the nominative case is unmarked and the other cases marked. In English, on the other hand, the objective case is unmarked and the nominative marked (see the second section of chap. 3).

The third aspect of markedness to be considered is its contextual variability. In addition to being contingent on the facts of particular languages, markedness values are also contextualized within a language. Values are not fixed, but rather are relative: cultural and linguistic structure acts as a context within which categories are evaluated, occasioning local reversals of general markedness values. As an example, consider the opposition masculine/feminine. In many contexts, including that of pronoun usage and many antonyms, the feature masculine is unmarked; in certain word pairs, however, the markedness values are reversed. The term *nurse*, for example, may be used to refer to nurses of either sex; the compound *male nurse*, on the other hand, is more specific. The usual markedness values of masculine and feminine have been reversed and, in the context of nursing, feminine is the unmarked feature and masculine is marked. There is, of course, an obvious cultural explanation for this markedness reversal in the social fact that nurses are most commonly female.

The contextual nature of markedness is perhaps even more evident in markedness reversals in phonology. The markedness values of phonological features frequently reverse according to the context of co-occurring features: what is marked in one phonological context is unmarked in another. For example, the distinctive feature [+voice], which refers to the vibration of the vocal cords, is generally taken to be unmarked in vowel sounds but marked in consonants; voiceless vowels (such as occur when one whispers a vowel sound) are marked as contrasted to voiced vowels (vowels with their ordinary musical articulation), but voiceless consonants such as *p, t,* and *k* are unmarked as contrasted to their respective voiced counterparts *b, d,* and *g.* Markedness reversals are quite common in phonology, probably as a means of reinforcing the differentiation of other features. We will see later that reversals are also common in the evaluation of grammatical features and categories as well. Their pervasiveness in both semantics and phonology gives markedness a contextual as well as a general nature.

Markedness and Markedness Values

Let us begin with a few observations aimed at clarifying the nature of the markedness relation. Markedness is taken to be an axiomatic property of oppositions, a theoretical primitive that follows from the definition of opposition. The thesis of Jakobsonian markedness is the proposition that all oppositions have an inherent nonequivalence defined in terms of the presence or absence of a feature. But although markedness is defined as an abstract relation between feature values, it is not intended that the determination of markedness relations be a priori; rather they should be grounded in the analysis of linguistic data that determine the features of the language. Jakobson's own work, for example, appeals to the facts of language to uncover its abstract relational structure; facts of semantic inclusion and dominance and of phonological distribution underlie his analysis of signs as marked and unmarked.

Viewing markedness as a property of oppositions, while true to the spirit of Prague School structuralism, presents difficulties in cases where the nature of oppositions is obscure. Since markedness relations correlate to empirical properties of language structure as well as to abstract oppositions, various diagnostic criteria have been suggested for ascertaining markedness values. The task of sorting out the proper criteria is complicated by the fact that markedness theory has developed in several ways since originally conceived. Jakobson's work at different times emphasized both the language-particular aspect of markedness (cf. 1984, especially pp. 71, 126, 130) and the possibility of universal asymmetries (cf. 1968 [1941], 1971 [1956]).

In later work, some linguists have focused their attention on markedness as a universal hierarchical relation between categories (or in some cases, between rules and constructions), while others have focused on markedness as a functional relation between opposed categories. The criteria selected to determine markedness values reflect these differences: for some, the emphasis has been on criteria that can be applied to a variety of languages; for others, the emphasis has been on the structure of particular systems.

The problem of determining markedness values is complicated further by the fact that the various diagnostics of markedness are not perfect. Though correlations have been suggested between markedness and a number of properties of linguistic structure, these correlations are not compulsory.[1] There is no single correlative property that can serve as an automatic diagnostic for markedness values, though some work better than others, as we shall see.

As Moravcsik and Wirth (1986:3) observe, a "classical" version of markedness can be defined that relies on three types of criteria: the distribution of elements, the amount of structure they have, and their elaboration in terms of subtypes. *Distribution of elements* and *amount of structure* are cover terms for sets of related and overlapping diagnostics. Criteria having to do with the amount of structure that a category has include indeterminacy of semantic structure, complexity of articulation, and complexity of grammatical or morphological form. Criteria having to do with the distribution of elements include optimality across languages, breadth of use within a language, and frequency of use within a language. As I examine these criteria in more detail, I will define a version of markedness in which markedness values in a particular language can be determined by a coalescence of properties—optimality, breadth of distribution, syncretization, indeterminateness, simplicity, and prototypicality.

Optimality refers to facts of cross-linguistic typology and implication that have constituted an especially important criterion in determining universal markedness values. Though it can of course be applied to grammatical and lexical features, this criterion plays a major role in many studies of phonological markedness, as is perhaps natural, since the concern with cross-linguistic typology began with the search for phonological universals. When certain segments or certain feature values imply others in language after language, those values are taken to be unmarked. For example, many languages lack /ü/, but far fewer lack /i/; /i/ is taken to have priority over /ü/ (i.e., to be unmarked with respect to /ü/). This means that the distinctive feature that distinguishes /i/ and /ü/ (namely, the feature rounded/unrounded or grave/acute) will find its marked value in /ü/ and its unmarked value in /i/. The feature values that are the implieds in implicational relationships are marked; the feature values that are implying are unmarked.[2]

Distribution within a language plays an important role in the determination of language-particular markedness values. Unmarked terms are distinguished from their marked counterparts by having a greater freedom of occurrence and a greater ability to combine with other linguistic elements. Included as part of the criterion of distribution is the phenomenon of neutralization, according to which phonological and semantic markedness can be determined by which term of an opposition occurs in positions of absolute neutralization. These are defined as positions in which an opposition is suspended and only one of its poles can occur. It should be emphasized that wider distribution does not simply mean having a greater frequency in the language than the opposed category, since the frequency of a token depends on such factors as lexical, grammatical, and discourse function. For the

determination of markedness values, the relevant criterion of wider distri
bution and greater productivity is understood as the ability to occur in a
wider range of contexts.

Distributional breadth concerns the ability of a feature to combine
with other features. The term *syncretization* is sometimes used to refer to
the elaboration of a category by a greater or fewer number of subdistinc-
tions. Jakobson (1984:154 [1939]), following an observation of Viggo Brøndal, proposes that unmarked categories tend to be more differentiated than
marked ones.

Indeterminateness refers to the semantic criterion that marked elements are characteristically specific and determinate in meaning while the
opposed unmarked elements are characteristically indeterminate, a factor
that follows from the definition of semantic markedness as having both a
general meaning and a meaning opposite from that of the marked term. The
indeterminateness of the unmarked has been likened to a meaning inclusion
relation: since the unmarked is capable of having a general interpretation, it
may be substitutable for the meaning of the marked term in some contexts.
It need not, however, be substitutable for the marked term in all instances.

Simplicity refers to the idea that unmarked elements are less elaborate
in form than their counterparts. Jakobson, for example, notes that, "A
marked category tends to be interpreted in relation to the unmarked one as
a compound complex category opposed to a simple one" (1962:266
[1937]). Simplicity has been invoked at both the phonological level, where
it refers to the acoustic or articulatory complexity of a sound, and at the
semantic level, where it refers to the morphological or syntactic complexity
of a category. Most concisely stated, the criterion of simplicity posits that
the physically or formally simpler element is the unmarked one.

To these tests originating in linguistics can be added a further test
having its origins in psychology. This is the criterion of prototypicality, best
known from the work of Rosch (1977). It has been suggested by Lakoff
(1987), Mayerthaler (1988 [1981]), and others that properties are less conceptually complex, and hence less marked, the more closely and clearly
they reflect attributes of prototypical or experientially more basic categories.

The tentative criteria for the assignment of markedness values can be
summarized and classified as follows:

(1)   a. Distributional criteria
                 optimality
                 breadth of use (neutralization)

             b. Amount of structure criteria
                 indeterminateness

simplicity
syncretization

c. Prototypicality

Part of my task in this chapter is to clarify these criteria as answers to
the question of which element is marked and which is unmarked. I will also
explore the logical connection among these criteria and whether the criteria
apply to language-particular markedness or to universal markedness relations.

Semantic Markedness: Nonequivalence of Signifieds

The application of markedness to semantic oppositions finds its origin
in the grammatical analyses of Russian undertaken by Jakobson in his
Prague days. During the 1930s Jakobson's interest in finding unifying principles for the organization of linguistic structure first led him to extend the
principle of phonological markedness to oppositions between lexical and
grammatical oppositions. In his first work on semantic markedness, "The
Structure of the Russian Verb," Jakobson states:

> One of the essential properties of phonological correlations is the fact
> that the two members of a correlational pair are not equivalent: one
> member possesses the mark in question, the other does not; the first
> is designated as unmarked (see N. Trubetzkoy in TCLP (Travaux du
> Cercle Linguistique de Prague) IV, 97). Morphological correlations
> may be characterized on the basis of the same definition. [1984:1
> (1932)]

In that article Jakobson introduced the concept of semantic markedness with the lexical example *ošël/oslíca* discussed in the last chapter, and
he went on to analyze marked/unmarked relations in the Russian verbal
system. The markedness values he ascribed to some of the categories of the
Russian verb appear in table 2.1.[3]

Some of the discussion with which Jakobson justifies the assignment
of markedness values is given below:

> The so-called "third person" form functions as a grammatical imper-
> sonal form, which as such does not indicate the relationship of the
> action to a subject; . . . The personal forms have at their disposal the
> following correlation: "first person" form (marked)~a form which
> does not indicate the relationship of the action to the speaker. [6]

Table 2.1

Markedness Values of the Russian Verbal Categories

Person Oppositions

Personal is marked as opposed to impersonal (unmarked).
(Within the category personal) first person is marked as opposed to second person.
(Within the category second person) inclusive is marked as opposed to exclusive.

Gender Oppositions

Subjective gender is marked as opposed to neuter.
(Within the category subjective) feminine is marked as opposed to masculine.

Number Oppositions

Plural is marked as opposed to singular.

Finiteness Oppositions

Finite verbs are marked as opposed to infinitives.

Tense Oppositions

The preterit is marked as opposed to the present tense.

Aspect Oppositions

Perfective verbs are marked as opposed to imperfective.
(Within the category imperfective) determinate verbs are marked as opposed to indeterminate.
(Within the categories imperfective and indeterminate) iterative verbs are marked as opposed to noniterative.

Mood Oppositions

Conditional mood is marked as opposed to indicative.
Injunctive mood is marked as opposed to indicative.

The "infinitive" was characterized by Karcevskij as a zero-form of the verb, as to its "syntactic" value, since it contains "the expression of a process outside of any syntagmatic relation." [18, 158] The remaining verbal forms indicate the presence of syntagmatic relations, and thereby function as the marked member of the correlation, in opposition to the infinitive. [4–5]

The indicative has already been defined several times as the negative or zero mood: "it is simply an action—one which has not been complicated by any specific modal shading, just as the nominative simply denotes an object without any shading of causality" (Peškovskij, I, 126; cf. Karcevskij, 141). Opposed to the unmarked indicative is a mood which indicates the arbitrary impact of the action. . . . [5] The unmarked character of the imperfective is apparently generally recognized. . . . the perfective, as opposed to the imperfective, indicates the absolute limit of the action. [3]

These sketches of the semantic properties of the verbal categories highlight the interpretive character of semantic markedness assignments for Jakobson. His analysis of the Russian verbal system relies on "generally recognized" interpretations of the meanings of the verbal categories analyzed in terms of the presence of semantic features versus their absence. Thus in characterizing the infinitive as the zero form of the verb, Jakobson refers to its indeterminate semantic content: the meaning of the infinitive is nonspecification of tense; the finite forms indicate the presence of tense. Similarly, Jakobson interprets the indicative as defined by the absence of any determination of modality, and the third person as the absence of "relationship to a subject," and so on. One of a pair of opposed categories is characterized by the presence of a feature and the other by its absence, which is realized as indeterminateness.

The characterization of which element is marked and which is unmarked reflects Jakobson's concern with the meanings and functions of linguistic categories. It is worth emphasizing here that the semantic oppositions into which grammatical categories are analyzed are not always the traditional ones like singular/plural, present/past, masculine/feminine, and so on. Sometimes a traditional category will be broken down into more minimal and abstract semantic features. The markedness values are discovered, in principle, by considering the meaning of a category within the system of semantic relations in the language and then by determining whether this meaning best reflects the presence or absence of a property. The semantic perspective Jakobson employs in analyzing traditional categories reflects his search for what he calls the invariant semantic properties of languages. The method is to extract the meaning of a category (the invariant) by considering the semantic property that is common to all its uses in a particular language.[4] The analysis of the system of meanings is carried out by defining semantic categories in terms of a smaller number of features, essentially the same method employed in the reduction of phonemes to distinctive features. A particularly important illustration of Jakobson's method of determining semantic relations and their markedness relations is found in his analysis of the Russian case system (1984 [1935, 1958]). Jakobson decomposes the cases of Russian into the properties of quantification, directionality, and marginality, each traditional case being a bundle of feature values from this set of properties and each having a composite markedness value. Jakobson argues, for example, that the general semantic property of the Russian accusative is its directionality: the accusative direct object is the target of the action, the case that "always indicates that some action to some extent affects, is directed at, or is manifested on, the stated entity" (1984:66 [1936]). The nominative, he suggests, is opposed to the accusative in being unmarked for the feature of directionality. It is the case of pure naming.

> In comparing the Russian nominative and accusative, the first is frequently defined as a case denoting the subject of some action, and the second, the object of the action. Such a definition of the accusative is by and large correct. The accusative always indicates that some action to some extent affects, is directed at, or is manifested on, the stated entity. . . . [Jakobson 1984:66–67]

Each of the other case distinctions in Russian is treated similarly. The instrumental case is characterized by the property of marginality: an instrumental object or time expression touches the action described only peripherally: the instrumental stipulates concepts that aid in the unfolding of the central verbal event, such as source, motive, implement, mode, and space through. The dative case is likewise characterized by marginality, since the dative object is only peripherally (indirectly) involved in the action described. While the dative and instrumental are both marginal cases, they may be distinguished by the same directionality correlation that distinguishes the nominative and accusative. The instrumental is unspecified for directionality, while the dative is marked for this feature.

> Like the A, the D also indicates that its referent is involved in an action, whereas the I, like the N, says nothing about this, and nothing about whether its referent itself exerts an action or participates in an action. [Jakobson 1984:77 (1936)]

The feature of quantification characterizes the genitive and locative cases. Jakobson finds that the genitive "always indicates **the limit of the referent's involvement in the context of the utterance** [emphasis in original]" (1984:72 [1936]), which manifests itself in a partitive bounding sense or in a broadly defined negative sense (the genitive of negation). The locative case Jakobson analyzes as indicating peripheral status in contrast to a dominant point in the utterance and also as indicating quantification in that the locative referent is "not represented in the utterance to its full extent" (1984:89). Thus the locative and genitive are both marked for quantification, and the locative is distinguished from the genitive by being marked for peripherality as well. The structure of the Russian case system is summarized below, where M indicates the presence of a feature and U indicates the absence of that feature:[5]

(2)   Russian Case System

	Nom.	Acc.	Dat.	Inst.	Gen.	Loc.
Directedness	U	M	M	U	U	U
Quantification	U	U	U	U	M	M
Marginality	U	U	M	M	U	M

Jakobson's method of semantic analysis consists, as we have seen, in reducing the meanings of a category (case, in this example) to a common denominator. Each category (each case) is distinguished from the other categories of the system (the rest of the declensional system) by the presence or absence of a feature (the marked or unmarked value). It is, however, unclear what the ultimate empirical basis is for determining the relevant semantic properties and the assignments of marked versus unmarked value. The markedness assignments of the Russian conjugational and declensional systems discussed above might be viewed as resting primarily on Jakobson's intuitions about the meanings and relations that make up the systems of verbal and nominal categories. While the establishment of general semantic properties and relations can provide a convincing intersubjective criterion for markedness assignments, the problem remains that such analyses are ultimately based in arguments about meanings, which are by their very nature open to various interpretations and therefore inconclusive. Will the meanings and the markedness values of features not differ from linguist to linguist? Consider, for example, the distinction between finite and infinitive verbs discussed earlier: could we not say that the finite verb should be the unmarked term because it is unspecified for any syntactic connection with a higher verb, whereas infinitives indicate subordination to a higher predicate? Are abstract semantic properties so subject to interpretation as to invalidate assignments of markedness values?

Despite its basis in semantic interpretation, I think that Jakobson's method of semantic analysis is not arbitrarily subjective. Judgements about meanings and semantic relations can be supported by appealing to a category's range of uses, and markedness values can be supported by appealing to facts of semantic inclusion that show the ability of the unmarked term to subsume its opposite. Here the logical connection between indeterminateness and distribution becomes apparent. Since the unmarked term has a double meaning, a diagnostic of semantic unmarkedness will be the presence of a more generic meaning. The featural distinction between the presence and absence of a feature has a correlation in the subsuming character of the unmarked term. This is the primary empirical correlate of semantic unmarkedness.

On a strict Jakobsonian interpretation, it might be argued that semantic analysis should be the only defining principle for markedness relations.[6] But as I have pointed out, the correct semantic properties are not always clear. Where the semantic facts are clear they may be given pride of place, but it is desirable in general to develop connections to other, nonsemantic, criteria in order to ground markedness more firmly in the objective substance of language.

The semantic indeterminacy of the unmarked is one facet of the grounding of markedness in the material aspect of language. We now turn to other potential evidence for semantic markedness relations. Before moving on, however, it should be pointed out that semantic indeterminateness is not a problem-free diagnostic. Though this criterion is perhaps the most widespread and the most intimately connected with the Prague School definition of semantic markedness, oppositions do exist in which the prediction that the unmarked term carries both the zero interpretation and the opposite interpretation is not borne out.

The opposition positive/negative is a case in point. Positive and negative are quite obviously polar and, according to Greenberg (1966:25–26), the positive is unmarked. But there is no real sense in which a positive sentence or verb can be used to indicate a negative one (or vice versa). The definition of the unmarked term as the nonsignalization of a property does not, strictly speaking, always translate into semantic indeterminacy. The opposition between *boy* and *girl* is another example. Though the terms are semantically opposed by the opposition masculine/feminine, neither may be used to refer to a general group of nonadults (compare the opposition *guys* vs. *gals,* or *guys* vs. *girls,* in which *guys* has the zero interpretation for many speakers). In the opposition between *boy* and *girl,* neither masculine nor feminine is the indeterminate feature. Such facts as these highlight the difference between equipollent and privative oppositions. If all oppositions were privative—if they could all be analyzed as oppositions of A versus not A—then it should always be the case that one term of an opposition would be indeterminate. But since some oppositions are characterized by equipollent opposites (as A vs. B rather than A vs. not A), we must expect that there will be cases in which indeterminacy does not hold. It is nevertheless natural and common to extend the notion of markedness to equipollent oppositions, since one term is often evaluatively dominant over the other. So, although semantic indeterminateness is a sufficient condition for determining the unmarked, it is not a necessary reflex of unmarkedness.

Formal Marking and Distribution

Markedness at the semantic level characterizes relations at that level (the level of signifieds), and I have suggested in the last section that the opposition between the signalization and nonsignalization of a semantic feature can be reflected in the semantic indeterminacy and wider range of the unmarked term. But semantic relations have morphological and syntactic expressions as well, which invite correlations between markedness as a semantic property and the syntactic and morphological properties of linguistic forms. Some writers on markedness—most notably Joseph Greenberg (1966), John Lyons (1977), Bernard Comrie (1976), and Willi Mayerthaler (1988 [1981])—have proposed nonsemantic tests for determining markedness relations, and in this section I consider these.[7] Properties of form and syntactic distribution sometimes show a correlation with semantic markedness, but it is a correlation attenuated by other factors. I argue below that form and syntactic distribution may, with appropriate caution exercised, be secondary heuristics for determining marked and unmarked status but are not alone sufficient to serve as defining principles.

Consider first what has been called formal markedness in the literature (Lyons 1977). Formal markedness, or better, formal marking is the relation between two opposed units of linguistic expression such that one is characterized by an augmentation, compounding, or complexity of form that the other lacks. Formal marking is solely a property of linguistic expression: the unmarked term is the basic one—that which is unaffixed (as opposed to affixed) or simple (as opposed to compound). The following pairs illustrate formal marking:

(3)   Formal Markedness

	Unmarked	Marked
a.	host	hostess
b.	go	is going
c.	cat	cats
d.	possible	impossible
e.	see	sees

The correlation between formal marking and semantic markedness informs much of Jakobson's work. In his address to the 1961 Dobbs Ferry Conference on Language Universals, Jakobson characterized the relationship between form and meaning:

In general, the 'iconic symbols' of language display a particularly clear-cut universalistic propensity. Thus, within a grammatical correlation the zero affix cannot be steadily assigned to the marked category and a 'nonzero' (real) affix to the unmarked category. For example, according to Greenberg, ''There is no language in which the plural does not have some nonzero allomorphs, whereas there are languages in which the singular is expressed only by zero. The dual and the trial are almost never expressed only by zero.'' In a declensional pattern, the zero case (''which includes among its meanings that of the subject of the intransitive verb'') is treated like the singular in respect to the other numbers. Briefly, language tends to avoid any chiasmus between pairs of unmarked/marked categories, on the one hand, and pairs of zero/nonzero affixes (or of simple/compound grammatical forms), on the other hand. [1971:585–86 (1963)]

The correlation of semantic markedness and formal marking is plausible a priori. A principle of economy can be appealed to, the argument being that it is communicatively natural for the conceptually basic member of an opposition to be the formal base of the paradigm and for the more conceptually narrow term to be constructed by a formal augmentation or complication of the basic term.[8] The relation between marked and unmarked might be compared, in this respect, to the relation between common and uncommon vocabulary. Just as words that are used habitually tend to be reduced morphologically by processes such as clipping and acronymy *(taxicab* and *video cassette recorder* are reduced formally to *taxi*—or *cab*—and *VCR),* unmarked items might tend to be more compact than marked items.

This is not to say that there will be no mismatch between formal and semantic markedness values. In fact, one can be found among the examples cited above. If we follow Jakobson in analyzing the verbal category third person as semantically unmarked (being, in his terms, impersonal as opposed to personal), then we must conclude that formal marking and semantic markedness are misaligned in example (3e). *Sees* bears the formal marking (the suffix -*s*), yet it is semantically unmarked.[9] Other examples are not difficult to find. In Russian, for example, masculine nouns in the nominative case consist of the base only while feminine and neuter nouns consist of the base plus a vowel. Yet, according to Jakobson, neuter gender is the least marked semantically. If complexity corresponds to markedness we would expect the neuter to be the base form. But this is not so.

There is also another reason, suggested by Lyons (1977), why formal marking cannot be taken as the definition of marked/unmarked semantic status: semantic relations do not correspond to pairs of formally marked and unmarked items, and semantic distinctions between marked and unmarked elements are not always implemented formally. In English, for example, the distinction between first and second person forms of verbs exhibits no formal inflection (the verb *be* excepted), but the opposition first person/second person presumably exists at the semantic level. Moreover, formal markedness is not always correlated with a single semantic opposition (cf. Lyons 1977). Consider pairs of items such as *master/mistress, governor/governess;* though these items are formally paired, their meanings are not opposed by any single feature in present-day usage. In fact, it is possible for semantically marked and unmarked terms to show a variety of formal relations, as can be seen in the following pairs of antonyms (from Lehrer 1985):

(4)		Unmarked	Marked
	a.	happy	unhappy
		accurate	inaccurate
		friendly	unfriendly
		pure	impure
		important	unimportant
		honest	dishonest
		fair	unfair
		even	uneven
		clean	unclean
	b.	long	short
		tall	short
		big	little
		large	small
		happy	sad
		clean	dirty
		friendly	mean
		far	near
		old	young
		old	new
		smart	dumb

The alignment of formal marking and semantic markedness is a tendency, and one which may hold to different degrees in different parts of the grammar and in different languages. However, there is no compulsory alignment between semantic markedness and formal markedness[10]—there is no reason why the formally augmented term of an opposition must correspond to the semantically marked one. As mentioned earlier, one might try to appeal to a principle of economy. But since language is not always sensitive to economic motivation as an organizing principle (see Haiman 1983), such an appeal is not convincing motivation for an absolute connection. We must reject formal complexity as a definitional criterion for markedness.

The next correlate of semantic markedness to be considered is syntactic distribution. This concept refers to the fact that pairs of opposed items never have equivalent distributions: one item occurs in a wider, less restricted set of contexts than the other. As with formal marking, there is a correlation between semantic markedness and distribution. The semantically unmarked term tends to occur in a wider range of contexts than its opposite. As a simple illustration, consider again the lexical opposition *tall/ short* mentioned in chapter 1 and exemplified below:

(5)   a. Mary is very tall.

         b. George is very short.

         c. How tall is Fred?

         d. How short is Fred?

The range of contexts in which *tall* may be used normally (that is, with no special implication) is wider than that in which *short* may be normally used. Though *short* can be used grammatically in (d) and similar examples, its use has a specially constrained sense that (c) lacks: (d) implies that Fred is in fact short, and it could not normally be answered by replying *Fred's six foot five;* (c), on the other hand, could be answered with either *Fred's six foot five* or *Fred's five foot seven. Short* signals the property shortness; *tall* is the nonsignalization of shortness, reflected as either tallness or the zero interpretation. The signalization of a property, the marked value, can only be used where that property is implied; the nonsignalization of the property, the unmarked value, can be used to imply either the opposite of *tall* or the general property of height. Nonsignalization thus has a wider range of use.[11]

The correlation of the unmarked value with a wider syntactic distribution requires some further discussion and clarification. The notion of wider distribution can be understood in basically three ways: as text frequency, type frequency, or occurrence in positions of neutralization. In the first case, the diagnostic predicts that the unmarked term occurs more frequently than the marked term in representative corpora of a language. In the second case, it predicts that the unmarked is the more freely combinable, productive element and occurs in a greater number of different grammatical contexts than the marked. In the last case, the expectation is that there are certain contexts in which the contrast between opposed elements is neutralized in favor of the unmarked term.

Consider text frequency first. Greenberg (1966:65ff.) has suggested that other diagnostic criteria will generally correlate with text frequency and that it may be possible to use text frequency alone to determine markedness assignments. However, others have noted that while greater text frequency may be viewed in part as a consequence of the broader meaning and wider distribution of the unmarked category, other factors impinge on this correlation. As Linda Schwartz (1980) points out, it is necessary to assume that we refer equally to all points in a semantic range in order to conclude that text frequency correlates with semantic unmarkedness. If such an assumption is not made, we invite a type/token fallacy since greater text frequency could be due to the frequency with which we use a particular category rather than to its semantic properties. Since text frequency can be a function of other factors besides the asymmetry of semantic category, I will avoid text frequency as a test for markedness.[12]

The second distributional criterion to be considered is occurrence in a wider range of contexts in a language. Above we considered a simple example of this criterion involving the lexical items *tall* and *short*. As we shall see in the next chapter, the criterion of broader distribution is also applicable to grammatical categories. The correlation of semantic markedness and distribution is extremely plausible given the double semantic value of an unmarked feature. The semantic indeterminacy of the unmarked term will result in its being used in a greater number of contexts than the marked member, all else being equal. The unmarked term will be the category used when a choice between opposites unnecessary or impossible.

The third distributional criterion, neutralization, can actually be viewed as a special type of distributional breadth in which one term of an opposition is used to the exclusion of the other in some environment. Originally developed in Prague School phonology, neutralization occurs when the marked term is excluded from some context and the unmarked term stands for both poles of the opposition.[13] As a simple illustration, consider the following uses of the word pair *host/hostess:*

(6)   a.   Your hosts are Mr. and Mrs. Hill.

        b. *Your hostesses are Mr. and Mrs. Hill.

As the asterisk indicates, (b) is impossible. In the plural, the masculine/feminine distinction between *host* and *hostess* may be neutralized; the only possible choice is the term that can stand for a mixed host and hostess pair. The word *hosts,* then, here signals neither masculine nor feminine. Since *host* occurs in the position of neutralization but *hostess* cannot, we take *host* to be the unmarked term.[14]

The hypothesis that unmarkedness is revealed by occurrence in positions of neutralization is undercut, however, by situations in which neutralization is to the marked term. As Sidney Greenbaum (1976) observes, such a situation arises in the English complementizer system. The complementizer *that*, which signals a following finite subordinate clause, is in opposition with a zero complementizer (that is, with the deletion of the overt function word). In semantic terms, we might consider *that* to be the marked form, since it specifically signals a following clause, while the omission of *that* signals nothing about what is to follow. And formally *that* is, of course, the more complex element, since it has a phonological representation, which ∅ lacks. Yet, the superficial distribution of these elements requires us to conclude that ∅ is the marked element. In environments in which the contrast between *that* and ∅ is neutralized (subject position, post-adverbial position, and after certain classes of verbs), neutralization is in favor of *that*, not ∅, as is indicated by the following:

(7)   a. John believes $\left\{ \begin{array}{c} \text{that} \\ \text{∅} \end{array} \right\}$ he is crazy.

    b. I hope very much $\left\{ \begin{array}{c} \text{that} \\ \text{*∅} \end{array} \right\}$ you will win.

    c. Mary snapped $\left\{ \begin{array}{c} \text{that} \\ \text{*∅} \end{array} \right\}$ she'd be right back.

    d. $\left\{ \begin{array}{c} \text{That} \\ \text{*∅} \end{array} \right\}$ he's crazy surprised us all.

We see here that there are no positions in which ∅ occurs but *that* does not occur, although the reverse is not true. On the grounds of neutralization alone, *that* should be the unmarked term and ∅ the marked, contrary to semantic and formal criteria. Here then, neutralization proves to be at odds with semantic and formal tests. We will see later that oppositions are neutralized sometimes to the unmarked pole of an opposition and sometimes to the marked pole.[15]

The connection between markedness and range of distribution is attenuated in a similar fashion. Above I remarked that we might expect unmarked terms to be used in a wider range of contexts because of their broader meaning, "all else being equal." The "all else" here is, of course, context. Notice, for example, that context was a hidden factor in the discussion of range of distribution of the lexical items *tall* and *short*. *Tall* has the broader distribution in the neutral context of a request for height. *Short* cannot be used in this neutral context, but it can be used in what might be considered a special context in which the supposition is that Fred is *short*. If there are cases in which such special contexts are particularly common, it could turn out that a marked term's distribution would be as wide or wider than that of the unmarked term.

The expectation that unmarked elements occur in positions of neutralization or in the wider range of environments is not an automatic diagnostic but one that requires that notion of context to be taken into account. In the next chapter I will suggest that neutralization and distributional breadth reflect the coherence of units and contexts whereby marked elements occur in place of unmarked elements in marked context. For now, suffice it to say that the criteria of neutralization and syntactic distribution must be framed within the analysis of language as a complete system of units and contexts rather than in terms of isolated contextless elements. If follows, of course, that neutralization and syntactic distribution cannot by themselves determine which units are marked and which are unmarked.

Syncretization

A further correlate of markedness that has often been suggested has to do not with freedom of combination with other categories but with an element's differentiation into subcategories.[16] Jakobson describes this criterion:

> V. Brøndal has brought out the fact that languages tend to avoid an excessive complexity in the aggregate of one morphological formation, and that, frequently, forms which are complex with respect to one category are relatively simple with respect to others. [1984;154 (1939)]

Jakobson gives the following examples:

> in Russian, the present tense (zero tense) distinguishes persons, in contradistinction to the past which has only one form for all the persons; the singular (zero grammatical number) distinguishes grammatical genders, in contrast to the plural, which has totally effaced them. But, even though the grammatical system limits the "accumulation of meanings" *[cumul des signifíes]* (term and notion introduced by Bally), it does not by any means exclude it.

The logic of syncretization is that the unmarked category, perhaps by virtue of its greater familiarity or frequency or syntactic distribution, lends itself to greater differentiation. But though this criterion is plausible and correct in many cases, there are, as Jakobson's comments imply, cases where the marked category shows an accumulation of further marks. Consider, for example, the present tense in English. While it is true that the present tense has retained distinct person forms, it is also true that the past tense shows a greater subdivision of verbs into conjugational classes. And while finite verbs are subdivided into the categories indicative, subjunctive, and imperative, nonfinite verbs are subdivided into infinitives, present participles, and past participles. So just as syntactic distribution is not sufficient to automatically ascertain markedness relations, neither is syncretization of one category or the other.

Prototypes and Best Examples

A final correlate of semantic markedness is defined neither by form, distribution, or differentiation, but rather is based on the idea that certain categories are conceptually and psychologically more basic than others. Such prototypical categories or prototypes have been explicity related to unmarked categories by some writers.[17] John R. Ross remarks, for example, that "the notion *prototype* . . . is essentially an outgrowth of the fundamental notion of markedness," adding that "in general one way of recognizing prototypical elements is by the fact that they combine more freely and productively than do elements which are far removed from prototypes" (1987:307). And George Lakoff, in his recent book *Women, Fire, and Dangerous Things,* treats markedness as a kind of prototype effect:

> In general markedness is a term used by linguists to describe a kind of prototype effect—an asymmetry in a category, where one member or subcategory is taken to be somehow more basic than the other (or others). Correspondingly, the unmarked member is the default value—the member of the category that occurs when only one member of the category can occur and all other things are equal. [1987:60–61]

Following the work of Eleanor Rosch (1973, 1977, 1978), Lakoff sees prototypes as cognitive reference points, as category members that serve as a "best example" of some category or set. The psychological criteria for determining what constitutes a prototypical physical category include direct rating by subjects, tests of reaction time, the production of examples, and asymmetries in the use of categories (cf. Lakoff 1987:41–42). In addition to psychological criteria for prototypes, there have also been specific suggestions for uncovering linguistic prototypes, such as that of Ross given above. Margaret Winters (1990) develops a set of diagnostics for defining syntactic prototypes that includes type frequency, productivity, salience, autonomy, and transparency as potential indicators of syntactic prototypes.

Type frequency and productivity are features that have already been discussed in connection with distribution. Salience can be defined as "extra emphasis to mark some emotionally motivated reaction to the information being conveyed," which Winters suggests will be correlated with less prototypical syntax.[18] Transparency refers to ease of production and clarity of perception of a syntactic construction, while autonomy indicates the ability of a category to stand alone in discourse.

The diagnostics suggested by Winters are, like the linguistic correlates of markedness, stated in terms of properties of language. Other linguists, however, have proposed criteria for markedness and prototypes that are linked more to the experiences of speakers than to the structure of language. Willy van Langendonck (1986:47), for example, suggests that unmarked categories and structures can be tied to "certain prototypical properties of a biological, perceptual, interactional or cultural nature." Van Langendonck suggests an "experientialist" orientation whereby unmarkedness is identified with contextually given elements and perceptually accessible categories. Some examples of markedness relations suggested by experiential prototypes are given below (taken from van Langendonck):

(8)   Prototypical   Nonprototypical

        a.   concrete   abstract
        b.   positive   negative
        c.   singular   nonsingular
        d.   front   back

Van Langendonck's basis for these markedness assignments is as follows: concrete things are more "perceptually accessible" than abstract ones; the notion positive, which he sees as associated with the concept of existence, is unmarked because it is "perceptually more conspicuous and psychologically and culturally more important that nonexistence"; singularity is more natural because "the prototypical speaker does not act in a group, but rather individually"; the concept front is prototypical because "the prototypical speaker has his eyes in the front of his head and not at the back of his head."

The assignment of markedness relations based on prototypical speaker properties adopted by van Langendonck seems to be based on the practice of Mayerthaler, who remarks that certain categories

> form the gestalt background of the speech situation, that is, the given with which we begin and against which the gestalt of the marked stands out: the speaker is animate, definite, is understood as the sub-

ject and agent of the action; his action is formulated according to the content of dynamic verbs, takes place in the present and is unfinished (imperfective aspect). . . . Categories from this class will be unmarked, where 'unmarked' means 'in agreement with the typical attributes of the speaker'. [1988:8 (1981)]

Mayerthaler sums up his definition of markedness in terms of prototypes:

> There are many areas that require recourse to biological and neurological [sic] determined speaker attributes. We can therefore say: *'A semantically less marked category (sem (K_i))' = def category K_i that reflects prototypical speaker attributes* [emphasis in original]. [ibid.:9][19]

Although the psychological notion of prototypes and the linguistic principle of markedness are similar in certain respects, they differ sufficiently to be kept distinct, at least until their relation can be further explored and better understood. Markedness is a structural relation, defined in terms of featural asymmetry and correlated with semantic breadth, distribution, form, and syncretization. Like markedness, the notion of prototype is easier to describe than to define. Linguistic prototypes, like unmarked categories, correlate with various diagnostics based on the uses and distribution that the best example of a category could be expected to have. But in fact, the grammatical properties that serve as diagnostics for prototypes are so similar to those for unmarkedness that they provide no new help in determining unmarkedness. Psychological tests might be useful, but it is impractical to carry them out for all of the syntactic, semantic, and phonological categories to be considered in the following chapters. For our present purposes, the most useful working definition of prototypicality is that it is the central member or best example of a category, where centrality or bestness is determined by our experience as speakers of a language.

The correlation of markedness with prototypes seems to have a reasonable basis in that categories that are more basic, obvious, and easily connected to our everyday experience can be expected to serve as a conceptual background. The role of prototypes as conceptual background corresponds to that of the unmarked feature value when it represents both terms of an opposition:

> Closer familiarity tends to be paired with simpler structure and greater variability; less frequent occurrence in human experience goes with increased structural complexity and diminished variability. People tend to see familiar objects as simpler in structure and more var-

ied in kind than less familiar objects; and they tend to make things
that are in common use to be simpler in structure and more varie-
gated than those in less common use. [Moravcsik and Wirth 1986:2]

In the chapters that follow, I will rely on the notion of prototype at times,
though I will try to use it carefully since its definition is uncomfortably
close to that of unmarked. Where a particular category serves as the best
example of an opposition, prototypicality will be taken as a criterion of
unmarkedness.

Correlating the central member of a category with the unmarked may
help to resolve cases in which clear-cut feature analysis is opaque, such as
the oppositions between positive/negative and *boy/girl* mentioned earlier.
Positive and *boy* might be assigned unmarked status on the basis of cultural
dominance rather than featural properties. Though recourse to prototypes
distances us from the Jakobsonian view of markedness as based on a logic
of binary relations, it has the advantage of allowing markedness values to
be determined in cases where oppositions are clear but the feature analysis
is obscure.

The notion of prototype may also be useful in allowing us to extend
the concept of markedness to categories that are bundles of features, such
as the categories of grammatical subject and object. As van Langendonck
(1986) notes (see also Silverstein 1976, Bates and MacWhinney 1982, and
van Oosten 1986) prototypical subjects are animate, topical, agentive, singular, and definite. The prototypical combination of features can be understood as the unmarked feature combination, the unmarked subject being
animate, topical, agentive, singular, and definite. Subjects that vary in one
or more of these features are marked in opposition to the prototypical combination. In a similar vein, Hopper and Thompson (1984) have observed that
prototypical nouns and verbs can be defined in terms of their semantic and
discourse functions. Various categories of nouns and verbs can be ranked as
more or less marked according to their relation to prototypical functions.

Summary: Diagnostics of the Breadth of Meaning

This brings me to the end of my survey of criteria for determining
markedness relations in semantics. Having introduced various linguistic criteria that serve as heuristics for determining markedness values, I can now
sum up to what extent these can be used to determine which member of an
opposition is marked and which is unmarked. While syntactic distribution,
formal simplicity, and syncretization *tend* to reinforce the criterion of semantic indeterminateness, we cannot simply replace semantic analysis with
distributional and formal accounting. We should keep in mind that the
markedness relation in grammar and lexical analysis was originally con-

ceived of as a semantic relation and that the semantic criterion of indeterminateness expressed in Jakobson's definition should be given priority. The criterion of prototypicality provides a useful means to determine markedness relations where purely semantic means fail and in cases where the semantic relation appears to be equipollent rather than privative (i.e., where the relation is of the type A/B rather than A/not A). The remaining criteria discussed—distribution, neutralization, simplicity, and syncretization—are more problematic. Breadth of distribution and neutralization appear to be closely connected to unmarkedness in some cases, though the effect of context remains to be elaborated. And as we have seen, simplicity and syncretization have only an imperfect connection with unmarkedness, reflecting the incomplete overlap between unmarkedness and economy.

No single diagnostic is a fully reliable indicator of marked/unmarked status for every opposition. We cannot count on all indicators pointing to the same conclusion. This state of affairs, however, should not worry us too much. Though they cannot serve as an algorithm for determining unmarked status, the criteria of semantic breadth and prototypicality taken together are a reasonably reliable heuristic with which we may assign markedness values and investigate the role of markedness in the organization of language. In many cases, those criteria will be joined by distribution, syncretization, and simplicity, though alone they are not a test of markedness. Overall, the diagnostic criteria provide guidelines for determining which of a pair of opposed elements is the more dominant, unmarked term.

I want to conclude this section by emphasizing that the analytic and heuristic (as opposed to algorithmic) nature of markedness values is no cause for worry. The fact that we cannot define the notions marked and unmarked perfectly is no more surprising than the fact that we cannot define the notion verb perfectly. Try as we might to reduce the concept verb to more primitive notions or criteria (such as "occurs with tense and aspectual endings," "can occur with a direct object," "functions logically as a predicate," "indicates an action or state"), there are always exceptions to and misalignments of the criteria. Yet this does not lead us to abandon the definition of verb (in favor of what?) or keep us from formulating generalizations about the behavior of verbs and their properties. To be sure, our goals should include improving the definitions wherever possible, but this can only happen if we attempt to apply the theory to actual data. This is the task of the following chapters. First, however, let us turn to the phonological aspect of markedness in order to complete the picture.

Phonological Markedness

Markedness is a concept of evaluation imposed upon both phonological structure and semantic structure. As such we naturally wish to consider

ways in which the criteria that play a role in the evaluation of phonological
features as marked and unmarked may be related to the criteria that define
markedness at the semantic level.[20] Since semantics and phonology are distinct levels of language, making up its inner meaning and outer form, parallelism between phonological markedness and semantic markedness bears
on the hypothesis that markedness is a primitive concept of linguistic structure. To the extent that phonological and semantic markedness *are* identified, the pursuit of unifying principles of linguistic structure is redeemed.

Some initial parallels between phonological and semantic markedness
are evident, as are some differences that arise. In the Prague School tradition, phonological markedness values have historically been defined by
principles of neutralization, syncretization and simplicity similar to those
that we saw at the semantic level. Phonological markedness relations
have also been defined, by implicational universals and cross-linguistic
optimality, though these considerations did not play a role in the study of
semantic markedness in the first part of this chapter. We begin our
discussion of phonological markedness with the familiar criteria of neutralization, syncretization, and simplicity, turning afterward to the criterion of
optimality.

Consider again the notion of neutralization, this time as a criterion of
phonological markedness. As I noted earlier, the use of neutralization as a
test of phonological markedness values derives from the work of Trubetzkoy. Though Trubetzkoy originally relegated the decision as to which
features were marked and which were unmarked to the "linguistic consciousness" of speakers (Baltaxe 1978:41), he later supplemented this with
other criteria, culminating in the proposal that neutralization be used as a
test of markedness:

> Two phonemes or, as may be the case, two phoneme classes between
> which a neutralizable contrast exists, are said to be especially close-
> ly related as to one another, and, when this neutralizable contrast is
> one which can be described as presence or absence of a particular
> feature, the phonemes in question are respectively the 'marked' form
> and the 'unmarked' form. The unmarked form here is always that
> phoneme which, where the contrast in question has been neutralized,
> appears as the sole representative of the relevant pair of phonemes—
> provided of course that the situation is not obscured by assimilation.
> [1968:27–28]

According to this criterion, the unmarked feature is determined in the
following way: where the contrast between a pair (or set) of phonemes is
neutralized, the unmarked feature is the one which is realized in the posi-

tion of neutralization, and the marked feature the one which is excluded. As an example, consider the stop consonants of English.

(9)   Bilabial   Alveolar   Velar

   a. tense (and voiceless)   p   t   k
   b. lax (and voiced)   b   d   g

There are two series of stops, the tense (and, redundantly, voiceless) stops in (a) and the lax (and, redundantly, voiced) stops in (b). (I assume here that tense/lax opposition is the distinctive opposition for English rather than voiced/voiceless.) In many positions these series of stops are in contrastive distribution, that is, they can occur in the same phonological environment; *pit* contrasts with *bit, tin* with *din*, and so on. After *s* however, this contrast is neutralized: we find *spit, stun*, and *skunk* but no *sbit, sdun*, or *sgunk*. Since the contrast is neutralized in favor of the tense series (i.e., since the tense series is the one that occurs in the positions of neutralization), tense will be the unmarked feature value and lax will be the marked feature value.

While many phonologists who discuss markedness treat neutralization as an important criterion, problems do arise.[21] Brakel (1984:14) points out that there are situations in which an opposition is neutralized to different phonemes in different contexts. He points out, for example, that in Portuguese /r/ and /r̄/ contrast intervocalically, but are neutralized elsewhere; in some environments the neutralization is to /r/, in others it is to /r̄/ (cf. Gundel, Houlihan, and Sanders 1986). In light of such examples, we must conclude either that markedness values fluctuate with phonological context or that neutralization does not tell the whole story. As Trubetzkoy suggested, neutralization plays a role primarily where it is possible to view neutralization absolutely rather than as influenced by contextual factors. This parallels what we have seen in the domain of meaning.

The criterion of broader distribution fares better as a criterion of phonological markedness. But as Gundel, Houlihan, and Sanders (1986) point out, there are cases in which the distribution of opposed phonemes is defective in the sense that the features do not contrast in any environment. In such cases it might be expected that the unmarked sound would occur in the wider range of environments. An example provided by Gundel, Houlihan, and Sanders (1986) concerns lax voiced and voiceless stops in Korean. Lax voiced stops occur between voiced sounds only, and lax voiceless stops occur in word-initial and word-final position or adjacent to a voiceless sound. Although neutralization does not enter into the picture, lax voiceless stops have a wider distribution, and so voicelessness would be considered the unmarked feature.

Once again I want to stress that broader distribution refers to frequency of contexts rather than text frequency. As Schwartz (1980:319)
notes, the plausibility of a connection between text frequency and phonological markedness is clearly more tenuous than that of text frequency and
semantic markedness. She points out that the frequency of a phoneme depends on the frequency of the lexical items in which it occurs, which is
largely arbitrary. She gives as an example the voiced interdental fricative
/ð/, as in *either,* which is marked, as opposed to its voiceless counterpart
/θ/, as *ether,* which, however, has a higher text frequency by virtue of occurring in function words such as *this, that, the,* and *them.*[22]

The criterion of syncretization is also useful as a diagnostic of phonological markedness. Greenberg (1966:59) equates syncretization with the
idea that "the number of phonemes with the marked feature is always less
than or equal to the number with the unmarked feature but never greater,"
citing as an example the fact that the number of nasal vowels is never greater
than the number of nonnasal vowels. Linda Waugh echoes this opinion:

> Another commonly recognized phenomenon I will call "the tendency
> not to accumulate marks—or the tendency to combine markedness
> with non-markedness." This correlates with the observation that cer-
> tain phonological sub-systems tend to be more differentiated than oth-
> ers. For example, since in the consonantal system, nasality is a mark,
> there is a general tendency not to elaborate the nasal consonants more
> than or even equally to the oral consonants. . . . a *noncontinuant~*
> continuant distinction is often missing in the nasals while it is most
> often present in the orals . . . the *tense~*lax or *voiceless~*voiced dis-
> tinction may be missing in the nasals and present in the orals . . . the
> nasals may evidence less 'points of articulation' than the correspond-
> ing stops/fricatives and in particular velars and palatals may be miss-
> ing since they are marked (compact) vis-a-vis the dentals and labials.
> [1979:158][23]

The role that neutralization, distribution, and syncretization play in
both phonological and semantic markedness is one point of parallel. A second parallel arises in the idea that marked elements are distinguished by
greater complexity. At the phonological level, complexity cannot, of
course, be interpreted as affixation or compoundedness, since distinctive
features are not the sort of objects that take affixes or occur in compounds.
The complexity of sound features must be weighed in another way. Since
features have a certain complexity or simplicity in terms of natural articulatory and acoustic properties, the relevant notion of simplicity in phonology will be one that takes articulatory and acoustic naturalness into account

where articulatorily simple features will be those whose articulation requires the minimal deformation of the vocal tract from a neutral rest position and acoustically simple ones will be those that are most easily perceived.

This idea too finds its origin in Prague School phonology. Trubetzkoy had incorporated the notion of articulatory naturalness into his theory of markedness: "In any correlation . . . a 'natural absence of marking' is attributed to that opposition member whose production requires the least deviation from normal breathing" (1969:146). Charles Cairns develops this idea more fully:

[I]t is possible to characterize every M [marked feature] as representing a deviation from the ideal, archetypal string: Each M represents either a complication of the program for driving the vocal tract, or some attenuation of perceptual distinctions. [1969:878]

Of course, features do not occur in isolation, but rather always occur in a context of other features. Since phonemes are feature bundles, each feature is coarticulated with the other features present in a segment itself (its simultaneous context), as well as with features in neighboring phonemes (its sequential context), articulatory and acoustic simplicity will be relative concepts. A feature is articulatorily simple if the associated articulatory command is physically natural from the point of view of the other features of the phonemes. A feature is acoustically natural if its correlated acoustic properties reinforce, or at least do not conflict with, the acoustic correlates of its cofeatures.[24] Again, Cairns illustrates this notion:

An example of an interpretive convention which seems to find its explanation in perceptual properties of speech is the universal tendency for high front vowels to be unrounded and high back vowels to be rounded. Jakobson argues that flatness (lip-rounding) is marked for acute non-compact vowels, and unmarked for grave non-compact vowels, because flatness and gravity are what he calls 'tonality features,' which tend to reinforce each other when they have the same value. When they are opposite valued they tend to obscure each other.

The connection of phonological simplicity with the physical and biological world in terms of general properties of sounds and of the human vocal apparatus is suggestive from the point of view of universal properties of phonological systems. In fact, the notion of simplicity might be equated with the idea of biological naturalness that arose in connection with prototypes.[25] If certain sound features and combinations of features are sim-

pler than others, in articulatory and acoustic terms, then these feature combinations may be considered prototypical for language in general, and it
may be expected that the feature combinations that produce such sounds
will be found in relatively many languages, whereas feature combinations
that yield complexities will be found in relatively fewer languages.[26] Cross-
linguistic studies of sound systems should provide evidence about which
phonemes are universally unmarked.

In addition to simplicity and universality, implicational universals are
also used as evidence of markedness relations. Consider again the example
of flatness in high front vowels that was discussed above. The well-known
fact that the presence of flat high front vowels (like /ü/) presupposes the
presence of nonflat high front ones (like /i/) suggests that nonflat is the
more basic feature value and that the feature flat (round), which distinguishes /ü/ from /i/, is marked in high front vowels.

Although Trubetzkoy took the position that phonological markedness
relations were ultimately language-particular phenomena,[27] the view of
phonological markedness as determined by universal laws seems to be basic
to Jakobson's view of phonological markedness, as well as to that of
Chomsky and Halle (1968) and Greenberg (1966). As we see from the following excerpt from *Fundamentals of Language,* Jakobson and Halle see
the optimality of features as being reflected through implicational universals found in acquisition, aphasia, frequency, and cross-linguistic phonological typology:

> The comparative description of the phonemic systems of manifold
> languages and their confrontation with the order of phonemic acqui-
> sitions by infants learning to speak, as well as with the gradual dis-
> mantling of language and of its phonemic pattern in aphasia, gives us
> important insights into the interrelationship and classification of the
> distinctive features. The linguistic, especially phonemic, progress of
> the child and the regression of the aphasic obey the same laws of
> implication. If the child's acquisition of distinction B implies his ac-
> quisition of distinction A, the loss of A in aphasia implies the absence
> of B, and the rehabilitation of the aphasic follows the same order as
> the child's phonemic development. *The same laws of implication un-
> derlie the languages of the world both in their static and dynamic
> aspects. The presence of B implies the presence of A, and correspond-
> ingly, B cannot emerge in the phonemic pattern of a language unless
> A is there; likewise, A cannot disappear from a language as long as B
> exists.* The more limited the number of languages possessing a certain
> phonemic feature or combination of features, the later it is acquired
> by the native children and the earlier it is lost by the native aphasics.
> [1971:38; emphasis added]

Implicit here is the idea that the optimality of sounds is basic: sounds are not optimal because they are learned early and universal, but rather they are learned early and universal because they are optimal.

Jakobson and Halle's remarks apply equally to features and to feature values. More basic features are superordinate to less basic ones. Languages will universally make use of the features high on the hierarchy, but some subordinate feature distinctions may or may not be implemented. The situation is parallel for unmarked and marked feature values: the unmarked feature values will be used by all languages employing a certain feature; however, some languages may choose not to use the marked value of a feature or to use it only in a limited way. So, for example, the feature nasal is often only employed to differentiate stops, and only more rarely does it distinguish vowels or fricatives.

The criteria of neutralization, syncretization, simplicity, and cross-linguistic optimality do not exhaust the proposals that have been advanced for determining phonological markedness values. They do, however, reflect the major proposals in the literature and illustrate the division of criteria into language-particular ones (neutralization, syncretization) and universal ones (simplicity, optimality). Parallels between phonological and semantic markedness are also apparent, though in phonology the criteria for markedness are oriented toward language-independent diagnostics much more than the criteria for semantic markedness are.

What of the criterion of indeterminateness that played such a major role in determining markedness values at the semantic level? This criterion is irrelevant in phonology, since phonological features have no semantic function other than to distinguish phonemes. It makes no sense for one phoneme to have a zero interpretation. Yet the conceptual indeterminacy of unmarked semantic elements finds a metaphorical analogue in the role of the unmarked phonological category as the basic value of a phonological opposition in positions of neutralization and in implicational statements. The unmarked value is the default value, the value that stands for the opposition itself.

The Phonological Features and Markedness Reversals in Phonology

Now it is time to be more specific about the nature of phonological features. Besides providing a brief introduction to the phonological features that will play a role in the discussion of English phonology in chapter 4, this section will also introduce the importance of context in determining markedness values, a theme that will also be raised with regard to semantic markedness in the next section.

In *Fundamentals of Language,* Jakobson and Halle elaborate a set of twelve distinctive features defined in both articulatory and acoustic terms, which they assert are central to the description of the world's phonemic systems. At the heart of the Jakobson and Halle feature system is their attempt to exploit typological facts in order to simplify the set of distinctive features needed to describe the languages of the world:

> The supposed multiplicity of features proves to be largely illusory. If two or more allegedly different features never co-occur in a language, and if they, furthermore, yield a common property that distinguishes them from all other features, then they are to be interpreted as different interpretations of the same feature, each occurring to the exclusion of the others, each presenting a particular case of complementary distribution. The study of invariances within the phonemic pattern of a given language must be supplemented by a search for universal invariances in the phonemic patterning of language in general. [1971:39 (1956)]

In a feature system, the traditional classification of sounds by such descriptors as labial, alveolar, fricative, affricate, plosive, high, mid, low, rounded, and so on is not only reduced to a more minimal descriptive framework, but the correspondences between vocalic and consonantal sounds are directly expressed since the same features are used for vowels and consonants. Listed below are the twelve features presented by Jakobson and Halle. I will briefly identify the traditional articulatory correspondents of each feature, focusing on the aspects of the definition that are most relevant to English phonology. For a fuller discussion of the articulatory and acoustic properties of each feature see Jakobson and Halle 1971:40–44 [1956]. For discussion of other feature systems, see Brakel 1984, Chomsky and Halle 1968, Donegan 1985 [1978], Ladefoged 1971, and Lass 1984.

Jakobson and Halle Distinctive Features

Sonority features
1. vocalic/nonvocalic
2. consonantal/nonconsonantal
3. nasal/oral (or nasalized/nonnasalized)
4. compact/diffuse
5. abrupt/continuant
6. strident/nonstrident (mellow)
7. checked/unchecked
8. voiced/voiceless

Protensity features
9. tense/lax

Tonality features
10. grave/acute
11. flat/nonflat
12. sharp/nonsharp   [1971:40-44]

Of these twelve features, the first three require no special comment. Vowels are vocalic and nonconsonantal; the nasals and the obstruent consonants are consonantal and nonvocalic. Liquid consonants and glides may be classified by combining the remaining feature values: liquids are vocalic and consonantal, and glides are nonvocalic and nonconsonantal. This classificatory scheme is summarized below:

(11) | | Vocalic | Consonantal |
|---|---|---|
| Vowels | + | − |
| Liquids | + | + |
| Glides | − | − |
| Obstruent consonants and nasals | − | + |

The opposition compact/diffuse opposes "forward-flanged" and "backward-flanged" segments, the former constituting low (or "wide") vowels along with velar and palatal consonants, and the latter constituting high ("close") vowels and labial, dental, and alveolar consonants. Jakobson and Halle point out that in vowel systems the compact/diffuse opposition is sometimes split into two separate features, compact/noncompact and diffuse/nondiffuse, a split which is necessary in order to distinguish three heights of vowels:

(12) | | Compact | Diffuse |
|---|---|---|
| High vowel | − | + |
| Mid vowel | − | − |
| Low vowel | + | − |

The opposition abrupt/continuant opposes a rapid closure or opening of the vocal tract to the absence of such a rapid turning on or off. Plosive or stop consonants like /p/, /t/, /k/, /b/, /d/, and /g/ and affricate consonants like /ǰ/ and /č/ are abrupt; fricative consonants like /f/, /v/, /θ/, /ð/, /s/, /z/, /š/, and /ž/ are continuant (or nonabrupt), as are all vowels.

The opposition strident/mellow opposes "rough-edged" consonants with a high-intensity noise to "smooth-edged" low-intensity consonants.

Labiodental, sibilant, and uvular fricatives are strident; labial, interdental, and velar fricatives are mellow.

Checked/unchecked opposes the presence of the compression of the glottis to the absence of compression. The feature checked is implemented in glottalized, implosive or click consonants, and hence plays a marginal role in a discussion of English phonology.

Voiced/voiceless opposes the periodic vibration of the vocal cords to the lack of such vibration. The consonants /b/, /d/, /g/, /ǰ/, /v/, /z/, /d/, /ž/ are (redundantly) voiced, as are vowels, sonorant consonants, and glides.

Tense/lax opposes a longer and stronger articulation to a shorter and weaker one. Long vowels and fortis or aspirated consonants are tense; short vowels and lenis or unaspirated consonants are lax. The English consonants /b/, /d/, /g/, /ǰ/, /v/, /z/, /d/, /ž/ are lax, while /p/, /t/, /k/, /č/, /f/, /s/, /θ/, and /š/ are tense.

Grave/acute opposes a peripheral articulation and concentration of energy in the low frequencies (as in labial and velar consonants and back vowels) to a medial articulation with a concentration in higher frequencies (as in palatal and dental consonants and front vowels).

Flat/nonflat opposes "narrowed-slit" phonemes to "wider-slit" ones. Flatness results in a velarization, pharyngealization, retroflection, and labialization, and in English is associated with rounded vowels as opposed to unrounded ones.

Sharp/nonsharp opposes phonemes produced with a "dilated back orifice (pharyngeal pass)" to those without such dilation. The result is that sharp phonemes carry a secondary palatalization.

The purpose thus far has been to introduce the features and their correlates with traditional articulatory features. Let us now turn to the question of the markedness relations of the phonological features. Two considerations are important with respect to phonological markedness relations: context sensitivity and universality. With respect to the first, it is important to recognize the markedness relations between phonological features are contextual in nature; the markedness values of phonological features are not immutable within a phonological system, but instead are determined according to the co-occurring features of a phoneme (its simultaneous context) and according to the surrounding phonetic environment (its sequential or syllable-structure context). To see an example of simultaneous context, let me reiterate the earlier example of the voiced/voiceless opposition. Most linguists take the feature value voiced to be unmarked in vowels and sonorants but marked in obstruents. Conversely, the feature value voiceless is unmarked in obstruent consonants but marked in vowels and sonorants.[28]

The markedness value of a feature can also be affected by sequential context—by the features of neighboring sounds. For example, although the

consonant /t/ is a relatively unmarked consonant in any analysis of markedness relations, there are contexts in which the occurrence of /t/ would be
quite unusual and unexpected (for example, adjacent to /d/, /l/, or another
/t/). In such contexts, features of /t/ that are unmarked in isolation may be
evaluated as marked.

A further contextual factor is syllable structure. Just as the syntax of
a sentence can affect the markedness values of grammatical categories, so
too can the structure of syllables play a role in determining a sound's
markedness value.

Implicit here is the idea that what is optimal for one subsystem might
be nonoptimal for another. One plausible reason for such variation is the
connection between optimality and a feature's ability to heighten other feature contrasts. Thus, for some features inherent acoustic or articulatory
properties are such that their optimal values in a vocalic context are the
reverse of their optimal value in the perceptually opposite (consonantal)
context. This is the case with voicing in vowels, for example. We might
expect to find a reversal in cases where complementarity of values enhances
contrasts. Waugh emphasizes the role of feature values in maintaining perceptual contrasts and the role of context in determining markedness value:

> If we turn to the phonological system *per se,* it is evident that the
> system—at least in its most basic patterning—is founded on the uni-
> versal and perceptually most prominent distinction consonant-vowel.
> As a first approximation, one may say that non-marks tend to be
> those values of features which enhance this opposition, while marks
> tend to be those which attenuate it. Thus, for example, the feature of
> nasality is a mark in the consonants since it brings the consonants
> perceptually closer to the vowels (by prolonging the consonant . . .);
> it is also a mark in the vowels since it brings them closer to the con-
> sonants. . . . Likewise the feature of continuancy is a mark in the
> consonants since it makes the consonants more vowel-like. [1979:156]

Later in the same article she adds (1979:157):

> One aspect of markedness which has been pointed out is its "context-
> sensitivity." . . . It is not at all the case that a given value of a given
> feature is always the marked one, but rather that it depends on the
> rest of the context (i.e., the bundle, the *Gestalt*) in which the given
> feature occurs. One major such context in phonological systems is the
> difference between consonants and vowels: in the vowels diffuseness
> (high vowels) is the mark, while in the consonants compactness (back
> consonants) is the mark. . . . Other contexts define other sub-systems

of phonological systems: e.g., in the compact (back) consonants, acuteness (palatality) is the mark, while in diffuse (front) consonants, gravity (labiality) is the mark.

We may speak, in such cases, of "markedness reversals," of the "switching" of the weighting from one pole to the other of the opposition as it enters into various combinations. Thus, one cannot simply talk about markedness in isolation. [ibid.:157]

Reversals are not limited to switches conditioned by the division of sounds into vowels and consonants.[29] Recall my earlier discussion of the optimality of flatness in noncompact vowels. Among high and mid vowels, the markedness value of lip rounding (flatness) is commonly viewed as reversed according to whether the vowel in question is grave (back) or acute (front). Thus, among nonlow vowels, front unrounded vowels are considered to be unmarked with respect to front rounded vowels, but back rounded vowels are unmarked with respect to back unrounded ones. The division between front and back reverses the optimality of the feature rounded/unrounded.

We can expect therefore to find that the markedness values of features undergo reversals in particular phonological contexts. The extent of such phonological markedness reversals remains to be determined, and various proposals have been made for the markedness values of phonological features. See the hierarchies encoded in Chomsky and Halle 1968, Cairns 1969, Shapiro 1972, Jakobson and Waugh 1979, Kean 1980 [1975], Gamkrelidze 1975, and Brakel 1984; for discussion of markedness hierarchies with specific reference to syllable structure, see Bailey (1973, 1977, 1978), Cairns and Feinstein 1982, and Cairns (1986, 1988).

A second important point to be made regarding phonological markedness has to do with universality. It is commonly assumed in studies of phonological markedness that markedness values and the hierarchy of phonological features are universals of language, having their basis in general properties of acoustics, articulation, and perception. There is, however, an alternative view of phonological markedness in which markedness relations can be language-internal, language-particular, evaluations of phonological categories.

As has already been pointed out, the language-particular status of markedness relations was first emphasized by Trubetzkoy in his phonological studies.[30] But Trubetzkoy was, of course, also sensitive to the existence of phonological universals, and his perspective on markedness suggests a potential unification of universal and language-particular approaches. Discussing the oppositions between fortis and lenis, heavy and light, voiceless and voiced, aspirated and unaspirated, infraglottal and recursive, and explosive and injective sounds, which he collectively referred to as "correlations based on the manner of overcoming an obstruction of the second degree," Trubetzkoy says,

> The question whether the "strong" or the "weak" opposition member of a correlation . . . is unmarked can, in the final analysis, be determined objectively only from the functioning of the particular phonemic system. However, in any correlation based on the manner of overcoming an obstruction a "natural" absence of marking is attributable to that opposition member whose production requires the least deviation from normal breathing. The opposing member is then of course the marked member. From this general or "natural" point of view the marked member in the correlation of tension is the fortis consonant, in the correlation of intensity the heavy consonant, in the correlation of aspiration the aspirated member. . . . Only in cases where the given phonemic system contains direct proof for another ("unnatural") distribution of markedness or unmarkedness of the opposition members can this "natural" way of evaluation be ignored. [1969:146–47]

Trubetzkoy's comments suggest that he saw the evaluation of oppositions to be both language-particular and universal. The cross-linguistic solidarity of sound systems leaves no doubt that universal nonequivalences are grounded in an inherent system and that phonological oppositions possess a natural ranking in terms of their inherent characteristics. But the facts of a particular language may override cross-linguistic naturalness, and the evaluation of an opposition in a given language may in some cases differ from the cross-linguistic norm. So while phonological markedness values of specific languages can be expected to often correspond to the universal norms, this need not always be the case. Trubetzkoy's insightful comment gives us both a good working principle for unclear cases and a reminder that cross-linguistic norms are not sufficient to determine markedness in every instance.

Markedness Reversals in Semantics

In the previous section I introduced the idea that markedness values of phonological features can be reversed in certain contexts. Such reversals are not limited to phonological features, however. Reversals at the lexical and grammatical levels also show the contingent nature of markedness. Recall that in the first section of this chapter the example *male nurse* was given as an instance of a reversal of markedness at the lexical level. Why, we must ask, does *nurse* become the unmarked item and *male nurse* the marked term? In contrast to phonological reversals, which appear to be motivated by acoustic and articulatory considerations, lexical markedness reversals are motivated by the connection between the semantic features of lexical items and the cultural importance, prototypicality, or frequency of their referents. Semantic markedness reversals are a locus of "real world" influence on linguistic structure: markedness values reverse when a marked term's referent comes to be the expected or general member of an opposition and the unmarked term's referent becomes the unexpected. When this happens, the feature value distinguishing the marked element becomes the new unmarked value, reversing its previous status. In the example cited above, then, the facts of sex differentiation in occupations are such that our expectations are for nurses to be women; male nurses are the exception to the rule, so they stand out as figure to ground.

Markedness reversals are sometimes treated as evidence of linguistic changes in progress. Stanley Witkowski and Cecil Brown (1983) in particular emphasize the role of cultural importance in markedness values, giving several examples in which the introduction of previously unknown referents, such as new domestic plants and animals, have led to shifts in cultural importance and hence to lexical changes in formal marking. One of their examples deals with Tenejapa Tzeltel, a Mayan language spoken in Mexico. In this language lexical markings have reversed in the words referring to deer (native) and sheep (which were introduced into Mayan culture). At the time of the Spanish conquest, the word for deer was *čih*. When sheep were introduced into the culture they were referred to as *tunim čih* 'cotton deer'. The markedness values assigned to these items have reversed, however, due to the increased cultural importance of sheep. Today the Tenejapa term for sheep is the unmarked *čih,* and the term for deer is *te?tikil čih* 'wild sheep'. The cultural importance of the sheep to the Tenejapa Tzeltels, who live in the highlands of the state of Chiapas, where sheep and the manufacture of woolen products are common, is contrasted by the situation in Bachajon Tzeltel, which is spoken in the lowlands, where sheep are uncommon. In Bachajon Tzeltel, deer are still referred to as *čih* and sheep are still referred to by the compound 'cotton deer'. Witkowski and Brown sum up their discussion of this and other examples by suggesting a connection between frequency of use and formal marking:

> The marking principles discussed above underlie these reversals. Thus an increase in the cultural importance of a referent typically leads to

an increase in the frequency of the label for that referent in everyday speech. Increased frequency in turn leads to simplicity of form, through label abbreviation or substitution. As cultural importance changes, lexical marking-values change. . . . [1983:575]

Markedness reversals occur not only in the coding of lexical oppositions as in the above examples, but in the evaluation of grammatical oppositions as well. Both linguistic context (syntax, semantics, discourse) and cultural expectations can occasion differences of evaluation of such grammatical features as animate/inanimate and singular/plural. Michael Silverstein (1976), for example, has argued that the markedness of the animate/inanimate opposition depends on whether nouns are subjects or objects. Since subjects are typically agentive and volitional, animate is the unmarked value for subjects; but since direct objects are more often affected patients of an action, inanimate is the unmarked value for objects (cf. Silverstein 1976, Bates and MacWhinney 1982, van Langendonck 1986).

Grammatical markedness reversals conditioned by cultural context are also discussed by Peter Tiersma (1982), who introduces a useful terminological distinction between general markedness values (the markedness values that categories exhibit in general in a language) and local markedness values (reversals of the general markedness relations). He suggests that reversals of markedness values in grammar can be characterized by aspects of real-world context that cause the usually marked term to be the more typical one. Tiersma's clearest example concerns the opposition singular/plural. While the plural is generally marked and the singular generally unmarked, Tiersma found that nouns whose referents "naturally occur[ ] in pairs or groups" or that are "generally referred to collectively" (1982:835) exhibit characteristics associated with unmarked values in the plural rather than the singular. He designates such nouns as having a reversed local markedness relation as distinguished from the general markedness relationship that exists between singular and plural in other types of nouns. Treating unmarkedness as revealed through historical and synchronic dominance, Tiersma shows, for example, that locally unmarked plurals are used as base forms in borrowing situations and in generalizations found in child language. In the general case, the singular forms have these dominant functions. Furthermore, in situations in which different singular and plural base forms are leveled out by analogy, locally unmarked nouns differ from the general case in that leveling favors the plural stem; for generally marked nouns, leveling favors the singular stem.

Tiersma provides another nice example from the language Frisian. The first set of forms below illustrates the general leveling process, in which the singular stem is extended to the plural; the second set of forms illustrates leveling in favor of the plural stem. For words that come in pairs or groups, then, the general markedness of singular and plural is reversed: plural is locally unmarked and singular is marked.

(13)   General Markedness

Conservative Dialect	Innovative Dialect	Gloss
(sg/pl)	(sg/pl)	
hoer/hworren	hoer/hoeren	'whore'
koal/kwallen	koal/koalen	'coal'
miel/mjillen	miel/mielen	'meal, milking'
poel/pwollen	poel/poelen	'pool'

(14)   Local Markedness

Conservative Dialect	Innovative Dialect	Gloss
(sg/pl)	(sg/pl)	
earm/jermen	jerm/jermen	'arm'
goes/gwozzen	gwos/gwozzen	'goose'
hoarn/hwarnen	hwarne/hwarnen	'(animal horn'
hoas/vjazzen	vjazze/vjazzen	'stocking'
kies/kjizzen	kjizze/kjizzen	'tooth'
spoen/spwonnen	spwon/spwonnen	'shaving, splinter'
toarn/twarnen	twarne/twarnen	'thorn'
trien/trjinnen	trjin/trjinnen	'tear'

As we see, forms in which the singular stem is leveled out in favor of the plural are consistent with Tiersma's principle.

Markedness reversals in lexical and grammatical structure further confirm the contingent nature of evaluation. In addition, reversals in semantics and in phonology illuminate the connection between markedness and foregrounding. Reversals occur when, for biological, cultural, or social reasons, some feature becomes dominant in a certain context, though in other contexts the feature is evaluated in the opposite way. But why do markedness values differ in different contexts? The evaluation of categories depends largely on the real-world properties of the referents of features. Social, cultural, and biological facts—such as sex differentiation in occupations in the case of *nurse* versus *male nurse,* occurrence in groups or pairs in locally unmarked plurals, typical discourse function of grammatical features in the animate versus inanimate distinction, cultural utility in the lexical opposition between deer and sheep, acoustic and articulatory properties in phonology—all play a role in the evaluation of features. Elements that are usual in a particular context—elements that are frequent and natural enough in that context to function as a conceptual background and therefore to serve as best examples of category—are likely to be unmarked elements in the context in question.

Differences between semantic markedness and phonological markedness arise in the factors that determine how a category is evaluated. In phonology a feature will be expected (in a particular context) if it is the acoustically or articulatorily natural choice in that context. These are physical factors rooted in the biology of articulation and sound perception. In the lexicon and perhaps also in grammar, a category's evaluation is based more on use and convention than on biology. A feature will be unmarked in part because it is the prototypical choice in a context; but which element is prototypical in the lexical and grammatical oppositions will depend to some degree on the background of social, cultural, and discourse expectations.

Social, cultural, and biological influences may not influence the different levels of language structure equally. Given its connection with social and cultural influences, semantic markedness can be expected to vary from cross-linguistic tendencies more than phonological markedness does. Conversely, phonological relations, which are rooted in the biology of speech production and perception, should be expected to exhibit less language-particular variability. Of course we should not rule out the possibility that some aspects of semantic markedness follow from biological principles of language structure, but it should be kept in mind that many aspects of semantic evaluation can be influenced by social and cultural factors. A useful terminological distinction will be to distinguish markedness as universal or as language-particular with the understanding that these terms may coincide, though they need not. Universal markedness relations are defined independent of individual languages. Language-particular values are those assigned on the basis of the facts of an individual language system.

Syntactic Markedness

Thus far I have treated the markedness of grammatical and morphological categories as part of semantic markedness. In this, I am adhering to the conception of language in which the basic division is between expression (sounds and sequences of sounds) and meaning. According to such a view, the markedness of a grammatical category is determined by its semantic relation to opposed categories in the language, and syntactic markedness is purely a derivative of semantic markedness. In such a framework, the term *syntactic markedness* might be a useful synonym for *formal marking,* used to refer to syntactic or morphological structures that are augmentations or permutations of other more basic structures: the idea would be that structures expressing unmarked categories will tend to be syntactically unmarked; those expressing marked categories will tend to be syntactically marked (cf. chap. 3).

The term *syntactic markedness* is, however, used in the literature in another sense, one in which a universal syntactic hierarchy is posited parallel to the universal phonological hierarchy. In this sense *syntactic markedness* refers to a language-independent ranking of syntactic constructs (rules, categories, constraints, etc.). Cross-linguistic markedness can be defined in several different ways. Chomskyan linguistics has developed notions of syntactic markedness embedded within the technical proposals of recent theories of Universal Grammar. In addition, there are approaches to syntactic markedness within a more general descriptive typology of language. A strong theory of universal markedness is proposed by Fred Eckman, who adopts a cross-linguistic definition of "typological markedness" (both syntactic and phonological): "A is typologically marked relative to B (and B is typologically unmarked relative to A) if and only if every language that has A also has B but not every language that has B also has A" (1977:320). Eckman's proposal parallels Greenberg's suggestion that

> whenever a statement of one of the above five types [neutralization, frequency, variability, syncretization, and independence] can be put in terms of a universal implication, it is the unmarked member which is the implied or basic term and the marked which is the implying or secondary. [1966:60]

Of course both Eckman's and Greenberg's suggestions have their origins in Jakobson's study of phonological universals. However, Greenberg also advances a weaker definition of cross-linguistic syntactic markedness. In his discussion of markedness in grammar and the lexicon, he equates markedness of grammatical categories with a convergence of criteria in a substantial number of languages, implying that the universally unmarked category will be that which has unmarked status in a wide number of languages:

> the evidence for the marked or unmarked character of a number of generic grammatical categories will not be considered. It will appear that the various criteria tend to converge in a large number of cases so that particular categories can be said to be marked or unmarked on a cross-linguistic basis. [1966:32]

In this weaker view, the syntactically unmarked category would be that which has unmarked status in a sufficiently wide number of languages.

Note that both the weak and the strong view allow the possibility that the universally marked element might be unmarked with respect to a particular language. We shall return to this possibility in chapter 4.

A related, though technically more opaque, development of syntactic markedness can be found in the syntactic theory associated with Noam Chomsky's recent work. The current Government and Binding framework emphasizes the role of innate principles and parameters of Universal Grammar as an explanation of linguistic data and a characterization of the problem of language acquisition. Acquisition is modeled as an idealized mapping of data to modular grammars, and the rapidity and uniformity of language acquisition is attributed to the richness of innate knowledge and the paucity of language-particular choices.

Within generative syntax different conceptions of markedness can be distinguished, as Nina Hyams has observed:

> As typically conceived, the theory of markedness is a function which maps linguistic data onto a particular grammar. That is to say, the theory specifies the "least marked" or "most highly valued" grammar consistent with the data of a particular language. If we consider only the final state achieved, i.e., the adult grammar, the relationship between acquisition and the theory of markedness is straightforward; the particular adult grammar is taken to be the least marked or most highly valued grammar consistent with the data. [1986:156–57]

The theory of markedness described in the above quote was first introduced to generative linguistics as the epilogue to Chomsky and Halle's *Sound Pattern of English* (1968) and imported to syntax in Lakoff's *Irregularity in Syntax* (1970). In the Standard Theory and Extended Standard Theory versions of generative grammar, markedness was sometimes associated with an evaluation metric to select the correct grammar for a language. Markedness was, in effect, a complexity hierarchy among grammars for different languages.[31]

Recent generative grammar has put aside the concept of evaluation metric in favor of a "principles and parameters" approach to grammar selection, and Hyams observes that some proposals, such as those of Alain Rouveret and Jean-Roger Vergnaud (1980:196, n. 71) and Edwin Williams (1981:8) now associate markedness with degrees of difference from the initial state of the language acquisition sequence, in other words, with the child's initial hypotheses about language. Hyams also points out a second way of viewing markedness within the Chomskyan tradition. In this view, which is suggested by Chomsky and Howard Lasnik (1977), unmarkedness is associated with a set of adult "core grammars" that are made available biologically. Markedness is the relation of a particular construction in a language to the core grammar of that language, where the core grammar is one of the systems defined by Universal Grammar. This assumes that actual grammars of languages may differ somewhat from the core grammars provided by Universal Grammar. This area of difference will be that of marked constructions. A particular language will consist of both unmarked (core) constructions and marked (peripheral) ones. Hyams comments:

> The view of markedness outlined above is closely related to the distinction made within Government-Binding Theory between "core" and "peripheral" grammar (Chomsky, 1981). Core grammar is defined as the grammar which results from fixing the parameters of UG in one or another of the permitted ways. Peripheral processes are those which involve an extension or relaxation of some principle of core grammar. . . . a rule or construction is identified as marked on strictly formal grounds; that is, by virtue of its relationship with (or distance from) principles of Core Grammar. To the extent that different languages have different core grammars (within obvious limits), markedness is a relative notion. [1986:160]

No one approach to markedness in generative grammar can be singled out. On the one hand there is a universalist view in which markedness is part of an evaluation metric determining the distance of a grammar from a cross-linguistic ideal or in which markedness is a grammar's distance from the initial state given by Universal Grammar. On the other hand, there is the core grammar view, which links language-particular and universalist elements and which defines markedness as the distance of a construction in the actual grammar of a language from the core grammar for that language.

Since the primary focus of this book is on markedness as a language-particular phenomenon and on its manifestation in English, universal markedness schemes will not be a major concern.[32] The promise of these approaches is a better understanding of cross-linguistic hierarchies in syntax and of the correlation of various syntactic properties within a language.

The notion of relative markedness associated with the distinction between core and periphery in generative grammar is of potential relevance to the language particular markedness values we are interested in. Of course, core grammar is a matter of current research and debate rather than a fixed body of knowledge, so syntactic markedness defined as difference from the core is difficult to test. I should point out, however, that the diagnostics of markedness given by Chomsky and Lasnik (1977) and by Lydia White (1982:95ff.) overlap with the classical view of marked categories as less broadly defined. Chomsky and Lasnik, for example, characterize marked rules of grammar as "the syntactic analogue of irregular verbs." And White gives the grammatical diagnostics of marked rules and constructions as irregularity, exceptionality, complexity, and nongenerality, which are similar in spirit to Greenberg's criteria; she also equates unmarked constructions with those that are "most common" (1982:101).

A Theory of Markedness

Before turning in the next chapter to the grammatical structure of English, I will summarize the main lines of discussion that have emerged so far.

In what we may call its classical version, markedness is an asymmetry in the evaluation of conceptual and phonological oppositions, and hence of the categories that oppositions define. It is a nonequivalence of structure that is imposed by both culture and biology on every linguistic sign—that is, on every unit and context of phonology or semantics. Every element has a markedness value with respect to opposed categories.

It is worth reemphasizing that in the Prague School framework, which was the precursor to the classical version, markedness was defined as an axiomatic structural relation between terms of an opposition such that

> the general meaning of the marked category states the presence of a certain (whether positive or negative) property A; the general meaning of the corresponding unmarked category states nothing about the presence of A, and is used chiefly, but not exclusively, to indicate the absence of A. [Jakobson 1984:47]

Translating this relation into specifics having to do with the material side of language, I have analyzed certain criteria for diagnosing markedness values that, taken together, reveal the dominant nature of the unmarked term as opposed to its marked counterpart. The criteria are similar to those used to define markedness relations in the work of Greenberg and others. First is the semantic indeterminateness of the unmarked term, a criterion which shows up as a broader, enveloping meaning. Second is that the unmarked category frequently serves as the prototype, or best example of an opposition. Third is that the unmarked is often revealed through its greater freedom of distribution or use, a freedom which is *sometimes* manifest as occurrence in positions of neutralization. This criterion, however, remains to be clarified.

A fourth criterion is syncretization: the unmarked sometimes shows a larger number of subcategorial distinctions, though this is not a perfect test. The fifth criterion is that the unmarked semantic category is often signaled by formal simplicity, though it has been pointed out that the tendency for the unmarked element to be formally simpler cannot be taken as a fully reliable test of unmarkedness. The final criterion is cross-linguistic optimality. The unmarked may be revealed by the status of a feature as the implied in implicational universals, though this criterion is mainly useful at the phonological level, where there seems to be less potential for mismatch between universal and language-particular evaluation (and perhaps where the set of oppositions is better understood as well).

It should be noted that determining markedness values by such criteria allows us to extend the application of the concept of markedness in certain ways. While a strict Jakobsonian framework takes oppositions to be uniformly privative and assigns markedness values in conjunction with the reduction of categories into features, expanding the criteria allows us to explore markedness relations between opposed elements without committing ourselves to a complete semantic analysis in every case.

These criteria provide a powerful and global means, though not an infallible one, to determine the evaluation of opposition. In exploring these criteria, the organization or markedness values—their patterning—has come to center stage as well. We have seen that markedness values are relative to background context within a language and that what is marked in one context may be unmarked in another. And we have seen that markedness can be construed as a language-particular relation or a universal one.

I conclude this section, and this chapter, with a summary of the ideas that have emerged so far:

(15)   a. In its Prague School version, semantic markedness is a relation between features whereby the marked feature signals the presence of a property and the unmarked feature signals either its absence or has a more general interpretation covering both terms of the opposition. Phonological markedness is the relation between the presence and absence of a phonological property.

          b. In many later versions, markedness is extended to apply to relations where the oppositions are not strictly privative— that is, not strictly of the form A/not A.

          c. The more broadly defined nature of the unmarked term is revealed by heuristics such as indeterminateness, prototypicality, neutralization, syncretization, complexity, and optimality.

d. Markedness values can be determined by factors intrinsic to the biology of language and can be determined by social and cultural factors.

e. Since different systems may impose different evaluations on concepts and categories, markedness values may vary cross-linguistically and they may change over time.

f. Since context can determine evaluation, markedness values may be contextually reversed within a language.

3

Markedness Principles and the Values of Grammatical Categories

Introduction: The Alignment of Units and Contexts

In the last chapter we saw that markedness relations are sometimes reversed within the subdivisions of language structure and use. In the present chapter, we will consider the contingent nature of markedness from another structural perspective, elaborating the markedness values of the features that characterize some areas of English grammar and advancing the thesis that these values are to some degree organized by principles of markedness assimilation and complementarity.

The principle of markedness complementarity will be introduced below. I begin the discussion in this chapter with the broader principle of markedness assimilation. Markedness assimilation proposes an overall coherence between the markedness values of linguistic units and the markedness values of their contexts. The effect of markedness assimilation is that marked units will tend to be found in marked contexts and, conversely, that unmarked units will tend to be found in unmarked contexts. Just as inherent perceptual properties, prototypical communicative function, and cultural importance can reverse markedness values, linguistic or sociolinguistic contexts also affect the distributions of marked and unmarked units by markedness assimilation. The relevant linguistic contexts for markedness assimilation can be any contextual opposition in which a markedness relation can hold: syntactic contexts such as subject versus object, prenominal position versus postnominal position, subordinate versus main clause; semantic contexts such as subjunctive mood versus indicative, positive versus negative, interrogative versus noninterrogative; and sociocultural contexts such as style of speech (formal vs. colloquial, informal vs. colloquial) or the lexical status of an item (specialized items vs. common ones, infrequent items vs. frequent ones).

Markedness assimilation represents a sharpening of the criterion of neutralization discussed in the last chapter. Recall that an important distributional criterion of the unmarked was occurrence in positions of neutralization. Markedness assimilation refines this criterion by connecting neutralization to context: in unmarked contexts, the expected neutralization will be to the unmarked term; in marked contexts, the expected neutralization will be to the marked term.

The attenuation of neutralization in light of markedness assimilation is nicely illustrated in the following example from Henning Andersen, who first proposed the term *markedness assimilation:*

> in the marked subjunctive mood, the past vs. present opposition *(they knew* vs. *they know)* is neutralized, and the normally marked past tense is used to the exclusion of the present *(I wish they knew).* Here too, the number opposition *(they were* vs. *he was)* is neutralized, the normally marked member being used to the exclusion of the unmarked number *(I wish he were).* [1972:45, n.23]

The standard forms of the subjunctive use the past tense form: *If I were you, I'd get back to work.* Viewed in terms of markedness assimilation, the use of the past form as opposed to the present form in the subjunctive is an assimilation of the markedness of the past (vs. the present) to the markedness of the subjunctive (vs. the indicative). Similarly, the use of the plural rather than the singular is an assimilation of the markedness of the plural (vs. the singular) to the markedness of the subjunctive.

As a notational convention, I will represent the assimilation of marked units to marked contexts by a proportion or analogy, the opposition between marked (M) and unmarked (U) categories being designated by a single colon and the alignment (or misalignment, in some cases) of markedness values being indicated by double colons. Thus the representation

(1)   *were* (M number) : *was* (U) ::
         subjunctive (M mood) : indicative (U)

says that the relationship between the marked form *(were)* and the unmarked form *(was)* is aligned with the relationship of the marked subjunctive mood and the unmarked indicative. The representation

(2)   past form (M tense) : present form (U) ::
         subjunctive (M mood) : indicative (U)

likewise indicates that the markedness relation of the tense forms parallels the markedness relation of mood.

In cases of markedness assimilation the use of the marked form rather than the unmarked is a sign of the marked context. The markedness of an element—its value vis à vis its opposite—takes part in an overall diagramming of evaluative relationships between units and contexts: an evaluative superstructure, to use a term introduced by Michael Shapiro (1976). Markedness assimilation, and other principles to be discussed below, reflects the functional, semiotic side of the study of markedness. This aspect of markedness theory, pioneered by Henning Andersen and Shapiro, has as its goal to understand the role of markedness in the formal expression of conceptual relations. Put more simply, it is an inquiry into the role of markedness in the patterning between expression and meaning. One of the main ideas of this line of investigation is that language structure can be seen as iconic rather than arbitrary—that is, as motivated by resemblances between expression and meaning rather than as essentially unmotivated pairings of sounds and meanings. John Haiman describes the study of iconicity as exploring

> one kind of functional explanation for various aspects of linguistic form: that linguistic forms are frequently the way they are because, like diagrams, they resemble the conceptual structures they are used to convey; or that linguistic structures resemble each other because the different conceptual domains they represent are thought of in the same way. [1985:1]

As Haiman observes, these ideas are not new. In modern times, the notion of diagrammatic linguistic relations has its origins in the sign classification system of the American philosopher Charles Sanders Peirce, whose ideas were merged with structural linguistics first, it seems, in an address given by Jakobson to the American Academy of Arts and Sciences and published in *Diogenes* (1965).[1] Though Peirce classified signs into sixty-six different subtypes, the most fundamental and influential part of his system is the division of signs into icons, indexes, and symbols.[2] Icons show a factual resemblance between a sign and its object, such as the similarity between a color chip and the color it stands for; indexes show a factual contingency between sign and object, such as a weather vane as an index of the wind's direction or smoke as an index of fire; symbols reflect a conventional contiguity that does not depend on resemblance or factual contingency, such as the way in which the color red symbolizes the command "stop" in the context of a traffic signal.

Peirce subdivided iconic signs into a further triad that has also been influential in studies of linguistic signs: images, diagrams, and metaphors. These three types are distinguished by the way in which they iconically represent their objects. Images, according to Peirce, "partake of simple qualities" of their objects. Diagrams are those which represent the "relations, mainly dyadic, or so regarded, of the parts of one thing by analogous relations in their own parts." Metaphors are icons that "represent the representative character of a representamen [i.e., a sign] by representing a parallelism in something else" (1965–1966, vol. 2, sec. 227).

The program of treating language patterns in iconic terms that developed from this combined Peircean and Jakobsonian tradition has sought to reveal and demarcate the iconic motivation of linguistic form (in the sense described by Haiman) through studies of, among other things, conceptual closeness reflected in the closeness of verbal stems and affixes (Bybee 1985); linear order as a diagram of temporal order (Tai 1985); intonation as part of an iconic gestural system reflecting meanings (Bolinger 1985); the iconic relation between information structure (predictable information, typical semantic structures); and syntactic properties such as reduced expression, word order, and feature hierarchies (Givòn 1985).[3] Prague School markedness and principles, such as markedness assimilation, that grow out of it fit into this general study of iconism in language. Though markedness assimilation is a specific form of iconism (one in which the relations are markedness relations rather than conceptual relations), we shall see that it is a very general and flexible type of iconism, since markedness theory expands to include complementary diagrams that would fall outside the scope of strictly iconic approaches. An additional advantage of markedness-based approaches to iconism lies in the fact that markedness is a global property of relations, rather than a semantic or phonological quality itself. This globality makes it possible for diagrams to be stated between levels of language whose qualities would not ordinarily be comparable. By defining diagrams in terms of values rather than semantic or phonological qualities themselves the relation between levels of language can be examined.

The remainder of this chapter will be devoted to the establishment of markedness values for selected categories of English grammar and to an exploration of the types of markedness principles, diagrammatic and otherwise, that have been defined for treating grammatical structures as motivated systems of relations.

Case Oppositions

The next few sections analyze the nominal and pronominal categories of English in order to establish the markedness values of the nominal categories and their role in the overall structuring of units and contexts via markedness assimilation. While English distinguishes two basic types of declensions, nominal and pronominal, the nominal declension makes inflectional distinctions only with respect to number and case (common case and genitive), and hence will be of relatively minor interest. The pronominal declension, on which we will focus most of our attention, inflects pronouns for person, number, case, gender, animacy, and reflexivity.

Within the pronominal paradigms, each of these correlations exhibits the structural nonequivalence that is characteristic of markedness: one term of the opposition is always more broadly defined and its opposite relatively more focused and constrained. We shall see below that the meaning, function, and distribution of grammatical categories makes clear the markedness relationships among them and that these markedness relations reveal patterns which give a structural wholeness to units and contexts.

Nominative and Objective Cases

We may begin the discussion by considering the distinctions in the case system of English pronominals. English may be viewed as distinguishing four sets of overt case forms for pronouns (cf. Quirk and Greenbaum 1973:101): the objective case, the nominative case, and two types of genitive case, the "subjective" genitive forms (i.e., those that occur as the determiner of a following noun: *my, our,* etc.) and the "objective" genitive forms (those that occur after the head noun or where the head is deleted: *mine, ours,* etc.). In addition, the analysis of the infinitival and gerund constructions is simplified if a null pronoun is assumed to occur in those constructions *(Ø to win would be nice).* After Chomsky (1980), I take the null pronoun to be a caseless pronoun form.

In determining the markedness relations among the English case forms, the analysis of Russian cases developed by Jakobson is, unfortunately, of little direct help, since the number and interrelations among the English cases is fundamentally different from those of Russian. English, for example, possesses no morphologically distinct locative, dative, or instrumental cases, and the semantic and thematic relations expressed by case endings in Russian and other highly inflected languages are instead expressed in English by word order or by lexical items such as prepositions. So while the conceptual features of directionality, quantification, and marginality that characterize the Russian case system can be found in English (cf. Andrews 1984: chap. 7), their place is not necessarily in the case system.

In English the fundamental case opposition is between an unmarked objective case and a marked nominative case. Despite the intuitive primacy of the nominative as "the name of a noun," and despite the fairly general assumption that the nominative is universally unmarked,[4] the objective case is consistently more broadly defined than the nominative. On the one hand, the nominative indicates specifically the subjecthood of its referent; its functions as subject of a tensed clause (or nominative absolute) and as the complement of a predicate nominal bear out its "subjectness." The objective case, on the other hand, is unspecified for subjecthood: the objective can signal the object of a verb or a preposition or the subject of an infinitival. It can also serve, prescriptive shibboleths aside, as the subject of a gerund clause (as in *I disapprove of them building a reactor so near my home*), or as a predicate nominal *(It's me)*. Note that in both of the last examples, common colloquial usage appears to favor the objective case forms (cf. Quirk and Greenbaum 1973: 103, 311), rather than the more formal genitive and nominative forms.

   The stylistic aspect of the nominative/objective opposition is worth further discussion, as it illustrates the alignment of markedness values between units and discourse context that characterizes markedness assimilation.[5] The nominative, in addition to being marked for subjectness, is marked for formality of style. Use of the nominative in favor of the objective in constructions in which there is a choice (e.g., predicate nominal constructions and comparisons) specifically signals 'formal (correct) grammar' or 'prestige usage' as distinct from the unmarked colloquial usage. The assimilation of markedness relations can be represented by the generalization:

(3)   nominative (M case) : objective (U) ::
           formal (M style) : colloquial (U)

   The markedness of the nominative may also be what is appealed to in hypercorrect usages as *just between you and I*. The use of the nominative in compound noun phrases when a speaker is adopting the prestige style can be viewed as a markedness assimilation. In fact, the use of the nominative in such contexts shows an assimilation to grammatical context and to discourse context together. The assimilation of case to formal style has already been noted. In the colloquial style of speech, we generally find such expressions as *just between you and me*. Consciousness to "good grammar" can result in the incorrect substitution of the nominative for the objective in compound noun phrases. Assuming that compounds are a marked category (as opposed to noncompound noun phrases), what we have here is a markedness assimilation of nominative case to the combination of marked style and marked syntax.

The Genitive

   Taken together, the nominative and objective may be considered the direct cases, following classical usage. The genitive may be analyzed as marked for a feature of 'limitation' for which the direct cases are unspecified. The English genitive may be analyzed as being similar to the Russian genitive sketched by Jakobson (see chap. 2). The genitive signals the limitation of a referent's participation. A genitive pronoun (or noun) is only involved in the verbal predication in so far as it is connected with the head noun that it modifies. The direct cases, nominative and objective, on the other hand, give no indication of limitation of involvement. The genitive is the signalization of limitation; the direct cases are its nonsignalization.

The limited nature of the genitive is manifest in the somewhat narrowed range of nouns that occur in this case and, further, in the neutralization of the genitive to the objective in many instances.[6] The fact that the genitive is neutralized to the objective and not the nominative further confirms the unmarked status of the objective case. The neutralization of the genitive to the objective is manifest in two ways. One is the tendency for gerunds that are objects of verbs or prepositions to have either objective or genitive subjects, as, for example, in *I disapprove of your seeing her* and *I disapprove of you seeing her.* As Quirk and Greenbaum (1973:321) note, the variant with the genitive marking tends to be the more formal means of expression. As before, colloquial usage is signaled by objective case pronouns. Formality assimilates to the marked pronoun, confirming my earlier hypothesis:

(4)   genitive (M case) : objective (U) ::
        formal (M style) : colloquial (U)

The greater breadth of the objective versus the genitive is also shown by the fact that genitives tend to be either pronouns or animate (or animated) nouns. For strongly inanimate nouns, possession is usually indicated by an *of* plus objective construction or by bare noun used adjectivally. Compare, for example, (5) and (6):

(5)   his mother
        my book
        the man's hat
        the company's representative
        the university's policies
        ?the table's leg
        ?the door's handle

as opposed to

(6)   the representative of the company / the company representative
        the policies of the university / the university policies
        the leg of the table / the table leg
        the handle of the door / the door handle

In the first set of examples, genitives that are clearly inanimate are odd (as the prefixed question mark indicates); however if the genitive expression is animate (or refers to an entity such as a university or company that may be thought of as animate) the phrases seem more natural.[7] The second set of examples again illustrates the neutralization of the genitive in favor of a construction using the objective case. In these examples the broader function of the objective is revealed by its ability to express the possessive meaning of the genitive construction. The reverse is, of course, not true. In English, the genitive can never be used to express a purely objective case function (excluding instances of ellipsis, which will be discussed below).

As mentioned above, the genitive case is further divided by a correlation between the "subjective" genitive *(my book)* and the "objective" genitive *(a book of mine, That's mine)*. In this contrast, it is less clear as to which of the forms is more broadly defined, but an argument may be constructed that the subjective form enjoys the breadth of distribution and that the marked category is therefore the objective genitive. The objective genitive appears to carry with it a connotation of detachment lacked by the subjective genitive. Such examples as *I tried to collect my thoughts* and *John picked up his parents at the airport*, as contrasted with *I tried to collect thoughts of mine*, and *John picked up parents of his at the airport*, demonstrate one aspect of the semantic distinction between the two genitives: one signals the closeness of the relation while the other signals distance. The examples *parents of his* and *thoughts of his* are odd precisely because people are intrinsically connected to their parents and their thoughts. The oddness of the objective forms may be due to a separation of this intrinsic connection by using the objective genitive. It is not, however, obvious on the basis of such examples whether closeness or distance is the unmarked feature. Prototypicality might tempt us to view closeness as the unmarked feature since the subjective genitive is arguably the more prototypical form (using the case of body parts and family relationships as best examples of genitives). But this too is not fully convincing (since it could be that these forms are only prototypical for inalienable possession), and to decide the markedness values of the subjective and objective genitive forms it will be useful to have further evidence.

In addition to being able to signal the closeness of a relation, the subjective genitive also exhibits a potential ambiguity denied to the objective genitive. *Her picture* may mean either the picture that she owns or her image in a photograph or portrait. *A picture of hers*, on the other hand, has a narrower range of meanings. It can only mean 'a picture that she owns'. Here the additional meaning of the subjective genitive form must be rendered by an *of* plus objective case paraphrase: *a picture of her*. Similar examples are easy to find: *her son's loss, the policeman's arrest*, and so forth.

Besides having a broader semantic range, the subjective genitive also has a broader distribution in terms of word formation. Not only does it serve as the morphological base for the construction of the objective genitive forms in some instances *(yours, hers, ours, theirs)*, but it is also the base for the first and second person reflexive pronoun forms *(myself, ourselves, yourself, yourselves)*.[8] Here grammatical markedness correlates with formal marking: the marked objective forms are constructed by using the unmarked forms as a base. I conclude then that meaning, distribution, and form together suggest that the objective genitive forms are marked and the subjective genitive forms are unmarked.

(7)   Unmarked Subjective Forms   Marked Objective Forms

my	our	mine	ours
your	your	yours	yours
his		his	
her	their	hers	theirs
its		its	

Elliptical Contexts

My conclusions in the last section about subjective and objective forms of the genitive provoke a further inquiry into the markedness values of elliptical versus nonelliptical syntactic contexts. The subjective genitive forms are structurally determiners, occurring in complementary distribution with articles and demonstratives (as shown by the illformedness of structures with both genitives and other determiners: *my that hat*, *the his hat*, etc.). In addition to occurring postnominally as the object of the preposition *of*, objective genitives also occur in elliptical constructions like *That is your book and this is mine* and *Hers is on the table.* Such constructions may be analyzed as shown in (8) below, on the pattern of similar structures like *the richest* in which adjective modifies an elliptical noun.[9]

At this point, we may consider the status of the zero noun, to which we shall return in more detail below. As Jakobson pointed out in "Zero Sign" (1984:151–60 [1939]), languages frequently implement semantic oppositions not in a contrast between two overt signs, but in the contrast between something and nothing—between a zero sign and an overt one. At the level of word structure, for example, the zero sign is manifest as the lack of an inflection (in English, customarily an inflectional ending) to signal the opposite grammatical category from that signaled by some overt inflection. Singular nouns, for example, are indicated by a zero suffix that contrasts with the plural suffix -*s*. As Jakobson points out, zero signs also occur at the lexical level where zero forms of root morphemes (i.e., zero words) contrast with their phonologically realized forms. A common example of this is the null nominative pronoun of some Romance and

(8)

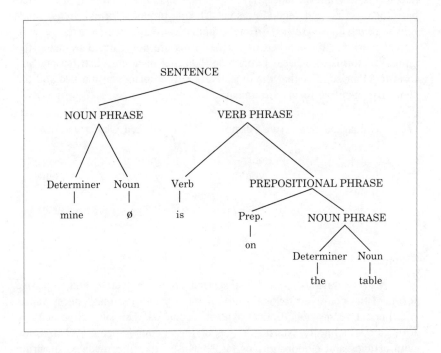

Slavic languages. In such languages as Spanish, Portuguese, Czech, and Polish, subject pronouns are freely omitted since the agreement inflection on the tensed verb indicates the grammatical features (person, number, gender) of the subject. The treatment of these zero pronouns is particularly interesting in that it is an area in which stylistic markedness values differ between languages. In Czech, for example, the stylistically neutral and hence unmarked form of the pronoun is the zero form; a phonologically overt pronoun signals emphasis. In Russian the reverse holds: phonologically realized forms are neutral and zero forms are marked for emphasis (cf. Jakobson 1984:156–57 [1939]). As noted in the last chapter, the alignment of unmarked/marked semantics and zero/nonzero form (formal marking) is a tendency subject to variability.

Returning now to the analysis of the zero element that occurs in construction with the objective genitive, we must ask why the pronoun left in ellipsis is the marked objective form rather than the unmarked subjective form. A possible answer is that we are dealing with a markedness assimilation. For this explanation to be convincing, we need to consider the contrast between elliptical noun phrases like [*mine Ø*] and nonelliptical ones like *[my book]*. Markedness assimilation implies that the elliptical variants are a marked context, since in that context the marked form replaces the unmarked. However, the assumption that ellipsis is marked as opposed to full forms is unlikely to be correct. As Fletcher (1985) has pointed out, the use of unmarked forms gives a continuity to discourse that is shown by the correlation of marked nominals with degree of topic shift and unmarked nominals with degree of topic continuity. Fletcher suggests that overt repetitions of nominals are marked as contrasted with ellipsis, and he proposes a scale of markedness correlated to degree of topic continuity. The contrast between elliptical noun phrases and nonelliptical ones can be viewed semantically as a contrast between reference to a noun phrase in the preceding linguistic context (or to a relevant topic in the real world situation) versus reference to something previously unmentioned or being reintroduced as the topic of discussion.

The question of markedness may then be recast in terms of the prototypical discourse situation. Is the typical discourse situation one of topic introduction of a topic continuation? A general answer to this question may not be possible since a prototypical discourse situation is probably impossible to define. We must treat the matter as a question of local evaluation, analyzing ellipsis as unmarked in the context of a shared topic and as marked in the context of topic shift or topic introduction. If so, then the zero pronoun of elliptical phrases like the following will be unmarked as opposed to the full noun phrases, since the first clause provides the appropriate context for topic continuity.

(9)   There were so many cars there that I had a hard time finding mine.
        John sent his parents on a cruise, and Sally gave hers a new car.
        I saw Bill's pictures of the wedding; now can I see yours?

The conclusion that the elliptical noun phrase construction is unmarked in such examples still raises an apparent problem with respect to the idea of markedness assimilation. If ellipsis is unmarked, why should the marked genitive forms be used rather than the unmarked ones? We should expect the unmarked forms and contexts to coincide. But while ellipsis is semantically unmarked in the above examples, it may not be the only factor that enters into the choice of pronouns. The critical factor in determining the selection of marked or unmarked genitives may instead lie in the typical use of the genitive as a modifier of a head noun. The unmarked genitive is chosen in the prototypical situation of modification—where the head is overtly present. In the atypical situations, in which the head is omitted and the genitive stands alone as a full noun phrase, the marked form occurs. If the opposition between 'occurring as part of a noun phrase' and 'occurring as a full noun phrase' is taken into account, then the choice of the objective forms in elliptical contexts can be viewed as a markedness assimilation, something like the following:

(10)   objective genitive (M case) : subjective genitive (U) ::
            use as a full noun phrase (M) : use as a modifier (U)

Another possible approach might be to interpret the marked genitive form as compensation for the unmarking (ellipsis) of the head noun. From the point of view of the concatenation of head nouns with genitive modifiers, both elliptical and nonelliptical constructions could be analyzed as a combining of a marked element and an unmarked one. However, it is not always clear how a particular opposition should be analyzed in terms of features and markedness. And the fact that the relevant opposition is not always apparent raises the possibility that markedness assimilation is neither a compulsory principle nor one that can be applied infallibly. These are issues that we will return to below.

Zero-Objective and Zero-Nominative Pronouns

We now turn our attention to a slightly different type of zero expression: the understood subject of infinitival and gerund clauses, the zero pronoun referred to in generative linguistics as PRO. PRO differs from the zero of ellipsis discussed above in both its conditions of occurrence and its interpretation: the zero of ellipsis replaces a noun (or sometimes a noun plus adjectival modifiers) and designates a specific referent outside its immediate clause. PRO, on the other hand, replaces a full noun phrase (a noun plus modifiers and determiners) and refers either anaphorically within its clause or arbitrarily. The two zero pronouns are distinct syntactic entities having distinct semantic properties and markedness values. The relevant opposition for understanding the zero of elliptical noun phrases is something like 'shared reference' versus 'new reference'. The context relevant for understanding PRO, on the other hand, is much more limited. The opposition between zero and overt noun phrases is restricted to positions in which the presence of objective case assignment is opposed to its absence—that is, to the subject position of a nonfinite clause. It is within that context that we must ask which form is the more broadly defined element. The following examples illustrate the opposition between PRO and overt noun phrases:

(11)   *Objective case positions without case marking*
            George expected [Ø to win]
            George enjoyed [Ø skiing]

(12)   *Objective case position with case marking*
George expected [himself to win]
George expected [him to win]

As contrasted with objective case pronouns or common case nouns that can occur in the same context, PRO is the conceptually unmarked element. In and of itself, PRO gives no clue as to its reference: its interpretation—whether it is arbitrary or controlled by an antecedent, and whether its controller is a higher subject or object—is determined by factors of the lexical and syntactic context (cf. Chomsky 1981, Manzini 1983). Thus, in *Mary promised George not to hurt herself*, PRO is controlled by the higher subject; in *Mary persuaded George not to hurt himself*, it is controlled by the higher object; and in *It is unclear what to do* and *Frightening oneself is no fun*, the referent is semantically equivalent to the arbitrary animate pronoun *one*. In such examples, replacement of PRO by an overt referent (where possible) would also result in a more narrowly focused meaning.

The broadly defined nature of the zero pronoun is further suggested in its relatively greater freedom of occurrence: PRO may occur generally in infinitival and gerund contexts (excluding those in which *for* immediately precedes and those governed by *believe*-type verbs). On the other hand, overt noun phrases require a *for* complementizer or the presence of what Chomsky calls exceptional case marking verbs.[10] Moreover, even in these contexts, the overt construction is sometimes quite marginal or ungrammatical, as in *It was fun for me to see you, John promised Mary for himself to visit*, or even *John wants himself to win*. I conclude then that in the contexts in which both are possible, PRO occurs more generally than objective noun phrases and is thus the unmarked element.

To the five case forms of English pronouns discussed so far, we might add a sixth: the zero pronoun that occurs in imperatives and in the reduced sentences (usually reduced questions such as *Going? Finished yet?*) of casual speech.[11] This zero element is not PRO, which is a zero-objective-case pronoun; the element in imperatives and reduced questions is rather a zero-nominative-case pronoun, differing from PRO in function (since the zero nominative signals grammatical mood or informal style) as well as in syntactic context. Unlike the zero objective, which functions as an unmarked case in opposition to the overt objective, the zero nominative may be treated as marked in opposition to the overt nominative,[12] which is the unmarked case for the subject of a finite clause in English. The markedness of the zero nominative may be treated as still another instance of markedness assimilation. The use of the zero nominative signals either imperative mood or casual style; the overt nominative, on the other hand, may be either indicative or imperative (cf. *You shut up!*) and may be either neutral or casual (cf. *You done yet?*). If we treat the imperative as a generally marked mood (Jakobson 1984), and if we assume that both very casual style and formal style are marked in contrast to a neutral colloquial style (cf. Shapiro 1986), then the restricted distribution of the zero nominative represents a markedness assimilation of mood to zero form and an assimilation of style to zero form. The fact that the zero nominative implements two distinct marked categories provides mutual reinforcement for the evaluation:

(13)   zero nominative (M) : overt nominative (U) ::
            casual (M style) : neutral (U)

(14)   zero nominative (M) : overt nominative (U) ::
            imperative (M mood) : indicative (U)

The distinction between the zero-objective and -nominative forms also provides us with a good example of a markedness complementarity in the context of the feature hierarchy. In the unmarked objective case subsystem, zero is unmarked and the overt case form is marked; in the marked nominative case subsystem, zero is marked and the overt case is unmarked. Just as we find reversals of markedness values in sequential contexts and in the context of cultural facts, we also find instances in which the form/content relation is reversed within a feature hierarchy.

The distinctions of the English case system are summarized in the hierarchy in (15) on the following page.

Reflexive versus Personal Pronouns

Like many other languages, English distinguishes personal forms of the pronouns from reflexive forms. While both personal and reflexive pronouns are pronominal categories, they differ in what are called their binding properties. Personal pronouns must be free (disjoint in reference) from other noun phrases in a certain domain, and reflexives must be bound (anaphorically related) to some noun phrases in (roughly) the same domain. See Chomsky (1982) for more details and an analysis of these categories in terms of features.

In the opposition between personal and reflexive pronouns, the reflexives are the marked member. Semantically they signal 'anaphoric relatedness' within a local syntactic domain as opposed to its nonsignalization in personal pronouns. The greater breadth of the personal forms is shown in their occasional use as bound forms in idiomatic expressions such as *Fred lost his cool* or *Mary craned her neck,* and in their use in place of reflex-

(15)

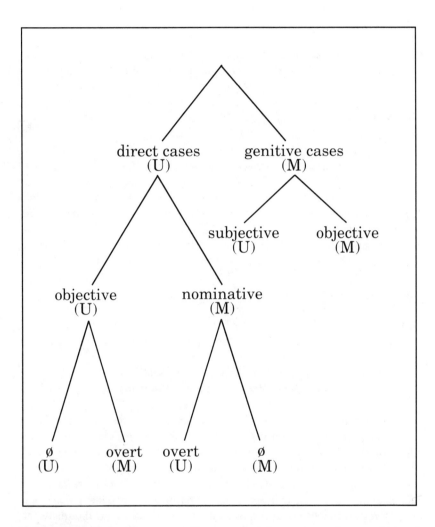

ives with certain locative prepositions, as in *John saw a snake near him* and *Sally had a gun on her.*

The narrowness of the reflexive is further pointed to by its distribution: reflexives do not occur as the subjects of tensed clauses. As is well known, there are no grammatical English sentences like **John believed himself was smart* or **One is unlikely to believe oneself is crazy.*

The markedness of the reflexive is revealed also in two markedness assimilations. I have already suggested that compound phrases are marked categories as opposed to noncompound ones. In compound expressions in formal style, we sometimes find the replacement of a personal pronoun with a reflexive in the first person singular. For example:

(16)   John and *myself* are going to the movies.
          Anyone interested should get in touch with Mary or *myself*.
          See Fred or *myself* about that.

The pattern is:

(17)   reflexive (M pronoun) : personal (U) ::
          compound (M syntax) : simple (U)

   Assimilation also occurs in the use of reflexives as emphatic forms: *Mary herself went to see the president* and *I saw the president himself*. The use of the reflexive as an emphatic is not uncommon cross-linguistically, and extensions of the reflexive to adverbial and emphatic status may be reinforced by the inherent specificity of the reflexive and its ability to signal a contrast.[13] Assuming the emphatic to be marked as opposed to the non-emphatic, we get the pattern:

(18)   reflexive (M) : personal (U) ::
          emphatic (M focus) : nonemphatic (U)

Singular and Plural in the Pronominal System:
The Markedness of Singular Pronouns

   With regard to the category of grammatical number, the singular is commonly taken to be unmarked and the plural to be marked (see Jakobson 1984:135 [1957]; Greenberg 1966:31ff.; Mayerthaler 1988:11 [1981]). This appears to be the correct analysis for nouns in general, given the ability of singular nouns to refer plurally, as, for example, in *The beaver builds dams* (see chap. 1). However, there is evidence that these markedness values undergo a reversal in the English personal pronoun system and that there the plural is the unmarked category and the singular is marked. The typical use of the personal pronouns points to the subsuming nature of the category of plurality and to the narrowness of singularity rather than the other way around. Plural pronouns may be thought of as 'unspecified for singularity' as opposed to singular pronouns, which are so specified.
   The clearest evidence for the unmarked status of the plural comes from the use of plural pronouns to refer to singular antecedents.[14] This is evident in all three categories of person, though in different ways. In the

first person, for example, we find the plural used to express group opinion, solidarity, or royalness, as in the editorial use of *we*, the hospital *we*, and the monarch's *we*. The singular use of *we* is also extended for some speakers in the South as a replacement for *I* in fixed expressions such as *We'll see you later*. In the third person, the unmarkedness of the plural is manifest by its ability to refer to indefinite singular antecedents in expressions like *Everyone should find their seat*. Here the use of the plural form *their* overlaps with that of the singular. It is worth noting that singular use of *their* has resisted more than two centuries of prescriptivist effort to replace it with the putatively more logical singular (see Bodine 1975), a fact that attests to the stability of this usage.

Next consider the second person, which in English has only one pronoun form, *you*. The unmarked nature of the plural is suggested by the structural fact that *you* is grammatically plural, not singular (as is demonstrated by agreement in examples like *You were alone, weren't you?*). The semantic opposition between singular and plural lacks a singular form, and the unmarked plural form expresses both the singular and plural meanings.

The loss of the second person singular forms historically brings out the diachronic nature of nonequivalence, an aspect of markedness that I will preview here and return to in chapter 5. Jakobson (1968 [1941]) suggests that, with respect to phonology, there is a diachronic tendency for unmarked categories to subsume marked ones. Analogously, at the semantic level, we might expect the merger of categories over time to favor the unmarked categories that are capable of expressing both terms of the opposition. The loss of the second person *thou* and *thee* forms, which I will refer to hereafter as TH forms, may be viewed in this way—as the dissolution of the opposition between singular and plural forms in favor of the unmarked term.[15]

The loss of the TH forms involves more than the neutralization of singular forms to plural forms, however. In the earliest period of English the distinction between TH and Y forms *(ye* and *you)* was a simple number distinction. In the thirteenth century, the plural forms came to be used in addressing superiors; in time, the Y forms became the generally polite form of address and the TH forms came to be used to address familiars and social inferiors; still later, the Y forms became usual regardless of situation, and by the sixteenth century the TH forms had largely disappeared. In the long run, the loss of the TH forms first involved a specialization of the Y forms and then later a generalization of the Y forms and specialization of the TH forms. If we treat specializations as secondary semantic markings added to the basic numerical meaning of the Y and TH forms and if we treat generalization as unmarking, a fairly interesting historical development involving markedness assimilation will become apparent. I return to this topic in chapter 5; suffice it to say for now that principle that unmarked forms subsume marked ones over time captures the loss of TH forms in a broad way only.

Person, Gender, and Animacy

I turn now to the contrasts among the categories of person, arguing first for the unmarkedness of the third person pronouns versus first and second persons, and then for the unmarkedness of the second person pronouns as opposed to the first person. The unmarked nature of the third person forms is shown by their enveloping nature, which is especially revealed in cases involving indefinite noun phrases such as: *One should always look both ways before crossing the street* or *If anyone gets in trouble with the police, he or she [they] should see a lawyer.* In such examples, the third person forms refer generally, including in their reference the speaker and hearer as well as unspecified others.

A similar observation holds for the subsuming nature of the second person with respect to the first person. Examples such as *You can never be too careful* demonstrate the ability of the second person forms to refer to the speaker's self, as well as to the hearers. First person is marked with respect to second person; first and second persons together are marked with respect to third person.[16]

Consider next the markedness relations among the third person singular pronoun forms *he, she, it,* and *one*. The content of the semantic correlations involved in these forms is not entirely clear, but it does seem reasonable that the pronouns *it* and *one* are both unmarked with respect to the pronouns *he* and *she*. *It*, which is used as a pronominal for infants, inanimate objects, and nonpersonified animals, and as a placeholder subject (for impersonal predicates and weather verbs), is indeterminate as contrasted to *he* and *she*. The pronoun may be used with inanimate referents or may be used with animate referents to provide a sense of impersonalness or objectification, deemphasizing the importance of the humanness of the referent: *It was Shakespeare who said. . . . , It's a girl [boy]!* By contrast, the forms *he* and *she* are marked for higher animacy: they attribute personhood to their referents.

The so-called impersonal pronoun *one* is also unmarked in contrast to *he* and *she*. The pronoun *one* may be used to refer to humans or as an anaphoric pronoun to refer generally. Compare its animate use in *One wonders about many things* and *John asked how to dress oneself appropriately* with its general use in *One of those is mine* and *I have one too.* But if *it* and *one* are both unmarked with respect to *he* and *she*, how do they differ? The exact nature of the distinction is elusive, since both pronouns may refer to animate and inanimate referents. However, note that *one* differs from *it* in that *one* refers to animate referents when they are indefinite (generic) and otherwise to referents that are unspecified for the feature animate/inanimate (but which are animate or inanimate according to context); *it*, on the other hand, refers to inanimates generally and to animate referents when depersonalization is intended.

One possible, though admittedly speculative, analysis is to treat the feature oppositions personal/nonpersonal and human/nonhuman as distinct. The feature personal would signify nouns whose referents may be said to have personality and the feature human will signify humanness. In this way it is possible to view the markedness values of the features personal/nonpersonal and human/nonhuman as complementary. The unmarked value of personal/nonpersonal would be the feature nonpersonal. This will reflect the ability of nonpersonal forms like *it* to refer either impersonally or personally. The unmarked value of human/nonhuman, on the other hand, would be human. This reflects the ability of human forms like *one* to refer to nonhumans. The pronoun *one* may be analyzed as doubly unmarked, both human and nonpersonal. The pronoun *it*, by contrast, would be marked as human but unmarked with respect to the personal/nonpersonal opposition. Thus *it* would refer to nonpersonal humans—that is, to humans in contexts where their personness is suppressed, as in expressions like *It's a girl!* The opposite side of this treatment is personification. Here the unmarked nature of the feature human in *he* or *she* allows those pronouns to be used to refer to nonhumans.

Despite being the maximally unmarked pronoun, *one* has a peculiar distribution in that the pronoun takes no part in depersonalization of personal referents or personification of nonhuman referents. When referring to human referents it assumes the general meaning of the feature nonpersonal—the sense of impersonality. When referring to nonhuman referents, on the other hand, *one* assumes a more specific sense of the feature nonpersonal, inanimacy.

Summary: Values, Assimilation, and Form-Content Alignment

Thus far I have shown how the oppositions of the nominal system are organized into pairs of marked and unmarked elements within an overall feature hierarchy. The relations between elements are not always transparent, and sometimes we have had to examine various perspectives in order to bring the more narrowly defined nature of the marked element to the surface.

A main theme that has emerged has been the role of markedness as a system of values that gives organization to linguistic forms and their meanings. Of particular interest have been instances in which marked linguistic and discourse contexts favor the use of the marked term rather than the unmarked term: the use of nominative and reflexive pronouns in formal contexts, the use of the reflexive as a marker of emphasis, the objective genitive in elliptical contexts. My focus has been on such markedness assimilation between units and contexts, but several variations on this theme have emerged as well. The relation between markedness at the level of expression and markedness at the level of meaning is essentially parallel to that between units and contexts, and the alignment of expression and meaning may be considered a special case of markedness assimilation. The tendency for the conceptually marked term to be an augmented version of the unmarked term is borne out by some of the examples we have considered. Among the marked pronouns we have examined, the reflexive and the objective genitive are, for example, formed by augmentation of the corresponding unmarked forms. However, the tendency of pronoun paradigms to have idiosyncratic alternations rather than regular productive ones makes that system a less likely place to find evidence than the system of noun forms. Within the noun declensions we do observe instances in which the marked category is an augmented form of the unmarked: consider, for example, plural number and genitive case, which are formed by suffixation to a noun base.

(19)   Unmarked   Marked

         singular: N + Ø   plural: N + s
         common case: N + Ø   genitive: N + $'s$

Some other oppositions discussed above also show formal augmentation correlated with conceptual markedness. The marked categories of emphasis and compounding are, for example, characterized by increased loudness and increased syntax respectively. The unmarked character of the zero pronoun PRO and the zero of ellipsis is also suggestive. However, the marked nature of the nominative zero pronoun provides a counterexample to this, since in that instance marked categories are implemented by the phonologically null term. Thus, no exceptionless law can be advanced about the status of zero at this point.

A further principle of markedness that has been illustrated so far, albeit tacitly, has been Brøndal's Principle of Compensation, mentioned in the previous chapter. Recall that this is the idea that the marked term tends not to accumulate further marks. The principle is borne out, for example, in the formation of the reflexive pronouns, where the unmarked subjective forms are chosen as the morphological base (*my* + *self* rather than *mine* + *self*, etc.). And note that where the reflexives vary from this pattern (in the third person), the morphological base is the unmarked objective case, rather than some other form.

The Verbal Categories: An Introduction

The remainder of this chapter takes up markedness relations within the English verb system. As in the discussion of nouns, there are two main issues: What are the markedness values of the verbal forms and of the semantic oppositions underlying the verbal categories? and What is the patterning of values between expression (forms) and semantic content? These are simple questions to state but difficult to answer because the meanings of verbal categories are quite complicated. In practical terms, a good way to begin is to first summarize the form categories of the verb system and their markedness values and then to turn to the analysis of the semantic categories.

Form Categories of the Verb

Traditional grammarians talk about the verb system in terms of conjugational classes like stem, past tense, present (or active) participle, and past (or passive) participle. Central to the analysis of the forms of the verb system in English is the bare verb stem, which I treat as a zero verbal ending. As shown below in the list of the forms of *do*, the zero ending occurs in the present tense (except in the third person singular) and in the infinitive, future, subjunctive, and imperative forms.

(20) Conjugational forms

Present:	(I, you, we, they)	do-Ø
	(he, she, it)	does
Past:		did
Future:		will do-Ø
		shall do-Ø
Past participle:		have done
		was done
Present participle:		was doing
Infinitive:		to do-Ø
Subjunctive:		do-Ø
Imperative:		do-Ø

In purely formal terms, we would assign markedness values to these categories in the following way. The past tense, formed by the dental ending (*-t, -d,* or *-ed*), as in the example above, or by ablaut in the case of historically strong verbs, is marked with respect to present tense forms, which are for the most part represented by the bare stem. Within the category of present tense verbs, the third person singular is, by virtue of its overt ending, marked as opposed to the other present tense forms. Graphically, the markedness of the form patterns is this:

(21)

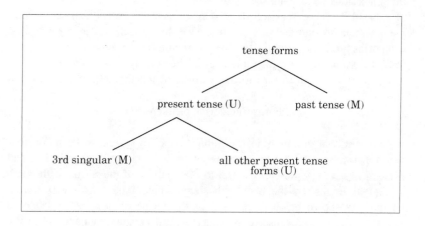

The other verbal forms listed above may be contrasted with the tensed verbs. The imperative and the subjunctive are each opposed to the indicative mood of the tensed verbs, while infinitives and participles are opposed to the finiteness of tensed verbs. Since the imperative and the subjunctive are invariant verb forms and do not show person or number alternations, they can be considered formally unmarked with respect to the present and past tense forms, which show various form alternations.[17] For the forms of nonfinite verbs, infinitives, and participles, the situation is more complex. While the infinitive has a zero suffix, it is constructed by adding the auxiliary element *to,* except after modals, *do,* and certain verbs of perception. Likewise, the participial verbal forms, in their aspectual use or in the passive voice, are preceded by an auxiliary *have* or *be.* If we think of syntactic augmentation as a formal marking, we are then led to analyze

(22)

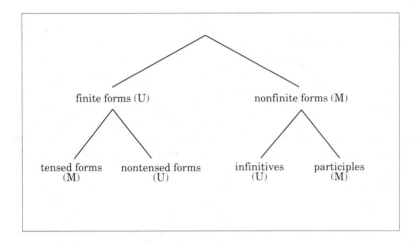

the participles and infinitives as formally marked in opposition to finite verbs, which do not require auxiliaries.

Within the set of nonfinite verbs, infinitives are the least marked category since they are overtly signaled only by *to*. The participial forms, which are signaled by suffixes as well as by auxiliaries, are more marked. We might also contrast the two participial forms themselves in hopes of ascertaining whether a formal markedness relation holds between them. However, since both types of participles are constructed with a nonzero ending plus an auxiliary verb, no simple zero/nonzero test can be applied, and so it may be best to eschew assignment of markedness values between these forms.

Before turning to semantics, a comment is required on the status of the modal auxiliaries, including those that indicate so-called future tense. Since we are taking the criteria for formal marking to include syntactic augmentation as well as morphological affixation and inflection, it is natural to consider modal auxiliaries as a formal marking on the main verb of a clause. Thus, the future tense forms *will* and *shall* are formally marked as opposed to their present tense counterparts.[18]

Semantics of the Verbal Categories

Having sketched the markedness relations of the verbal forms, I now turn to the semantic features of verbal meanings. First, however, some clarification may be useful concerning analysis of verbs into semantic oppositions. A categorization of the verbal system (or some other domain) into oppositions and features should not be construed as a complete semantic account of that system. Such a structural analysis is not semantics in the sense of a mapping from syntax to a model-theoretic formalism or to a Chomskyan logical form. But structural semantics is not inconsistent with such approaches either: a feature analysis may be viewed as a set of hypotheses that attempts to clarify a domain such as the verb system by giving a pseudosemantic representation of the relations among its categories. The *pseudo-* of pseudosemantics is not a pejorative; though such an analysis is not exhaustive and formalized it can play an important intermediate role in the process of giving a formalized semantics by providing a descriptive framework for semantic analysis.

This said, we turn with due diffidence to some aspects of the pseudo-semantics of the English verbal categories. As was the case with the verbal form classes, the meaning of the verbal categories can most easily be examined by explicating the traditional categories of mood (indicative, subjunctive, and imperative), finiteness (finite, infinitive, and participle), tense (the inflected past and present tenses and the periphrastic future tense), and aspect (perfect and progressive).

The categories of the verb system comprise several subsystems, as the list just given indicates. Keep in mind, however, that not all the verbal features participate in every subsystem; some features are restricted to certain domains and are irrelevant within others. Mood, for example, is distinguished only among finite verbs, and tense only among indicative verbs (it makes no sense to speak of a past tense imperative, for example). The category of aspect provides another example of such defective distribution, since the perfect and progressive occur only marginally in the imperative and subjunctive. Examples like the following are distinctly odd: *Have left by nine o'clock; Be going to the store when I get back; I insisted that he have left by nine o'clock; I demand that you be going to the store when I get back.*

The preliminary classification of verbal inflectional categories in (23) will serve as a basis for the discussion in this section.

In addition, tensed verbs and infinitives further distinguish perfect and progressive aspect and active and passive voice. These categories have been omitted from the diagram.

(23)

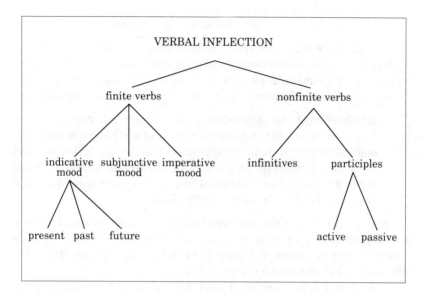

VERBAL INFLECTION

finite verbs   nonfinite verbs

indicative   subjunctive   imperative   infinitives   participles
mood   mood   mood

present   past   future   active   passive

Finite Indicative Verbs

In this section, I consider the subsystem of verbs that are finite and indicative, focusing first on the oppositions among tenses and then turning to the oppositions between aspectual verb forms and nonaspectual ones that cross-classify the system of tenses. What we are interested in are properties that characterize the oppositions among the categories past, present, and future tense and also the oppositions between simple tensed verbs and those in the progressive and perfect aspects. Consider, then, some examples of these oppositions:

(24)   Simple (past and present forms)
I write a lot of letters every year.
I wrote a lot of letters last year.

(25)   Progressive (past and present forms)
I am writing to my friend Mary.
I was writing to my friend Mary (when I was interrupted).

(26)   Perfect (past and present forms)
I have (just now, recently) written to the manufacturer.
I had (already) written to the manufacturer.

(27)   Future (past and present forms)
         I will write a lot of letters next year.
         I would write a lot of letters (if I had time).

While it is perhaps tempting to think of tense as a three-valued category with its center in the present moment and the past and future extending from this center, such a symmetrical approach glosses over some important differences between the past and the future. As Bernard Comrie observes, the past tense

> subsumes what may have already taken place and, barring science fiction, is immutable, beyond the control of our present actions. The future, however, is more speculative, in that any prediction we make about the future might be changed by intervening events, including our own conscious intervention. Thus, in a very real sense the past is more definite than the future. [1985:43–44]

He goes on to note that this conceptual difference might be a motivation to treat the future as a category of mood rather than tense. However, Comrie concludes that the future in English is in fact a tense category (1985:44–48), and I adopt that position here as well.

As a first approximation, I treat the feature past as indicating the 'specification of an action as taking place in the past (prior to the moment of speech)' as opposed to the nonspecification of past time reference that characterizes the present and future. Of course, the feature nonpast is the unmarked member of this opposition: the past tense is restricted to past time meaning while the present tense forms, as we have already seen in chapter 1, may refer to actions ranging over past, present, and future time.

Now let us consider the future/nonfuture opposition, which is realized by the presence or absence of a form of *will* (or *shall*). The future tense indicates that the verbal action follows some reference point. I take the future to be the marked semantic category and the nonfuture to be unmarked, since we find that the meaning of the simple present may impinge on that of the future, particularly when events are treated as scheduled in some sense as, for example, in *I leave for the coast next month*. Conversely, the future tense may only be used to indicate future time: *I will leave for the coast* has only a future meaning.[19]

We can schematize the tense oppositions and their markedness values as follows, sharpening our earlier classification of verbal categories:

(28)   Past   Future

         Past tense   + (M)   − (U)
         Present tense   − (U)   − (U)
         Future tense   − (U)   + (M)

Is there a form that is marked for both past and future? It is tempting to speculate that this is the analysis of the habitual past tense forms below (cf. Khlebnikova 1973):

(29)   He would always agree with you, no matter what you said.

However, this form does not appear to combine the general meanings of the past and future tenses. Rather, what may be going on is a type of markedness assimilation in which the marked form of the nonpast (namely, the future) is used to implement the marked category of the iterative (habitual) past tense.

Another possible candidate for a past future is the following conditional construction:

(30)   We would be healthier if we ate more oat bran.

But here again the meaning of the main verb is not a function of the meanings of the categories past and future. If we reverse the order of the clauses, the presence of the past tense morphology (the -d ending of would) can be seen to follow from the sequence of tenses rule illustrated below:

(31)   a. John said he was leaving.
            John says he is leaving.

          b. If I had time, I would go.
            If I have time, I will go.

          c. If Mary arrived today, the hotel wouldn't have her suite ready.
            If Mary arrives today, the hotel won't have her suite ready.

In such examples as these, the presence of a marked past tense verb in the main clause triggers the neutralization of the past and present forms in favor of the marked past tense forms rather than the unmarked present tense forms. The above examples are similar to the reversal mentioned by Andersen whereby the marked past tense form is used as an indicator of subjunctive mood (cf. the first section of this chapter). In this case, the context is syntagmatic, since the replacement of the unmarked tense by its marked counterpart is triggered by a marked element earlier in the sentence, while in Andersen's example the conditioning was paradigmatic, since it was due to the selection of one category, the subjunctive, rather than another.

Verbal Aspect

Now we turn our attention to the categories of aspect, which are represented in English by the perfect and progressive verbal forms. Aspect differs

from both the absolute tense of finite indicative clauses and from the
relative tense of nonfinite clauses and may be generally defined as "different ways of viewing the internal temporal constituency of a situation"
(Comrie 1976:3), or as "the manner in which the verbal action is experienced or regarded (for example as completed or in progress)" (Quirk and
Greenbaum 1973:40). The perfect and progressive aspects in English are
illustrated in (25) and (26) above.

The Perfect

While some aspectual systems are organized so as to directly oppose
categories of perfective and imperfective aspects, the relevant oppositions
for the aspectual system of English are between the simple forms and the
perfect and progressive ones, as Khlebnikova (1973) has pointed out.[20] I
begin by discussing the opposition between perfect and nonperfect verbs. As
has been suggested by Reichenbach (1947), perfect verbs indicate a past
that is relative to a reference point specified by the tense of a clause. Consequently, the perfect aspect shares with past tense the notion of anteriority,
but differs in that the anteriority is with respect to a reference point rather
than with respect to the moment of speech. Due to its ability to connect
some verbal state or action to a previous situation, the English perfect may
be used to indicate persistence of result, existence of an event in the time
prior to the reference point, persistence of a situation up to the reference
point, or actions taking place in the recent past (cf. Comrie 1975:56–61).
These uses are illustrated below:

(32)   John has arrived.
              Have you ever eaten shark's fin?
              We've lived here for ten years.
              Bill has just (this minute) arrived.

In each instance, the relation between the activity or state designated
by the main verb and the time reference designated by the tense can be
represented as follows:

(33)

------verbal activity------reference of tense--------------
past----------------------------present--------------future

For convenience, let us designate this opposition as perfectness versus nonperfectness. Which is the marked value of this opposition? As before, evidence comes from the meaning overlap between verbs characterized by these oppositions. Consider (34), where we find overlap between the simple and the perfect tense forms:

(34)   a. I read *War and Peace.*
           I have read *War and Peace.*

        b. I read *War and Peace* three times before I saw the movie.
           I had read *War and Peace* three times before I saw the movie.

        c. I ate shark's fin many times before I ever knew what it was.
           I had eaten shark's fin many times before I ever knew what it was.

        d. We saw this movie already!
           We have seen this movie already!

The simple tense forms and the perfect sometimes overlap in meaning, the simple forms of the past being used to express the sense of the perfect. Such examples suggest that 'nonperfectness' is unmarked and 'perfectness' is marked. Notice that I contrasted the past tense both with the past and present perfect forms. In simple sentences a direct contrast between tenseless perfect and nonperfect forms is impossible since simple sentences require a tensed verb; however, we can abstract away from the contribution of tense by using examples like the following:

(35)   a. For his plan to have worked so well is amazing.

        b. For his plan to work so well is amazing.

The meaning of these sentences can be clarified by considering paraphrases. The first sentence, but not the second, can be paraphrased as a sentence in which the subject clause is in the past tense: *That his plan worked so well is amazing.* The second sentence, however, can be paraphrased by a sentence with a present tense subject clause: *That his plan works so well is amazing.* Example (35b) is unspecified as to whether the plan's working is a present, past, or future state; the plan in question works well in general. In (35a), the plan worked on a particular occasion or occasions prior to the moment of speech. Such data, which parallel observations about past and present tense, confirm the suggestion that nonperfect is the more general, unmarked concept.

A further bit of evidence concerning the markedness of the perfect aspect in English comes from the sequence of tenses rule mentioned earlier. In indirect reports of speech, the past tense of a main verb conditions a change in the tense of the subordinate verb. So, for example, one can report John's announcement of his engagement as any of the following:

(36)   a. John said, "I'm getting married."

            b. John said he is getting married.

            c. John said he was getting married.

I suggest that in (36c) the markedness of the main verb conditions the use of the marked form of the subordinate verb. The question arises of what happens when the direct speech event is already in the past tense. As Comrie (1985:116–17) notes, in such a case the past tense verb can be replaced by the perfect form:

(37)   a. John said, "I arrived on Friday."

            b. John said he arrived on Friday.

            c. John said he had arrived on Friday.

The use of the perfect form in (37c) provides a nice parallel with the markedness assimilation of the present tense if the perfect forms are marked. In (36) the present tense alternates with the marked past, while in (37) the marked past tense alternates with the marked aspect. It is worth pointing out that Comrie also distinguishes a stylistic function in the example just given, "the version with the pluperfect being the more literary, the version with the simple past more colloquial" (1985:117). This style distinction corresponds with the general pattern we have seen of marked forms predominating in literary and formal language.

The Progressive

We turn now to the progressive aspect verb forms. The progressive aspect in English is a verb form that indicates a verbal activity or state of limited duration.[21] The notion of limited duration inherent in the progressive is sometimes manifest as temporariness versus permanence of the verbal state, as in (38a, b, and d), or as the division of an action into discrete subevents, as in (38c). In the subevent case, the meaning of the sentence requires that only some of the subevents be completed at the reference point fixed by the tense of the sentence. Thus, in (38c), only some of the book was completed at the past time indicated; consequently, the progressive is often used to indicate an activity during which some other event is interpolated.

(38)   a. The statue stood on the corner of Main and Elm.
               The statue was standing on the corner of Main and Elm.

            b. The engine runs well.
               The engine is running well.

            c. I read *Barriers.*
               I was reading *Barriers* when I was interrupted.

            d. I live in Birmingham.
               I am living in Birmingham.

What is the markedness relation between the progressive and the nonprogressive? It is tempting to follow the pattern of the perfect/nonperfect opposition and assign the value marked to the progressive and the value unmarked to the nonprogressive. On the face of things, the well-known restriction that stative verbs resist the progressive aspect, while dynamic verbs (activities, processes, and verbs of sensation and momentary action; cf. Quirk and Greenbaum 1973:46–47) allow it, suggests that the progressive is generally marked. This resistance to the progressive, which also holds of predicate adjective constructions in which the adjective describes a permanent state, is illustrated below:

(39)   ?I am owning a car these days.
            ?I am seeing the movie.
            ?I am understanding linguistics.
            ?I am resenting my situation.
            ?I am loving life.
            ?John is being blonde.
            ?Mary is being tall.
            ?Bob is being thin.

Such data suggest that the nonprogressive enjoys a broader distribution than the progressive, and they may be taken as partial evidence of the unmarked status of the nonprogressive. Despite the intuitive appeal of the idea that the simple forms are the unmarked ones, it is possible to argue that progressiveness is unmarked for certain verbs, especially when the present tense is involved. Verbs like *rain* and *snow*, for example, can only occur in the present tense with a general meaning, as in *It never rains when you need it.* Otherwise, such verbs are unable to take the simple present: *It is raining now,* but not **It rains now.* A preference for the present progressive over the simple present is also found in examples like the following:

(40)   a. I step through the door.
             I am stepping through the door.

           b. I mix the two solutions.
             I am mixing the two solutions.

           c. I place the coin in the slot.
             I am placing the coin in the slot.

Here the simple forms have an immediate future sense, in which one is commenting on what is about to happen or giving a running account of some event. The present progressive forms, on the other hand, indicate that the action described is taking place at the moment of speech. So in these examples, the limited duration meaning of the progressive allows it to refer to an action that is beginning at the moment of speech. If the simple present could also refer to actions of limited duration, we should expect the simple forms to have this use as well. But that is not the case.

One way to resolve this question is to treat the category progressive as being "the combination of progressive meaning and nonstative meaning" (Comrie 1976:35) and to take the markedness of progressive verbs to be local in the sense discussed in chapter 2, rather than being general for all verbs.[22] For verbs whose lexical meaning is closely tied to stativeness and permanent duration or general habit, the nonprogressive aspect will be unmarked. And for verbs whose typical lexical meaning strongly suggests dynamic activity, the feature of progressiveness will be unmarked.

There are verbs, however, that may be viewed either as a dynamic activity or as a state (or a habitual activity). Can a general markedness preference be defined for verbs that refer both to dynamic activities and states of being? It is not at all obvious that one can be. Moreover, tense seems to interact as well. The present tense is particularly prone to a state function, perhaps because of its lack of specific time reference. Some verbs can have either a state or an activity function; the simple present seems a little less natural than the present progressive if such verbs refer basically to activities:

(41) a. I teach three classes this quarter.
      I am teaching three classes this quarter.

      b. I read a lot of fiction these days.
      I am reading a lot of fiction these days.

      c. The engine runs well today.
      The engine is running well today.

The contrast between the state and activity orientation can be further brought out in the following examples, discussed by Kučera (1981). In (a) through (c) the progressive indicates a temporary habit spread over an interval determined by the adverbial; the simple present indicates a more permanent state or a long-term habit.

(42) a. I eat more now than I used to.
      I am eating more now than I used to.

      b. He drinks too much these days.
      He is drinking too much these days.

      c. Dad smokes a lot right now.
      Dad is smoking a lot right now.

      d. *Dad talks on the phone right now.
      Dad is talking on the phone right now.

      e. *Dad answers today's mail right now.
      Dad is answering today's mail right now.

Kučera remarks that

> the first sentence [of 42c] is quite acceptable; the adverbial *right now* must, of course, be interpreted here as designating an interval, not a point in time. . . . Clearly, smoking a lot can be quite naturally viewed as a state in Vendler's sense [cf. Vendler 1967]. Simple talking on the phone, on the other hand, is a very poor candidate for a state. Notice that an appropriate manner adverbial that forces the interpretation of [the first sentence of 42d] as a state makes this sentence much more respectable: *Dad talks on the phone a lot right now.*[188–189]

He goes on to point out that the only acceptable interpretation of the original example is where talking on the phone is a present characteristic, or state, of Dad's. Kučera's conclusion is that the English simple present "has basically a state function, although it can, in special usage, denote reported events" and that the progressive "although generally used to denote activities, is commonly used for limited duration states as well" (188). This conclusion is further supported by the fact that, in the past tense at least, the meaning of the simple verb form can be used to express events of a limited duration, overlapping with the progressive, as in the following examples:

(43)   a. I taught three classes last quarter.
               I was teaching three classes last quarter.

            b. I read a lot of fiction in college.
               I was reading a lot of fiction in college.

            c. The engine ran well.
               The engine was running well.

The simple tense form, which in the past implies an end to the activity described (cf. *John is smart,* vs. *John was smart*), permits the simple past tense forms to have the limited duration sense typical of the progressive. In the future as well, the meaning difference between the simple and progressive forms is reduced:

(44)   a. I will teach that next quarter.
               I will be teaching that next quarter.

            b. I will read a lot of fiction on my vacation.
               I will be reading a lot of fiction on my vacation.

   In the past and present then, the distinction between limited duration states and prolonged events is apparently reduced, and in these tenses the simple forms can be used to indicate continuous events. For the past and future tenses we can say that the general markedness value is that the progressive is marked and the simple forms unmarked. For the present tense the evaluation of the opposition depends on the status of the verbal meaning as an activity or a state. The hierarchy of features and values may be summed up as follows:

(45)

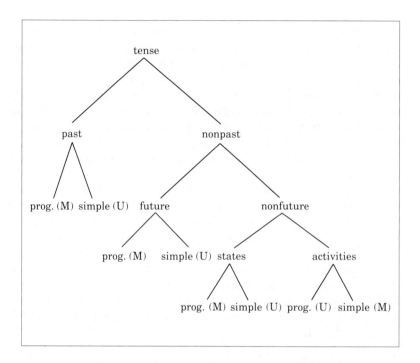

Having now introduced the features of aspect and their uses, we can summarize the semantic oppositions of aspect and their general markedness values as follows (abstracting away from reversals entailed by local markedness values):

(46)

	Perfectness/ Nonperfectness (relative anteriority)	Progressiveness/ Nonprogressiveness (limited duration)
Simple verbs	− (U)	− (U)
Perfect verbs	+ (M)	− (U)
Progressive verbs	− (U)	+ (M)
Perf. prog. verbs	+ (M)	+ (M)

Mood Distinctions

We turn now to the oppositions that make up the grammatical moods of English. The distinction here is traditionally among the indicative, the imperative, and the subjunctive, though it is perhaps possible to collapse the imperative and subjunctive as contextual variants of a single property that are in complementary distribution. For clarity's sake, I adopt the traditional three-way distinction, which opposes the subjunctive and the imperative to the indicative (cf. Quirk and Greenbaum 1973:38). The category imperative, of course, indicates a command (or a prohibition, a negative command). The category subjunctive basically expresses a counterfactual or unfulfilled wish or desire (cf. Harsh 1968). Putting aside the formulaic subjunctive, the main uses of the subjunctive are in mandative *that* clauses *(I insist that he go in my place)* and in hypothetical clauses containing *were (If I were you, I wouldn't do that)*. In both instances, of course, the choice of the subjunctive is an indicator of formal as opposed to colloquial usage.

The features 'imperative' and 'subjunctive' are marked as opposed to the features 'nonimperative' and 'nonsubjunctive', which characterize the indicative mood. Both of the posited marked moods have more restricted syntactic distribution than the indicative. The imperative, for example, is used only in main clauses, and the subjunctive is used only in subordinate clauses and some fixed formulaic expressions. Moreover, the indicative can subsume uses of both the subjunctive and the imperative. The moribund status of the present-day English subjunctive is prima facie evidence for the use of the indicative in its place. In colloquial usage the indicative frequently replaces the subjunctive:

(47)   If I was you, I wouldn't do that.
            (cf. If I were you, I wouldn't do that.)
            If he was rich, he wouldn't have that problem.
            (cf. Were he rich, he wouldn't have that problem.)
            I'd prefer (it) for him to come over here.
            (cf. I'd prefer that he come over here.
            I'd prefer that he comes over here.)
            I require everyone to be on time.
            (cf. I require that everyone be on time.
            I require that everyone is on time.)

Commands may be expressed by formally indicative structures, as with the perlocutionary main verbs in (48) and the interrogative forms in (49):

(48)   I order you to stop.
            I command you to obey.
            I require you to turn in your work on time.

(49)   You will turn your work in on time from now on, won't you.
            Would you be quiet please!
            Will you shut up!

Given both the syntactic and semantic breadth of the indicative as compared to the subjunctive and imperative, we evaluate the mood features as
below, where the labels of the columns are cover symbols for yet-unknown
semantic features:

(50)   Imperative   Subjunctive

            Indicative mood   − (U)   − (U)
            Imperative mood   + (M)   ——
            Subjunctive mood   ——   + (M)

Finiteness and Voice

The grammatical category of finiteness is traditionally taken to distinguish clauses that manifest tense and mood (the indicative, imperative, and
subjunctive) from those that do not (infinitives, participial clauses, and gerunds). Since the semantic tense distinctions are syncretized in the imperative and subjunctive in English, perhaps finiteness is more appropriately
designated as a feature of clauses that have either tense *or* mood. For our
purposes, however, the issue is the markedness relations among finite
verbs, participles, and infinitives.

There is both a conceptual and a grammatical basis for the distinctions between finite and nonfinite clauses. The grammatical basis is of
course that finite clauses exhibit a formal tense or mood distinction while
nonfinite clauses lack such distinctions. The conceptual basis is that nonfinite clauses manifest a relative tense—that is, a tense determined in part by
its grammatical and lexical context. The traditional labels for these types of
clauses, of course, suggest that nonfinite clauses lack tense, but there is
more to it than that.

Focusing first on tensed verbs and infinitives, we can make a useful
distinction between two perspectives: the perspective of the clause and the
perspective of the verb itself. On the one hand, tensed clauses are the prototypical clause type and infinitival clauses are marked clause types having,
let us say, a feature of 'subordination' for which finite clauses are unspecified (since they can occur either as main clauses or as subordinate clauses).
The dominance of finite clauses versus infinitives is demonstrated not only
in their ability to occur as both main and subordinate clauses, but also
by their occurrence with a wider range of adverbial subordinators than in-

finitives (we find, for example, *Since they left town, we hardly hear from John and Mary anymore* but not **Since to leave town, we hardly hear from John and Mary anymore*). The evidence that finite clauses are unmarked is not unequivocal, however. Infinitives are generally more accessible to a variety of syntactic processes than are tensed clauses (cf. Chomsky 1973 for a number of examples). And although finite clauses can occur in most contexts where infinitives can occur, certain types of predicates require infinitives, suggesting at least that there are some local reversals of markedness.[23] Consider the following examples:

(51)   a.   I like [to swim in the ocean].
              *I like [that I swim in the ocean].

         b.   [To go to the movies] is usually entertaining.
              *[That we go to the movies] is usually entertaining.

Tensed clauses with an overt *when* are possible, though perhaps somewhat stilted: *I like it when I swim in the ocean, It's usually entertaining when we go to the movies.* On the whole, it makes sense to treat tensed clauses as unmarked clause types; however, from the point of view of verbs as verbs, it is most natural to think of infinitives as unmarked. Tensed verbs are specified for some absolute tense. Infinitives are unspecified for absolute tense; rather, the temporal reference of infinitives is dependent on the higher verbs or complementizers with which they are in construction. For example, when subordinate to a tensed clause, an infinitive often has an interpretation in which the infinitive verbal action is unrealized at the time indicated by the higher clause (and thus functions as a 'possible future'). Similarly, in adverbial clauses and relative infinitivals, the 'possible future' interpretation of infinitives permits their use as purpose clauses:

(52)   Dave wants [to learn to speak Czech].
         Sally remembered [to lock the door].
         Frank forgot [to bring a gift].
         Alice is looking for someone [to paint her picture].
         George found a plumber [to fix the sink].
         Mary fired her secretary [to save money].
         Don worked hard [to make a good impression].

It may be that the finite/infinitive distinction is best treated as an instance of local markedness. The relative tense of the infinitives makes them the conceptually unmarked category with respect to the property of time reference. However, when language makes a specific time reference necessary, as in main clauses, tensed verbs are expected and hence unmarked. In other words, infinitive verbs are the generally unmarked verbal category, while tensed clauses represent the generally unmarked clause type. In main clauses, however, the requirement of independent time reference reverses this evaluation.

Now let us consider the other nonfinite verb forms: the active and the passive participles. Like infinitives these forms have a relative tense and can be treated as unmarked for absolute tense. Unlike infinitives, however, participles have additional semantic features signaling simultaneity with or anteriority to the verb of the main clause.[24] Thus, in (53a) the -*ing* participle indicates that the sitting was simultaneous with the reading and in (54a) the -*ed* participle indicates that the day was over before any leaving took place:

(53)   a. Sitting in the chair, Mary read the evening paper.

           b. Picking up her pen, Mary set to work.

(54)   a. Her workday finished, Mary went home.

           b. The project begun, Mary felt much better.

The markedness values of the tensed and nonfinite verbs is summarized in the hierarchy in (55) on the following page, which shows the interaction of context with markedness value. Needless to say, such a hierarchy is not intended as the final word on the markedness values of verbal categories in all contexts, but as a first approximation that might be extended in various ways, perhaps taking into account different factors that condition the local evaluation of tensed versus nonfinite clauses. Such factors might include the role of subject position versus object position, clause function as adjectival versus nominal, the stative or dynamic nature of an event, or the discourse function of verbal elements in foregrounding and backgrounding.[25]

Word Order

We have not yet considered the markedness of the active/passive opposition. Though it might seem natural to treat active and passive as an opposition between verb forms, it is more accurate to view it as an opposition between clause types since the opposition involves both verbal morphology and argument structure. Comrie (1981a) has pointed out some suggestive parallels between perfective aspect and passive voice that might serve as the basis for analysis of the difference between passive and active verb forms as verbs. However, the focus here will be whether the active or passive is the unmarked clause type, and in a more general vein, the question of how syntax and semantics are correlated in respect to word order variation and syntactic modification.

(55)

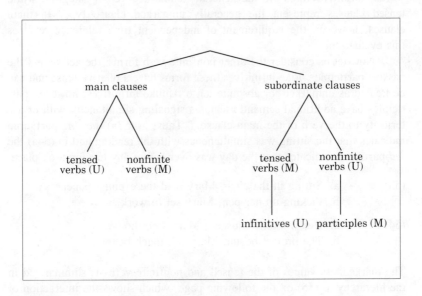

With respect to form alone, passive clauses are marked types. In addition to the "promotion" of the direct or indirect object to subject position and the "demotion" or suppression of the logical subject, the syntactic expression of the passive involves augmentation: adding the passive auxiliary *be*, putting the main verb in the passive participle form, and in some cases adding the preposition *by*. The passive is also the more restricted category distributionally, being impossible with relational predicates such as *resemble, cost, have* ('possess'); furthermore, the passive is precluded with many verbal idioms, such as *kick the bucket* and *shoot the breeze*. And of course the passive is typically treated as a nonprototypical clause type in traditional and descriptive grammar.[26] Moreover, with respect to information focus, the passive is the conceptually marked category since passivization in effect topicalizes the promoted object making it the information focus of the sentence.

The conclusion that passives are marked clause types both conceptually and formally raises the question of iconicity between expression and meaning at the clause level. The contrast between a prototypical clause type and nonprototypical types is a fairly common opposition in studies of word order function and word order variation. Such studies often assume the existence of a dominant word order type for a given language and treat variations from that order, especially those associated with some sort of information focusing, or associated with a particular semantic or stylistic effect, as marginal or marked word orders. Hopper and Thompson (1980) and Ross (1987), for example, give the prototypical form of an English sentence as:

(56)   agent subject + verb of action + patient (direct) object

In such a prototypical sentence the subject is the (usually animate) agent of a dynamic transitive verb and the object is the affected patient (usually inanimate) of the verb. The assumption that there is a cardinal or canonical word order for a language again raises the question of the alignment between element order and semantic and stylistic functions.[27] Iconicity and markedness assimilation will favor a closeness of fit between basic syntax and categories of meaning that are stylistically neutral and semantically cardinal (that is, categories with no special semantic function, information focus, emphasis, or dialectal flavor). Conversely, clauses that implement nonprototypical categories, such as nonassertions (questions, negations, exclamations, commands), special styles (formal language, dialectal speech, very casual speech), and special rhetorical or discourse functions (such as contrastive emphasis or the introduction of a new topic) should exhibit syntactic complications (marked expression). Constructions in English that reflect such conceptually marked processes seem to include the sentences in (57) which, tellingly, also involve syntactic permutations and augmentations.

(57)   *Questions*
         Is anyone interested in going to dinner?
         (inversion)
         What would you like to do?
         (*wh*-fronting and inversion)
         John went to the store?
         (rising intonation)

         Emphasis
         What a fascinating talk that was!
         (*wh*-fronting)
         Emily wanted to go to Harvard Law School, and go there she did!
         (verb fronting)

         Information focus
         It was New Hampshire that really decided the election.
         (clefting)
         On the corner was a wizened old gentleman.
         (prepositional phrase inversion)
         These books, everyone should read.

(topicalization)
As for these books, everyone should read them.
(topicalization)
The report was leaked to the press.
(passivization)
What today's results mean is that the election is much closer.
(pseudoclefting)

Dialectal
I asked what did he say.
(inversion)
These books, everyone should read.
(topicalization)

In a general way, such observations as these suggest the assimilation of marked syntactic expression and marked meaning. Such markedness assimilation between grammar and meaning is a fruitful area for future research. Note that meaning can be construed broadly here to include both traditional semantic functions of clauses and their stylistic function as well. From the perspective of style, the hypothesis to be tested is that in (58), while from the perspective of (traditional) semantic categories, the correlation to be tested is that in (59).

(58)   M syntax : U syntax :: M style : U style

(59)   M syntax : U syntax :: M semantics : U semantics

An investigation of markedness assimilation between syntactic expression and meaning might proceed on several fronts. To be sure, further analysis is needed to confirm the markedness and unmarkedness of syntactic patterns. Evidence for this confirmation might come from various sources: the distribution of word orders in various types of clauses or with types of intonation, the function and use of different types of word orders, the comments of traditional and descriptive grammars on the generality or restrictedness of various word orders. In addition, a hierarchy of word order types might be developed to permit more fine-grained distinctions among word order types. For example, if the form given in (56) is in fact the unmarked clause type for English, would any syntactic process that modifies this order be characterized as a semantic marking? In particular, we will want some way of distinguishing between simple sentences of different valences or argument structures and sentences with special semantic or stylistic function. I will not make further concrete proposals here for investigating markedness assimilation in syntax, since to do so would expand this book beyond a reasonable length. However, the discussion of the markedness analysis of the nominal and verbal categories should make it clear how markedness might be applied to word order and to grammatical domains other than those considered here.

The Complementarity of Form and Content

As must be evident by now, markedness relations determined by complexity of morphological or syntactic expression correlate sometimes with the conceptual complexity of categories, but not in every case. Though there are many cases where form and meaning line up, it is not at all difficult to find instances that show a complementarity of formal complexity and conceptual complexity. Examples include the marked categories of imperative and subjunctive, which are expressed by zero endings, and the marked person-number forms of present tense verbs, which are also expressed by zero. In this section, I consider further the idea that complementarity of markedness values, as well as assimilation of values, is relevant to the organization of grammatical expression and meaning, following a theme developed in Shapiro (1980, 1983).[28]

A good example to illustrate the role of complementarity is the present tense of verbs. Recall that the present tense is unmarked as opposed to the past and future tenses and that, in apparent alignment to this markedness relation, the forms of the present tense are *usually* represented by the bare verb stem, lacking endings for person and number. But within the present tense system, the exception to this rule is the third person singular, where the -*s* ending occurs. Why should the third person singular form be the one that is formally expressed and not some other person-number category? This pattern provides an interesting puzzle when we attempt to interpret it in light of the markedness relation between singular and plural and the markedness relation among the features that define first, second, and third person. Recall from the discussion of the pronoun features that third person is the conceptually least marked category. And if we adopt Jakobson's view of the markedness of singular and plural (namely, that singular is unmarked and plural is marked) then the values for the verbal person-number categories are:

(60) | | Singular | Plural |
|---|---|---|
| 1st person | M person U number | M person M number |
| 2nd person | M person U number | M person M number |
| 3rd person | U person U number | U person M number |

Earlier however, I suggested that the person-number categories for the pronominal system took plural as unmarked and singular as marked. If this
evaluation is correct for the *verbal* person-number categories as well, then
the markedness values are somewhat different:

(61)   Singular   Plural

    1st person   M person M number   M person U number
    2nd person   M person M number   M person U number
    3rd person   U person M number   U person U number

That it is singular that is unmarked for verbs is suggested by neutralizations such as the following, in which the singular is found rather than
the plural.

(62)   Where's my shoes?
           There's a few people coming over tonight.
           Who is going with us?
           Who is getting married?

Such examples suggest that the markedness value for number in verbs is the
reverse of its values in pronouns and that the markedness value of number
for verbs does in fact follow the pattern suggested by Jakobson. The
markedness values for person and number in (60) will hold for English
verbs and for nonpronominal nouns, while the values in (61) hold for English pronouns.

      Given that the third singular is the least marked person-number cate-
gory and the other person-number categories therefore have a composite
markedness value of at least one, we can make some sense of the formal
marking of the third person singular by positing that English encodes the
unmarkedness of the third singular by means of a formal marking, apparently reversing the expected pattern of alignment. This can be stated in the
following way:

(63)   In the unmarked category of third person singular present
           tense, the unmarked number has a marked expression and the
           marked number has an unmarked expression.

Such a complementarity of expression and meaning is not at all anomalous
with the structure of English. Note that in the genitive case paradigm,
which I discussed at the start of this chapter, the double markedness of the

genitive plural is expressed by zero rather than by an overt suffix. The complementarity of this pattern can be stated as follows:

(64)   For nouns, the marked category of genitive case has a marked expression in the unmarked singular number and an unmarked expression in the marked plural number.

We might even go on to relate the complementarity in (63) and (64) to the contrast between nouns and verbs. For nouns, the markedness relations between expression and meaning are aligned in the unmarked common case forms but are reversed in the marked possessive case. For verbs, on the other hand, the correlation of expression and meaning is complementary; the unmarked present tense shows formal marking in the category that is unmarked and shows zero expression in the marked categories. This complementarity of the correlation between expression and meaning also yields a syntagmatic complementarity as well in that -s and -$\emptyset$ alternate in the third person to signal singularity and plurality:

(65)   3rd person singular: N + $\emptyset$ V + s
                                (The student works hard.)

            3rd person plural   N + s   V + $\emptyset$
                                (The students work hard.)

Patterns such as these suggest that attempts to defend a strong thesis of markedness iconism between expressions and meanings will fail, at least in the domain of inflectional morphology.[29] What the existence of complementarities does suggest, however, is that a weaker version of iconicity might be in order in which markedness relations between expression and content are sometimes patterns of alignment and sometimes patterns of complementarity (reverse iconicity), perhaps with different areas of grammar organized according to different principles. Shapiro describes the markedness values in the system of Russian conjugation:

> as the analysis of Russian conjugation has repeatedly made manifest, the morphophonemic system of a language largely eschews the symmetrical, replicative patterns of semiosis which are favored by phonology. Indeed, morphophonemics systematically exploits a second, less-studied form of complementation; this is antisymmetrical in its effects, as an inversion, and can accordingly be called CHIASTIC. The predominant use of chiastic complementation is perfectly consistent with the semiotic nature of morphophonemics. . . . [1980:89]

Although Shapiro introduced the term *markedness complementarity* to characterize alternations of morpheme shape (such as vowel/zero alternations in Russian word formation), the principle appears relevant to the organization of English inflectional categories as well. The fundamental idea of introducing a principle of complementarity is that values of expressions and meanings can vary in coherent and uniform patterns (both syntagmatic and paradigmatic). The role of markedness is that of an organizing principle supplying an evaluative vocabulary for investigating the patterning of linguistic categories.

The difficulties of such a value-based, semiotic approach to grammar are not to be underestimated. One problem is that of determining markedness values, though I have tried to address this by showing how formal and semantic markedness values can be determined by a set of heuristics. A second problem that arises in analyses positing markedness assimilation and markedness complementarity is determining which principle applies when. If expressions and meaning can be either aligned or complementary, then won't one or the other principle be satisfied by any pattern? How is circularity to be avoided?

The circularity of the approach is vicious only if it is insisted that all linguistic patterns are compulsory diagrams of underlying relations. However, if the obligatoriness of iconic congruence is rejected, then markedness assimilation and complementarity can be seen not as an a priori dictum but as patterns—signs—that are either grounded in the facts of language or are not. Iconic diagrams are the result of the interpretation of the facts of language rather than imposed by theoretical axioms. Linguists interpreting the patterns of the language stand in for the community of speakers. Their posited analyses represent claims about the patterning of value in the surface system of the language. Markedness patterns must, for this reason, be thought of as interpretive products, and hence subject to dispute, rather than a set of facts to be memorized.[30] A particular pattern can be challenged, refuted, or corrected in various ways: by showing that the markedness values it is based on are incorrect; by showing that there is a better account of the same data based on other patterns or values; by showing that the system of data is basically incoherent or unpatterned.

It is worth pointing out that the method of analyzing language into patterns of markedness values is perhaps more similar to interpretative disciplines such as literary analysis or symbolic anthropology than to traditional American structural linguistics. Viewed in terms of markedness, a language is an artifact or text, made up of oppositions that have values in the overall system. The values of oppositions may play a role in defining assimilatory or complementary patterns of their associated categories. These patterns are real (though not compulsory), since they are based in the forms of the language, but are hidden and must be revealed through the analysis of the language in terms of assimilation and complementarity.

The interpretive, rather than deductive, focus of markedness assimilation and complementarity does not invalidate the search for patterns of markedness. What counts is that the patterns found explain something worth explaining. We must, therefore, ask what is accomplished in analyzing language as a system of values. In what way does such an enterprise help us to explain the structure of a language? The answer to such questions is at two levels, I believe. The significance of markedness relations lies first in the simple recognition of asymmetry in language from the point of view of language use. Understanding the choice between past and present, between *old* and *young*, between an overt pronoun and zero in terms of marked and unmarked value unifies stylistic and grammatical choices in terms of their information content, context, and unconscious evaluation: markedness is method of interpretation that allows us to understand the nuance—the communicative aesthetic—of a message and (in some cases) of the culture of which it is a part.

The second level of significance of markedness relations lies in the realization that the correlation between expression and meaning and between units and contexts is not totally arbitrary but rather patterned by diagrams of asymmetric relations. In allowing for the possibility that values build upon and reflect one another in patterns of assimilation or complementarity, the significance of markedness moves beyond a useful taxonomy of asymmetries to give language a superstructure of evaluation. The analysis of markedness relations supplements other methods of grammatical analysis by addressing the question of *why* certain forms express certain categories. In chapter 5 I will explore the possibility that the nonarbitrariness implied in markedness patterns plays a role in explaining aspects of language change—that is, in answering the question of *why* certain changes are selected from among competing possibilities. When grammar itself provides no push, why does language pattern one way and not another? These are the areas where an analysis in terms of markedness relations will be most revealing.

Summary: Determining Values and Finding Principles

In this chapter, we have considered the nature of the markedness relations between grammatical categories in English, illustrating how factors of meaning, use, and distribution may be used to argue for one or another assignment of markedness values. In the spirit of the Prague School approach to markedness, I have also raised the question of the alignment of expression and meaning and have illustrated the structural principles of markedness assimilation (categories of like markedness value co-occur) and markedness complementarity (co-occurrence of marked and unmarked categories). Together with Brøndal's principle of compensation, which states that unmarked categories tend to be more differentiated than marked categories, and the principle of markedness reversal, which allows that general markedness values may be locally reversed in specialized contexts, these principles make up an interpretive theory of markedness relations. Such an interpretive theory assumes that the facts of language are in most cases coherently patterned and that languages prefer a goodness of fit between expression and meaning that will be revealed in the assimilation or complementation of markedness values.

As for the markedness values themselves, the grammatical categories of English have illustrated several themes. The locality of markedness values has been illustrated in the aspect, case, and singular/plural number systems. The tendency for marked expression to correlate with marked concepts was illustrated in the syntax of word order. However this principle appears to be somewhat less applicable to the analysis of inflectional categories: for inflection complementarity of expression and meaning may be an equally important principle (perhaps because it allows a greater contrast between marked and unmarked semantic categories). The importance of a language-particular analysis was illustrated by the markedness of the English case system (in which objective turns out to be the unmarked term) and the pronominal number system (where plural is unmarked), which differ from cross-linguistic markedness values assumed in other studies.

4

Phonology, Morphology, and Morphophonemics

The Markedness Values of Phonological Features

The physical process of speaking involves more than a hundred muscles controlled by the nervous system. Actual spoken words, moreover, are physically continuous events articulated at a rapid rate. Yet speakers of languages have relatively little trouble dividing utterances into discrete sound segments. In part this is because the mind imposes an analysis on sound matter that divides it up into discrete, segment-sized feature matrices called phonemes. Phonemes are, in the classical view, sounds whose distinctiveness signals differences in meaning, as the distinctiveness of /I/ and /i/ in the pair of words *bit* and *beat* (/bIt/ and /bit/) differentiates the meaning of the words in question. The phonemes of a language may be viewed as the psychologically distinctive sound units of a language. Not all sound differences in a language are phonemic, of course; some, such as the difference between the /æ/ sounds in *bat* and in *bad,* are purely phonetic (or allophonic) differences that enhance distinctive differences. The difference in length between the two pronunciations of /æ/ does not function in English to distinguish the meaning of two different words but is instead predictable from qualities of the surrounding sounds, in this case from the voicing of the final consonant. The two pronunciations of /æ/ are different phones, i.e., they are physically distinctive sound units, but they are the same phoneme.

The phones and phonemes of a language are treated as feature matrices consisting of more minimal quanta of language—the features themselves. Phonological regularities of a language are expressed in terms of the feature values of segments. Allophonic variation (as between the pronunciations of /æ/ can be naturally treated as a process of phonological derivation by which phonetic entities are derived from phonemic ones by filling in predictable feature values. Similarly, change of a morpheme shape (a morphophonemic alternation) can often be treated as a process in which one phoneme changes to another by altering some feature values. Thus

when the /f/ of *knife* becomes /v/ in the plural, we treat this as a change in
the feature of voicing in a feature matrix that otherwise defines the class of
labiodental fricative consonants (/f/ and /v/).[1]

A question that will occupy us later in this chapter is the correlation
between markedness values of phonological units and the markedness values of the grammatical categories with which they are associated. The correlation between the values of forms and the values of their conceptual
objects was raised briefly in chapter 2, where it was pointed out that the
concern for the formal expression of conceptual structure was a recurrent
theme in the Jakobsonian tradition. This correlation was developed in more
detail in the last chapter, where I introduced the theme of diagrammaticity
pioneered by Peirce and Jakobson. In the second half of the present chapter,
I return to the question of how markedness mediates the relation between
expression and meaning. First, however, it is necessary to provide some
illustration of the markedness values of the various phonological features.

My method of exposition will be as follows: I first give some tentative markedness assignments for phonological features in isolation. These
assignments, which are given in the two following sections, are based on
the implicational relations between features assumed by Jakobson (1968
[1941]) and by Jakobson and Halle (1971 [1956]). I then look at the function and distribution of sounds in English phonotactics as a means of illustrating and supporting these markedness assignments. In connection with
the concatenation of sounds into syllables, I return to the topic of contextual reversal. As indicated in chapter 2, the values of features do not exist
in isolation; rather, a feature's value depends on such factors as its place in
the feature hierarchy and its simultaneous, sequential, or syllable context.

Like grammatical systems, sound systems are most insightfully
viewed as subdivisions of ranked features. Just as verbs are divided into
finite and nonfinite, indicative and nonindicative, and so on, sounds are
divided into consonantal and nonconsonantal, continuant and noncontinu-
ant, and so on. Before considering the markedness values of phonemes, let
me reemphasize the hierarchical organization of the phonological features,
since it has been suggested that the hierarchization of phonological distinctive features interacts with markedness in certain ways.[2] With respect to
paradigmatic context, Shapiro (1972, 1974) suggests that the context sensitivity of the markedness value in feature hierarchies is determined by patterns of replication and reversal that hold for (parts of) the feature
hierarchy. He has argued, for example, that in the vocalic subhierarchy the
presence of a positive specification in a superordinate feature entails the
replication of the markedness values of that feature in the subordinate feature, while in the consonantal subhierarchy the presence of a plus specification entails the opposite markedness value in the subordinate feature.[3]

According to Shapiro, such replications and reversals will universally determine the general values of features. However, such proposed universals are difficult to confirm, and Shapiro qualifies his scheme by exempting certain features and by positing a reversal of the principles when features are nondistinctive.[4] I nevertheless raise the issue to underscore the point that context may be paradigmatic (hierarchical) as well as syntagmatic (combinatorial).[5]

Returning now to the main theme, let us consider the markedness values of the hierarchy of phonological features introduced in chapter 2.

As might be expected, at the top of the hierarchy of phonological features are the features that define the major classes of sounds—the features consonantal/nonconsonantal and vocalic/nonvocalic.

The first question that arises is, Which opposition is superordinate, consonantal/nonconsonantal or vocalic/nonvocalic? I assume here, following Jakobson (1968 [1941]), Kuipers (1970), and others, that the consonantal opposition is generally superordinate to the vocalic one and the [+consonantal] is the unmarked value of the opposition (cf. Andersen 1974). This yields the following hierarchy:

(1)

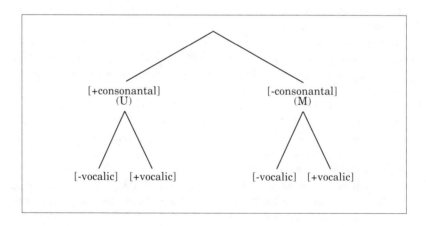

The subordinate opposition of vocalicness divides the consonantalness opposition to yield the four major classes of sounds: obstruents, resonants, glides, and vowels. Now we ask this: what are the markedness values of the features [+vocalic] and [-vocalic] in these contexts?

The markedness value of vocalicness is reversed depending on the feature value of [consonantal]. In [-consonantal] segments, the feature

[+vocalic] is unmarked. Hence vowels are marked with respect to the feature nonconsonantal, but unmarked with respect to the feature vocalic. Conversely, nonvocalicness is marked in the context [−consonantal], that is to say that glides are doubly marked as both nonconsonantal and nonvocalic. Within the [+consonantal] branch of the hierarchy, vocalicness is marked and nonvocalicness is unmarked; for obstruent consonants (including nasals), the features [+consonantal] and [−vocalic] are both unmarked. Liquid consonants are unmarked for the feature [+consonantal] and have the marked feature [+vocalic]. The overall patterning of markedness values for obstruents, vowels, glides, and liquids is as follows:

(2)

	Consonantal	Vocalic
Obstruents	+ (U)	− (U)
Vowels	− (M)	+ (U)
Liquids	+ (U)	+ (M)
Glides	− (M)	− (M)

Markedness Values of the English Consonants

Within the category of [+consonantal] segments, we first consider the markedness of stops versus fricatives. This contrast is defined by the opposition abrupt versus nonabrupt. Abrupt consonants—that is, affricates and stops (including resonant stops)—are unmarked for abruptness while fricatives are marked as nonabrupt. This assignment of markedness values is borne out by the fact that resonants resemble stops in their articulation rather than resembling fricatives. The unmarked value of abruptness is the one that the marked resonants have, in accordance with Brøndal's principle. Among nonconsonantal segments (vowels and glides) the opposition between abrupt and nonabrupt segments is canceled; vowels and glides are always nonabrupt, so nonabrupt is the unmarked (and in fact the only) value for those segments.

Note that the markedness values of abruptness are reversed for consonantal and nonconsonantal segments. Markedness values are also reversed for voicing, the division falling between obstruent consonants ([+consonantal, −vocalic]) and all other segments. The unmarked value for obstruents is [−voiced] and the marked value is [+voiced]. For resonants, vowels, and glides the unmarked value of voicing is [+voiced].

Reversal is not always the case for consonantal and nonconsonantal realizations of a feature. Sometimes the markedness values are the same in both types of segments. So, for example, nasality is marked in both consonants and vowels since both oral vowels and consonants are more broadly-defined than their nasal counterparts.[6]

In the opposition tense versus lax, tenseness is the unmarked feature and lax is marked. Since tenseness and laxness allow voicing to be predictable features of English consonants, the features for voicing are redundant. Another important set of features to be considered are those that distinguish the various places of articulation. Included among those features are the oppositions grave/acute and compact/noncompact. Acute consonants (dentals and alveolars) are unmarked as opposed to grave ones (labials and velars).[7] Noncompact consonants (labials and dentals) are unmarked as opposed to compact ones (palatals, velars, and retroflexed consonants such as English /r/ in many cases).[8] The markedness values of the alveolars, labials, palatals, and velars are given below:[9]

(3)   Grave   Compact

    Alveolar consonants   − (U)   − (U)
    Labial consonants   + (M)   − (U)
    Palatal, velar, and retroflex consonants   + (M)   + (M)

The feature of stridency distinguishes the sibilant fricatives from the nonsibilants and also distinguishes affricates from stops. Stridency is subordinate to the feature abrupt/nonabrupt; [+strident] is optimal in nonabrupt segments and [−strident] is optimal in abrupt ones. This situation can be represented by the branching diagram below:

(4)

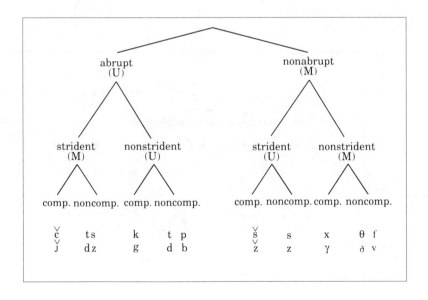

The affricates /č/, /ǰ/, /ts/, and /dz/ and the fricatives /x/, /γ/, /θ/, /ð/, /f/, and /v/ are marked. Stops and the sibilant fricatives are unmarked.

We are now in a position to summarize the markedness values of the consonants. The following tables give the traditional phonetic classification of phonemes; their distinctive feature analysis and the markedness values of these features in the context of the segment are indicated. Note that each segment in the consonant inventory can be given a composite value that is the sum of the markedness values of its features. The composite values of each segment are given as integers under the column for that segment.

Table 1

Articulatory Classification

	labial	labio-dental	dental	alveolar	alveo-palatal	palatal	velar	glottal
Stops								
voiceless	p			t			k	
voiced	b			d			g	
Affricates								
voiceless						č		
voiced						ǰ		
Fricatives								
voiceless		f	θ	s	š			h
voiced		v	ð	z	ž			
Nasals	m			n			ŋ	
Liquids				l	r			

Table 2

Distinctive Feature Classification

	p	t	č	k	b	d	ǰ	g	f	θ	s	š	h	v	ð	z	ž	m	n	ŋ	l	r
consonantal	+	+	+	+	+	+	+	+	+	+	+	+	+	+	+	+	+	+	+	+	+	+
vocalic	−	−	−	−	−	−	−	−	−	−	−	−	−	−	−	−	−	−	−	−	+	+
nasal	−	−	−	−	−	−	−	−	−	−	−	−	−	−	−	−	−	+	+	+	−	−
compact	−	−	+	+	−	−	+	+	−	−	−	+	+	−	−	−	+	−	−	+	−	+
abrupt	+	+	+	+	+	+	+	+	−	−	−	−	−	−	−	−	−	−	+	+	+	+
strident	−	−	+	−	−	−	+	−	−	−	+	+	−	−	−	+	+	−	−	−	−	−
tense	+	+	+	+	−	−	−	−	+	+	+	+	+	−	−	−	−	−	−	−	−	−
grave	+	−	−	+	+	−	−	+	+	−	−	−	+	+	−	−	−	+	−	+	−	−

Redundant features of voicing and flatness are omitted. Note also that the treatment of /h/ given here differs from that of Jakobson, who treated it as a glide rather than a consonant.

Table 3

Markedness Values of Consonants

	p	t	č	k	b	d	ǰ	g	f	θ	s	š	h	v	ð	z	ž	m	n	ŋ	l	r
consonantal	U	U	U	U	U	U	U	U	U	U	U	U	U	U	U	U	U	U	U	U	U	U
vocalic	U	U	U	U	U	U	U	U	U	U	U	U	U	U	U	U	U	U	U	U	M	M
nasal	U	U	U	U	U	U	U	U	U	U	U	U	U	U	U	U	U	M	M	M	U	U
compact	U	U	M	M	U	U	M	M	U	U	U	M	M	U	U	U	M	U	U	M	U	U
abrupt	U	U	U	U	U	U	U	U	M	M	U	U	M	M	M	U	U	U	U	U	U	U
strident	U	U	M	U	U	U	M	U	M	M	M	M	M	M	M	M	M	U	U	U	U	U
tense	U	U	U	U	M	M	M	M	U	U	U	U	U	M	M	M	M	U	U	U	U	U
grave	M	U	U	M	M	U	U	M	M	U	U	U	M	M	U	U	U	M	U	M	U	M
composite value	1	0	2	2	2	1	3	3	3	2	1	2	4	4	3	2	3	2	1	3	1	2

In terms of composite values, the consonants most unmarked are /t/, /p/, /d/, /l/, and /s/. The most marked segments are /h/, /v/, and /ŋ/.

Such tables of markedness values as that given above provide an overview of the markedness of a segment system. However, such composite markedness values as these give only a rough account of segment evaluation. In fact, in certain respects composite values are misleading since integer values lump together sounds that are otherwise quite disparate. Part of the problem is that tables like these abstract away from context, presenting the illusion that segments can be evaluated in isolation. Moreover, marked features do not all really have the same weight—some marked features count more heavily in segment evaluation. I do not propose to take up the technical problem of encoding such weightings to arrive at more accurate pictures of segmental markedness (if in fact this is possible; cf. Bailey 1973 and Vennemann 1972 for some early tries at this). My intention in supplying such tables is merely that they give the reader enough of a sense of the markedness of English consonant sounds to make the remainder of the discussion in this chapter comprehensible.

The Markedness Assignments of Vowels and Glides

The maximally unmarked vowel is taken by Jakobson and others to be a low central vowel approximating /a/. After /a/, the least marked vowels are high front unrounded and high back rounded vowels, yielding the classic vowel triangle of high front unrounded, high back rounded, and low central vowels: *i, u, a*. Both typologically and ontologically these may be regarded as the optimal vowels (cf. Jakobson and Halle 1971 [1956]). The feature matrices involved are as shown below:[10]

(5)   a   i   u

+compact	−compact	−compact
−diffuse	+diffuse	+diffuse
−flat	−flat	+flat
−tense	−tense	−tense
+grave	−grave	+grave

We might analyze the values [+diffuse] and [+compact] as generally unmarked for vowels, following Andersen (1974), Shapiro (1972), and Waugh (1979). According to this analysis, in the primary low vowel /a/, [+compact] will be unmarked and [−diffuse] marked. For high vowels, [+diffuse] is unmarked and [−compact] is marked. Mid vowels, which are [−diffuse, −compact], will have the value of [−compact] as marked and will be doubly marked, that is, marked for both diffuseness and compactness.

The feature compact appears to have a special status in the vowel system, one that is required in connection with the treatment of /a/ as the unmarked vowel. To capture the fact that low vowels other than /a/ are less optimal than high vowels, it must be assumed that [+compact] is marked for all low vowels other than /a/. This results in markedness values for high, mid, and low vowels as below (cf. Andersen 1974, Kean 1980 [1975]):

(6)   Compact   Diffuse

High	− (M)	+ (U)
Mid	− (M)	− (M)
Low	+ (M)	− (M)
/a/	+ (U)	− (M)

Let us now turn our attention to the values of the features [grave] and [flat]. For low vowels, I assume that the unmarked values of these features are [+grave] and [−flat], as in the vowel /a/. As pointed out in chapter 2, the typologically optimal values of these features are mutually dependent for high and mid (i.e., noncompact) vowels. For high and mid vowels, the unmarked combination of these features is for vowels to be grave and flat or to be nongrave and nonflat. Grave nonflat and flat nongrave vowels are cross-linguistically rarer and appear to be acquired later than vowels representing the other combinations of those features. What we therefore desire is that the composite markedness value of flat nongrave vowels like /ü/ and of grave nonflat vowels like /ɨ/ be greater than those of vowels like /i/ and /u/. One way to accommodate this is to make the markedness of [flat] subordinate to the value of [grave]:

(7)

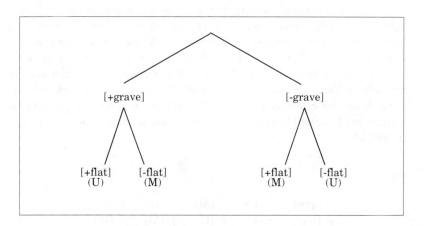

We could also take the approach of subordinating [grave] to [flat]:

(8)

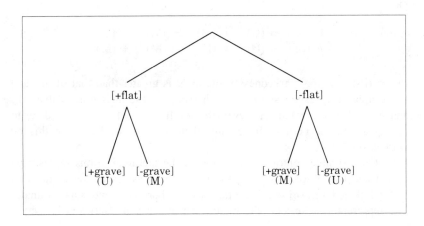

Either option achieves the desired result that the combination [−grave, +flat] will always be more highly marked than [+grave, +flat] and that the combination [+grave, −flat] will always be more highly marked than [−grave, −flat]. Languages treat the relationship between flat and grave in different ways. Some (such as Russian) have a distinctive flatness opposition and a redundant gravity opposition; others (such as Japanese) have a distinctive opposition of gravity and a redundant opposition of flatness (cf. Shapiro 1983, Waugh 1979). Assuming that distinctive oppositions dominate redundant ones, languages might have either the system in (7) or that in (8).

A problem arises, however, in that there is also a markedness relation between the superordinate features in (7) and (8). This skews the composite markedness values of the four combinations of feature values. What we desire is for /ü/ and /ɨ/ to be marked with respect to /u/ and /i/, but we don't want /u/ and /i/ to differ in markedness. But whichever way the values of the superordinate features are assigned, the composite values will be skewed. So, for example, consider (7) above and suppose that [+grave] is marked and [−grave] is unmarked. Then the markedness of /i/, /u/, /ü/, and /ɨ/ will be:

(9)   i   u   ü   ɨ

        grave   − (U)   + (M)   − (U)   + (M)
        flat   − (U)   + (U)   + (M)   − (M)

Similarly, if we take [flat] as the superordinate feature, as in (8), we have:

(10)   i   u   ü   ɨ

        flat   − (U)   + (M)   + (M)   − (U)
        grave   − (U)   + (U)   − (M)   + (M)

In the first case the markedness value of /i/ is greater than that of /u/, and /u/ is equal in markedness to /ü/; in the second case /i/ is greater than /u/, and /u/ and /ɨ/ are equal. However, the result we want is for /i/ and /u/ to be equal and for both to be greater than /ü/ and /ɨ/. How can this be worked out?

One possible solution is to combine the hierarchizations represented by (7) and (8) above, assigning the markedness values of the features so that [flat] and [grave] are simultaneously subordinate and superordinate. The representation reflects the mutual dependence of [flat] and [grave].[11]

(11)

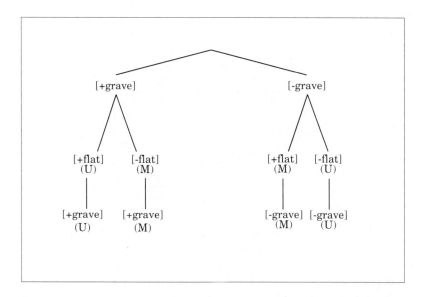

The markedness values of [grave] will be determined subordinately to flatness, and the markedness values of [flat] will be determined subordinately to gravity. The markedness values of /i/, /u/, /ü/, and /ɨ/ will be:

(12)   i   u   ü   ɨ

flat   − (U)   + (U)   + (M)   − (M)
grave   − (U)   + (U)   − (M)   + (M)

Now we turn to the feature [tense]. There is some reason to believe that distinctively tense vowels (/i/, /u/, /e/, and /o/) are marked and that lax vowels are unmarked. This is because tenseness is a more restricted feature in the vowel system, only functioning distinctively among the [−compact] vowels.[12] On the other hand, Shapiro (1983:87) has suggested that tenseness is unmarked among vowels and marked among consonants. This suggestion is supported by the freedom of distribution of tense vowels syntagmatically (thus, for example, we have words like *bee* /bi/ but not *bi* /bI/). One possible reconciliation of these facts is that tenseness among vowels is contextualized by vowel height, and that tenseness is unmarked for noncompact vowels, but marked for compact ones. I adopt this as a tentative hypothesis.

This completes our survey of markedness values for the vowel features. The tables below summarize the classification and markedness values of the English vowels and glides.

Table 4

Traditional Classification of English Vowels

	Front Unrounded	Central	Back Rounded
High	i		u
	I		U
Mid	e	ə	o
	ɛ		
Low	æ	a	ɔ

Table 5

Distinctive Feature Analysis of Vowels and Glides

	i	I	e	ɛ	æ	u	U	o	ɔ	a	ə	j	w
consonantal	−	−	−	−	−	−	−	−	−	−	−	−	−
vocalic	+	+	+	+	+	+	+	+	+	+	+	−	−
nasal	−	−	−	−	−	−	−	−	−	−	−	−	−
compact	−	−	−	−	+	−	−	−	+	+	−	−	−
diffuse	+	+	−	−	−	+	+	−	−	−	−	+	+
voiced	+	+	+	+	+	+	+	+	+	+	+	+	+
tense	+	−	+	−	−	+	−	+	−	−	−	−	−
grave	−	−	−	−	−	+	+	+	+	+	+	−	+
flat	−	−	−	−	−	+	+	+	+	−	−	−	+

Table 6

Markedness Values of Vowels and Glides

	i	I	e	ɛ	æ	u	U	o	ɔ	a	ə	j	w
consonantal	M	M	M	M	M	M	M	M	M	M	M	M	M
vocalic	U	U	U	U	U	U	U	U	U	U	U	M	M
nasal	U	U	U	U	U	U	U	U	U	U	U	U	U
compact	M	M	M	M	M	M	M	M	M	U	M	M	M
diffuse	U	U	M	M	M	U	U	M	M	U	M	U	U
voiced	U	U	U	U	U	U	U	U	U	U	U	U	U
tense	U	M	U	M	U	U	M	U	M	U	U	U	U
grave	U	U	U	U	M	U	U	U	U	U	U	U	U
flat	U	U	U	U	U	U	U	U	M	U	U	U	U
composite value	2	3	3	4	4	2	3	3	5	1	3	3	3

With respect to the composite markedness values in Table 6, I again note that such integer values abstract away from the weights and contexts of features, sometimes perhaps yielding counterintuitive results.

Marked and Unmarked Features in English Syllable Onsets and Codas

Having sketched the markedness values of the English phonemes, I now wish to consider in more detail how markedness values function in context. Broadly speaking, we are interested in determining how the categories of marked and unmarked are played out as (respectively) the more narrowly defined and more broadly defined feature values in English sound structure. As we have seen, nonequivalence of feature values can be looked at in various ways. In this section the focus will be on the combination of segments in consonant clusters that make up syllable onsets and codas in English, and I will illustrate the way in which marked segments are more narrowly defined phonotactically than their unmarked counterparts.

I choose to examine the syllable structure of onsets and codas in English for two reasons. The first is simply that interesting generalizations emerge that illustrate the distribution of marked and unmarked features with a minimum of theoretical background. We are able to see that certain feature oppositions are excluded in complex syllable positions such as consonant clusters and that it is usually marked terms of the oppositions that are excluded from clusters. The second reason for examining syllable structure is that the sequential makeup of clusters highlights the context sensitivity of markedness. Just as just as co-occurrence of features in the same segment can engender a reversal of values, so too can sequential and structural context in the syllable or cluster. In particular, we will see in this section that English sound structure has certain reversals of the general markedness values (given above) in the context of like features in a cluster.[13]

In the last section I developed some hypotheses concerning marked and unmarked feature values. Some background is now needed concerning the structure of consonant clusters and the positions in clusters that various segments and features may occupy. I therefore begin with a brief overview of the structure of the syllable onsets of English.

Three types of onsets are permitted in English: onsets consisting of single consonants (as in *pin, go, thin*), onsets consisting of two-consonant clusters (as in *preen, ski*, etc.), and onsets consisting of three-consonant clusters (as in *spray, stripe*, etc.). A simple onset can consist of *almost* any English consonant, the compact sounds /ž/ and /ŋ/ being excluded in native vocabulary. Clusters of two consonants (CC clusters) are restricted to: (a) a fricative plus an obstruent stop, (b) a fricative plus a resonant, and (c) a stop plus a resonant. These possibilities are illustrated below. The possible clusters are arranged in columns so as to exhibit the parallelism in point of articulation among the second consonants of each cluster, and blank spaces indicate gaps in the co-occurrence patterns:

(13)   CC Onsets

    (a) /sp/   /st/   /sk/
    (b) /sm/   /sn/   /sl/
                      /šr/
              /fl/   /fr/
                      /θr/
    (c) /pr/   /tr/   /kr/
        /br/   /dr/   /gr/
        /pl/   /kl/
        /bl/   /gl/

Onset clusters with three consonants (CCC clusters) have an even narrower range of possibilities: in CCC clusters, only the following sequences are permitted:

(13)   CCC Onsets

    (d) /spl/   /skl/
        /spr/   /str/   /skr/

Since CC and CCC onsets exhibit narrower options, we will consider these structures marked phonotactic structures in contrast to onsets consisting of single consonants, which are unmarked (cf. Shapiro 1972, Kean 1980 [1975], Kaye and Lowenstamm 1981).

    Two observations about the distribution of features in marked phonotactic structures are relevant to the patterning of markedness values. The first is that the major-class features and manner-of-articulation features combine in a complementary fashion. In row (13a), stops, which are unmarked for abruptness, combine with fricatives, which are marked for that feature. In (b) and (c), fricatives and stops, which as a class are unmarked for vocalicness, combine with resonants, which are marked for vocalicness. It appears that combinations of consonantal segments favor a dissimilarity or complementarity of segment types.

A second way in which features pattern in marked clusters is in terms of the exclusion of certain features (and thus of the segments those features define). In onset clusters we find a number of exclusions, and in all cases the features excluded from the cluster are marked with respect to the features permitted in the cluster.

Consider first the patterns in rows (13a) and (b). In (a) fricatives combine with obstruent stops, and in (b) fricatives combine with resonants. The fricative of choice in these patterns is /s/. (The exclusion of /s/ in CC onsets before /r/ is only apparent, I believe.) The absence of any /sr/ onsets and the lack of /š/ in any other onset clusters suggests that /šr/ is underlyingly /sr/ with /s/ assimilating to the compactness of /r/. Given this, we can view the patterns in the first two rows of (b) as uniformly involving /s/ (cf. Cairns 1988). Of course, /s/ is the maximally unmarked fricative, so it is natural that it occurs in most fricative plus stop clusters. There are also fricative plus resonant clusters with /f/, which, next to /s/, is the least marked fricative (/f/ is unmarked for voice and compactness). And there is just one cluster with /θ/, a fricative that is more marked than /f/. The relative markedness of /s/, /f/, and /θ/ thus reflects their occurrence in clusters.

In row (13a) we also note the exclusion of voiced obstruent stops from combining with /s/, [+voiced] being the marked value of the feature [voicing]. In the clusters in rows (a) and (b), then, we find a tendency to form clusters by combining the unmarked fricatives and stops. Confirmation of the markedness value of resonants can be found in the gap in the row in which /f/ combines with resonants: nasals, which are marked for nasality, are excluded, while the unmarked resonants /l/ and /r/ are permitted. The exclusion of nasals in favor of the liquids also shows up in the stop plus resonant pattern in (c). Also note that the major systematic exception to the patterning in (13a through c), fricative plus fricative patterns found in Greek borrowings like *sphere, Sphinx,* and *sphincter,* combines the two least marked fricatives, /s/ and /f/.

Phonotactic patterns like these can be viewed in terms of the exclusion of marked features in marked syllable structure contexts. Other phonotactic gaps in English, however, require further language-specific principles to be elaborated for contextual reversals of markedness values. Consider the pattern of stops plus liquids, repeated below:

(13)(c)	/pr/	/tr/	/kr/
	/br/	/dr/	/gr/
	/pl/		/kl/
	/bl/		/gl/

There are no CC clusters consisting of /tl/ or /dl/ (excluding the word *Tlingit*, which is of course borrowed from the Amerind language that it names). What accounts for this gap? The relevant factor appears to be that /t/, /d/, and /l/ are all alveolar. The phonotactics of English do not admit sequences of [+acute, −compact, −abrupt] consonants. This proscription may be understood as a contextual reversal of the markedness values of those features. While [+acute], [−compact], and [−abrupt] are generally unmarked features, they are contextually marked when they occur in a consonant cluster next to a segment with the same feature combination. This reversal can be expressed in the following way:[14]

(14)   Markedness Reversal in Alveolar Clusters
            [−compact] consonants are marked if adjacent to [−compact] consonants.
            [+acute] consonants are marked if adjacent to [+acute] consonants.
            [−abrupt] consonants are marked if adjacent to [−abrupt] consonants.

In other words, these feature values are marked when they occur in the context of identical feature values. The effect is to devalue clusters of alveolar stops. (14) is a descriptive generalization about markedness values that asserts that consonant sequences in which both elements are alveolar stops will be doubly marked (viz., /tl/, /dl/, /ld/, /lt/, /nd/, /nt/, /tn/, /dn/, /td/, /dt/).[15] This assignment of markedness values enables us to describe the lack of such clusters as part of the same bias against inherently marked consonants in clusters.[16] Note that /tr/ and /dr/ sequences will not be marked by this rule since /r/ is a compact resonant (i.e., [+compact]) in English. Similarly, fricative plus stop sequences will not be marked by this rule since they will differ in abruptness.

We can be reasonably certain of the validity of the reversal discussed above since it is confirmed by more widespread restrictions on pairs of adjacent consonants. The well-known prohibition on the consonantal allomorphs (/-t/ or /-d/, as opposed to /-Id/) of the past tense ending after roots ending in an alveolar stop reflects the markedness of alveolar sequences, as does the tendency for the past tense ending to be dropped in the context of alveolar resonants or stops (*I tol' you, I expec' to win*, etc.). In these situations the markedness reversal is extended across morpheme and word boundaries.

Markedness reversal of the major-class and manner-of-articulation features fits in well with the complementary structure of complex onsets. The exclusion of CC sequences in which both consonants are obstruent stops, for example, can be encoded as a reversal in which adjacent obstruent stops are devalued:

(15)   Markedness Reversal for Adjacent Stops
         In a [+consonantal, −vocalic] sequence, [+abrupt] is marked
         if adjacent to [+abrupt].

Similarly, the prohibitions involving fricative plus fricative sequences and resonant plus resonant sequences suggest that adjacent pairs of those segments are devalued as well:

(16)   Markedness Reversal for Adjacent Fricatives
         In a [+consonantal, −vocalic] sequence, [−abrupt] is marked
         if adjacent to [−abrupt].

(17)   Markedness Reversal for Adjacent Resonants
         In a [+consonantal, +vocalic] sequence, [+abrupt] is marked
         if adjacent to [+abrupt].

It should be pointed out that not all identical features become marked when adjacent. The feature compact, for example, seems to invite assimilation and therefore identity. Consider, for example, the observation made earlier, that an underlying phonotactic /sr/ is phonetically realized as [šr]. Here the compactness of /r/ is adopted by the fricative /s/. A similar assimilation of [+compact] is suggested by the pronunciation of /tr/ and /dr/ clusters with affricates, as in the pronunciation of *train* as [čren], *trip* as [črIp], *drain* as [ǰren], and *drip* as [ǰrIp].[17] So it is not always the case that adjacent identical features yield devaluations.

I now turn to coda clusters. The phonotactic patterns of English codas parallel those found in onsets, and we again find restrictions on consonant clusters that confirm the markedness assignments that have been proposed.

The structure of complex (mixed) codas is given below. We find clusters of (a) two obstruent stops, (b) an obstruent stop plus a fricative, (c) a fricative plus an obstruent stop, (d) a nasal plus a stop, (e) a nasal plus a fricative, (f) a liquid plus a stop, (g) a liquid plus a fricative. The table below indicates the permissible sequence of final consonant clusters (cf. Sommerstein 1977:50–51). Morphologically derived clusters have been omitted, and, as in (13) above, the columns indicate the point of articulation of the second consonant.

(18)   English Codas
        (a)   pt   kt
        (b)   ps   ts   ks
                           dz
        (c)   sp   st   sk
                           ft
        (d)   mp   nt   nč   ŋk
                           nd   nǰ
        (e)   mf   nθ   ns   nš
                           nz
        (f)   lp   lt   lč   lk
               lb   ld   lǰ
        (g)   lf   lθ   ls   lš
               lv

The glides /w/, /j/, and /h/ are excluded from final position, a situation that further confirms the markedness of the feature nonconsonantal as opposed to consonantal. Sommerstein treats postvocalic /r/ as part of the syllable peak and hence as excluded from codas.

Especially striking in coda clusters are the restrictions on voicing. A major prohibition is that voiced obstruents are largely missing from coda clusters. This is not due to a simple phonetic assimilation, of course, because the gaps in the pattern persist even when a voiced consonant such as a resonant precedes an obstruent (*/mb/, */mv/, */ŋg/, */nz/, etc.). The voicing restriction of coda clusters is parallel to that found in onset clusters (with the exception of the voiced cluster /dz/, which occurs only marginally in root words such as *adze* and *AIDS*). Another exception to the voicing pattern is the nasal plus voiced obstruent cluster /nd/, as in *hand* and *land* (compare the nonoccurring */mb/ and the nonstandard /ŋg/). It is quite interesting here that in the exceptional cases of /dz/ and /nd/, the permitted clusters are combinations of the unmarked place of articulation, namely alveolar.

The relaxation of the constraint on stop clusters is also revealing. As we see from (18a), stop clusters are possible in coda position, though they are excluded from onsets. We see again the dominance of alveolar consonants. All the allowable stop clusters have the unmarked segment /t/ as the second stop of the sequence. The relaxation of the restriction is a widening of the distribution of the unmarked consonant type, which is exactly what we expect to happen. Note however the absence of geminate stops—that is, clusters of identical stops. This absence reflects our earlier observation concerning the devaluation of adjacent alveolar consonants. The devaluation of adjacent stops is relaxed in codas, but the devaluation of adjacent alveolar stops is not. In the context of a preceding /p/ or /k/, /t/ has its usual unmarked status, but in the context of another /t/, it becomes a marked segment.

The above discussion of onset and coda phonotactics confirms many of the markedness relations asserted in the previous sections. The markedness values of segments, made on the basis of typological laws, are confirmed by restrictions on feature combinations in which marked features are more restricted in the marked syllable structures (complex onsets and codas), while unmarked segments occur more freely. The way in which features combine also illustrates the reversal of markedness values according to context: in some cases modifications of general markedness values can be understood as a contextualization in which features become marked when they co-occur in a cluster with similar features. In taking into account the contextualization of markedness, we can begin to see complementarity as a motif in phonotactic organization as well as syntactic organization.

The study of universals of syllable structure has been pioneered by Greenberg (1978 [1965]), who proposed a number of implicational universals for initial and final consonant clusters (see especially his Universals 1 through 7). Greenberg's generalizations, and their later elaboration by other researchers, confirm the complementary nature of the "syntax" of the syllable. To aid in illustrating this, let us adopt the terminological convention that the middle consonant of a three-consonant cluster is the cluster's core, the consonant closest to the vocalic nucleus is the adjunct, and the external consonant is the precore or postcore. Similarly, two-consonant clusters will consist of a core and an adjunct or a core and a precore (or postcore) segment. Given this terminology, which follows that of Cairns (1986), we can summarize the structure of English consonant clusters as follows:

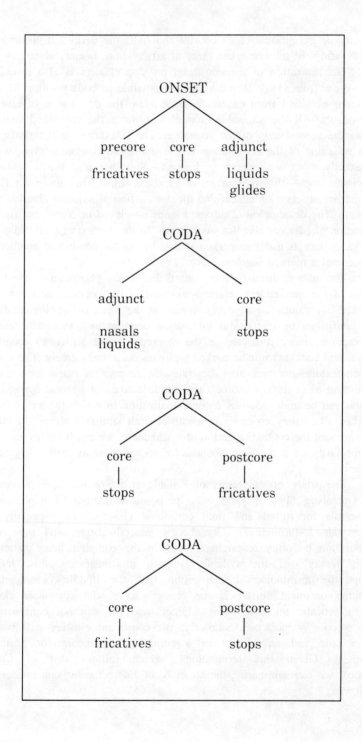

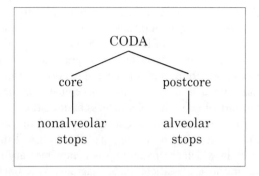

As noted, these templates illustrate the preferred English syllable structures, and it can be seen that these syllable structures are ones in which adjacent segments are generally of complementary types. In addition, the information supplied by such templates should allow us to refine the characterization of markedness values by taking syllable position into account. Such a sharpening of the evaluation scheme would remedy some of the problems noted in connection with tables 3 and 6 above. I will not pursue the contextualization of phonological features further in this book, but interested readers will find an extended coding of markedness values in different syllable positions in Cairns (1988). Relevant material can also be found in Vennemann (1988).

Sound-Meaning Diagrammatization in Morphology and Morphophonemics

In this section we turn our attention to the participation of phonological markedness values in iconic diagrams of conceptual markedness relations. A central theme will be markedness relations among the different shapes (allomorphs) of a morpheme, including the relationship between a zero allomorph and a phonologically overt one, mentioned in the last chapter. In discussing how semantic and phonological signs are related, I will consider the correlation of conceptual and phonological markedness, taking conceptually marked elements to be those that have a more narrow morphological, syntactic, and semantic function, and taking phonologically marked allomorphs to be those that express marked phonological features as contrasted with the phonological feature values of related allomorphs of the same paradigm. Examining the principles that organize the alternations among forms, we pursue the idea, introduced in the last chapter, that markedness assimilation is largely superseded in morphophonemics and morphology by a pattern of markedness complementarity, similar in some respects to the pattern of complementarity found in phonotactics.

Recall that the question of iconism centers on the view of language as a system of signs and particularly on the diagrammaticity of relations between conceptual oppositions and relations of expression (form and phonology). Such an approach inquires how conceptual relations are mapped coherently onto formal relations. Markedness assimilation is the situation in which the mapping of relations is one of alignment of values, a *strictly iconic* mapping.[18] But it has been suggested that coherent mappings of relations also exist in which the patterning is complementary rather than assimilatory, leading to a classification of diagrams as assimilative (strictly iconic) or complementary (reversed iconic).

Markedness assimilation between expression and meaning predicts the alignment of the conceptually basic form of a morphological paradigm with a relatively unmarked phonological form and an alignment of inflected or derived forms with relatively marked phonological forms. The notion of marked phonological form may be construed as including, in addition to affixation, such changes in stem shape as occur in the English strong verbs or in mutated plurals. The principle of markedness assimilation leads us to expect to find marked uses of a root (inflection, derivation) correlated to formal markedness (affixation, stem allomorphy). Consider, for example, the stem alternations in roots in which the voiceless fricatives of the singular become voiced in the plural:[19]

(20)   Singular   Plural

                  wife   wives
                  knife   knives
                  life   lives
                  leaf   leaves
                  staff   staves
                  half   halves
                  wolf   wolves
                  hoof   hooves
                  elf   elves
                  calf   calves
                  dwarf   dwarves
                  scarf   scarves

The relation between phonological and semantic markedness is not always straightforward, however. In other morphophonemic patterns, stems undergo unmarking in morphologically complex situations. Consider, for example, the derivational pattern *five, fifteen, fifty, fifth*. Here we find the unmarked member of the voiced/voiceless pair (/f/) occurring in the morphologically complex environments and the marked member (/v/) occurring in the morphologically simple environment.

As we see from the above examples, and from the discussion of zero versus nonzero inflections in the last chapter, it is easy to find examples in which inflected and derived words undergo unmarking, a result that suggests that markedness assimilation alone is too limited to provide a full understanding and interpretation of morphological diagrams. Instead I suggest that the phonological markedness value of a stem in English may be correlated to the relative conceptual markedness of its morphological function by a complementarity relation.

The principle of complementarity of markedness values allows that morphological expression can be implemented as either a marking or an unmarking depending on the morphological markedness value of the stem. If the stem of a particular morphological category is unmarked, then the derived form will undergo marking; if the stem form is already a marked form, then the derived form will undergo unmarking.

Before going on, a brief digression is perhaps in order concerning the conditions under which a stem or affix should be considered phonologically or conceptually marked. Since stems and affixes occur in the context of morphological paradigms that define a set of related forms or categories, we consider a morphological category more or less marked in relation to its particular set of paradigmatically related categories. The exact conceptual distinctions among categories, of course, depend on the nature of morphological paradigms. For example, in the noun paradigm, plural is conceptually marked as opposed to singular; similarly, genitive case is more marked than the common case of other nouns. Thus, in the noun paradigm the common case singular will be the least marked form, and the genitive plural the most marked. Likewise, for numerals the category cardinal numeral is unmarked with respect to the category ordinal numeral; and simple numerals are unmarked with respect to compound ones.

The phonological markedness of categories that is relevant to morphology is determined in the same fashion. The markedness value of a stem is not determined in an absolute sense (say, by adding the markedness values of all the phonological features), but in terms of the alternations in form that arise in a morphological paradigm. The stem allomorph *five* is phonologically marked with respect to the allomorph *fif-* because *v* is marked as opposed to *f*. A marked stem will often be one that terminates in a marked syllable type or segment—for example, a vowel as opposed to a consonant, a voiced obstruent as opposed to voiceless one, a fricative as opposed to a stop, and so on.

As a simple illustration of complementarity, consider again the English plural. The pattern for common case nouns is for the semantically unmarked term of the morphological paradigm (the singular) to use the bare noun stem form, while in the semantically marked plural either a suffix is added or the noun stem undergoes mutation of the vowel (*woman, man, foot, goose,* etc. are pluralized as *women, men, feet, geese,* etc.). The marked number is expressed by a formal marking of the stem. The pattern is one of alignment:

(21)   a. singular noun (U semantics) : plural noun (M semantics) ::
                [stem + ø] (U form) : [stem + *s*] (M form)

             b. singular noun (U semantics) : plural noun (M semantics) ::
                [stem + ø] (U form) : [mutated stem + ø] (M form)

In the genitive, the increased conceptual markedness is implemented by a further phonological marking in the singular (the -'*s* suffix). What is interesting in the genitive is that the plural forms only have one -*s* suffix, not two: *cat, cats, cat's, cats'* (not **cats's*). In the genitive plural, which is the most marked category conceptually, the plural stem ([noun + *s*]) undergoes a formal unmarking (to the shape [noun + ø]) and the '*s* is added to this unmarked stem. This pattern of markedness values can be represented as follows:

(22)   common case (U) plural (M) : genitive case (M) plural (M) ::
                [stem + -*s*] (M) : [[stem + ø] (U) + -*s*] (M)

The plural stem undergoes a formal unmarking when it is combined with the marked genitive affix. The markedness of the genitive plural is implemented by complementation—by an unmarking of the plural stem—rather than by supplementation with a further formal marking.

The reversal of formal and conceptual markedness values functions as a diagram in the same way that the alignment of values does. In assimilation, formal relations directly replicate conceptual ones. In complementarity, formal relations mirror conceptual ones indirectly through reversal. But in each case a diagrammatic relation exists as a coherent principle of interpretation that makes sense of expression/meaning patterns.

The interpretation of inflectional and derivational forms by complementarity can be extended to other examples as well. The above example was primarily morphological, concerned with the form of the plural suffix. But is is also possible to analyze morphophonemic alternations in terms of complementarity of markedness values. A particularly nice example illustrating the patterning of markedness values in both morphology and morphophonemics involves the suffix *-ion* and its allomorphs. The morphophonemics of the various root classes illustrates a pattern of complementarity of phonological markedness values within the conceptually marked classes of roots.

As described by Aronoff (1976), the suffix *-ion* has five main variants:

(23) a. +ation /ešyən/
      b. +tion   /šyən/
      c. +ion   /yən/
      d. +ition /Išyən/
      e. +ution /ušyən/

The allomorph in (a) is the unrestricted variant; it occurs with roots of various phonological shapes, as the following data indicate:[20]

(24)   Labial   Alveolar   Velar

            perturbation   cessation   evocation
            exhumation   degradation   expurgation
            formation   elicitation   prolongation
                            accusation
                            revelation
                            declaration
                            examination
                            representation
                            deportation
                            manifestation
                            consultation
                            affectation
                            commendation
                            sensation

In addition to the above consonant final stems, *-ation* attaches to vowel final stems: *continue/continuation, vary/variation*. The breadth of its occurrences makes it clearly the unmarked suffix allomorph in opposition to the allomorphs in (b) through (e), each of which is marked vis-à-vis (a) by being restricted only to certain types of roots. Note that in the (a) forms there is no secondary marking or unmarking of roots. There is only simple affixation. In the unmarked root class, the derived form is created by a simple affixation with no change in the root sound shape.

Before turning to the behavior of the marked root classes and marked allomorphs, we will examine a special subclass of roots within class (a). These are roots that end in the sequence *-ate* prior to the addition of *-ation*. Consider the following:

(25)   Stems in *-ate*

Stem	Derived Form	Non-occurring Form
equivocate	equivocation	(*equivocatation)
defecate	defecation	(*defecatation)
demonstrate	demonstration	(*demonstratation)
orate	oration	(*oratation)
inflate	inflation	(*inflatation)

What is happening of course is that the repeated *at(e)* is truncated, precisely as in the pattern that arose in the genitive plural of English nouns. While the addition of the ending *-ation* is generally unmarked, a reversal occurs when the stem and the suffix are formally similar, revaluing this combination as one in which the stems ending in *ate* and the suffix *-ation* are evaluated as marked. In such multiply marked situations, apparent truncation breaks up the combination of marked stem and marked suffix. A similar double markedness and truncation arises with adverbs formed from base adjectives that end in *-ly:* these adverbs have the same form as the adjective base, hence one of the *-ly* endings is omitted. Adjectives ending in *-ly* can be viewed as marked stems, as opposed to ordinary (non *-ly*) adjectives, and the truncation can be seen as a stem unmarking under suffixation.[21]

Returning now to the main example and to the marked allomorphs of the suffix in question, consider the class of stems that combines with allomorph (b), *-tion*. As we see from the list below, almost all of these forms have grave consonants as the root-final segment of the derived forms:

(26)   Stem   Derived Form

	Stem	Derived Form
i.	receive	reception
	deceive	deception
	conceive	conception
ii.	consume	consumption
	resume	resumption
	presume	presumption
	redeem	redemption
iii.	reduce	reduction
	deduce	deduction
	seduce	seduction
iv.	subscribe	subscription
	describe	description
	absorb	absorption
v.	destroy	destruction

Morphophonemics   143

Since -*tion* only occurs with roots ending in grave segments, we consider it to be a marked suffix allomorph, in contrast to the allomorph -*ation*, which occurs generally. A restricted allomorph such as -*tion* may be treated as the conceptually marked variant. Roots that add -*tion* are formally (hence phonologically) marked since they end in grave segments, which are marked as opposed to nongrave. Given the complementarity principle, we expect the derived forms to complement the markedness value of the stem form. And this is in fact what we find. Comparing the formal markedness values of the stem forms to those of the derived forms, we find that the derived forms, though formally marked in the sense that they undergo suffixation, exhibit a secondary phonological unmarking.

In each subcase above, the stem shape of the derived form ends in a segment that is less marked than the final segment of the unsuffixed stem form. In (i), a voiced fricative is found in the stem and a voiceless stop in the derived form; the /v/ is marked for voicing and nonabruptness while the /p/ is unmarked for both those features. In (ii) we find an epenthetic /p/ yielding a CCC cluster (/mps/) in the derived form; such a cluster is less marked than the CC cluster (/ms/) that would otherwise result, since the CCC cluster /mps/ conforms to the marking conventions of English coda phonotactics while /ms/ does not. In (iii) the unmarked stops of the derived form alternate with marked fricatives. In (iv) voicelessness in the derived form alternates with voicing in the stem. And in (v) consonantality alternates with nonconsonantality.

Now consider the stem allomorph -*ion*, listed as (23c) above. This allomorph is also conceptually marked in contrast to -*ation* since it, like -*tion*, is restricted to a specific subclass of roots: -*ion* occurs only with roots ending in nongrave consonants, as we see from the following list:

(27)	Stem	Derived Form	Alternation
	exert	exertion	t/š
	insert	insertion	
	desert	desertion	
	permit	permission	t/š
	admit	admission	
	convert	conversion	t/ž
	revert	reversion	
	digest	digestion	st/šč
	connect	connection	kt/kš
	decide	decision	d/ž
	explode	explosion	
	concede	concession	d/s

scan	scansion	n/nš
convene	convention	
retain	retention	
prevent	prevention	
coerce	coercion	r/rž (rš)
disperse	dispersion	
submerge	submersion	rǰ/rž
adhere	adhesion	r/ž
recur	recursion	r/rž
rebel	rebellion	l/l
expel	expulsion	l/lš
convulse	convulsion	
revise	revision	z/ž
percuss	percussion	s/š
admonish	admonition	s/š

Since we are again dealing with a marked situation we might expect a secondary complementarity between the stem and derived forms. In this case, the stem-final consonants are phonologically unmarked (ending in nongrave segments) and the derived forms are marked. In most instances, the suffixed forms have phonological shapes that differ from the bare stems in having a marked feature where the stem has an unmarked one: nonabruptness as opposed to abruptness, voicing as opposed to voicelessness, and nonacuteness as opposed to acuteness.

The class of roots associated with allomorph (23d), *-ition*, may be most efficiently treated as a marked variant of the already marked class (23c), giving this class a doubly marked value. Roots like *expose, compose,* and *repeat* require a stem extender morpheme *-it-* (realized as /Iš/) between the stem and the class (23c) suffix *-ion*. The addition of the stem extender can be viewed as a secondary marking of the underived stem, parallel to the marking of the stem that occurs in class (23c) above. In (23c) the marking was a morphophonemic alternation; here it is a morphological addition. Treating the addition of the stem extender as a marking aligns markedness values of derived forms like *exposition, composition,* and *repetition* with the markedness value of the derived roots in class (23c) above.

We now turn to class (23e), where we find that stems ending in *-olve* exhibit allomorphs that end in *-olution:*

(28)　　　　　　　Stem　　　　　Derived Form

	revolve	revolution
	evolve	evolution
	solve	solution
	dissolve	dissolution

These roots may be analyzed as variants of class (23b) above, since /v/, the final consonant of the stem, is grave. Morphologically, these forms add the suffix -*tion* to bases ending in /lv/. As in class (23b), we expect a secondary unmarking of the base stem, since grave is the phonologically marked feature. In this case, however, the unmarking of the base takes a slightly different form. Since direct addition of -*tion* to bases ending in /lv/ would result in a marked phonotactic situation (the CCC consonant cluster /lvt/), the unmarking takes the form of the vocalization of /v/ to /u/, yielding a more nearly optimal syllable structure: a CVC syllable /lut/. The change of the grave consonant to the grave vowel has the status of an unmarking due to a reversal of markedness values occasioned by the consonantal context: the feature [+consonantal] is marked in the environment of surrounding [+consonantal] features (cf. Chomsky and Halle 1968). That is, in the cluster /lvs/, the [+consonantal] specification of /v/ is a marked specification, and the change of /v/ to the [−consonantal] /u/ is an unmarking.

The overall pattern of markedness values can be summarized as follows:

(29)

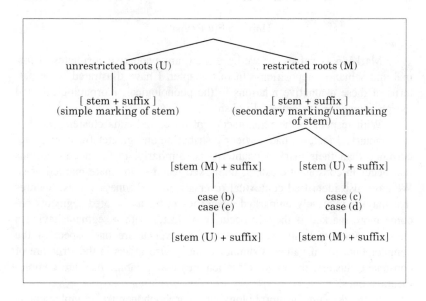

The pattern of markedness values of morphological processes in this example can now be seen as correlated with the markedness of root classes in a mutually defining but ultimately coherent arrangement. Suffix allomorphs are conceptually marked by distribution: the unmarked variant

-ation occurs with all types of roots; the marked variants (*-tion* and *-ion*) occur with only specified classes of roots. Roots themselves are marked for their paradigmatically relevant phonological properties (gravity or nongravity, etc.). In the unmarked class, derivation is simple addition of a suffix with no secondary marking or unmarking. In one subcase, however, that in which the base stem ends in *-ate*, this simple markedness yields a complementarity resulting in an unmarking of the stem.

Within the class of restricted or marked roots, morphophonemic alternations reveal a secondary pattern of markedness complementarity in which phonologically marked stems become unmarked when a restricted suffix is added and phonologically unmarked stems become marked. This pattern also is found in the truncation effect.

What is striking about the pattern of markedness values in *-ion* suffixation is how the morphophonemic facts pattern together as a unified whole. While the actual morphophonemic processes are quite disparate (devoicing, palatalization, vocalization, truncation, stem extension, assibilation, etc.), the principles of alignment and complementarity of markedness values make the overall pattern comprehensible. The patterning of markedness values is a structuring of phonological values signifying a related structure of morphological values—that is, a diagram of values by values.

Universality Revisited

Markedness values, as we have seen, are evaluative correlates of formal and semantic oppositions. In this chapter, I have illustrated some patterns of these evaluative relations in the phonological, morphological, and morphophonemic systems of English.

With respect to the phonotactics of onset and coda clusters, we saw that unmarked features had a wider distribution and greater freedom of occurrence than their marked counterparts. Similarly, in the neutralizations that occur in consonant clusters, unmarked features dominate marked ones. We have also identified contextual reversals of markedness values: features that may be relatively unmarked when they occur as isolated segments become more marked if they co-occur in a cluster with a segment having a similar feature makeup. Such patterns of reversal are one aspect of the complementarity of values. Complementarity also arises in the structure of consonant clusters: the major class features that combine best are complementary ones.

In the domains of morphology and morphophonemics, complementarity of values also serves as an organizing principle. Stems and affixes possess markedness values both in their phonological makeup and in their conceptual features.[22] Patterns arise in which markedness values of derived forms reflect the markedness values of their stems: marked stems show an unmarking in the process of word formation, and unmarked stems show a marking.

Having explicated markedness values in phonology and patterns of values in morphology, phonology, and morphophonemics, this is a good point to reconsider how markedness values are related to universal properties of language.

As should be clear by now, there is considerable agreement, even among linguists of different theoretical persuasions, that universal properties of languages can be described and studied. As noted in chapter 2, the relation of markedness to universals is particularly compelling with respect to phonological features, hierarchies, and inventories. Mary-Louise Kean gives a typical approach to phonological markedness:

> The theory of markedness is a theory of the distinctive features which characterize the segments of languages. . . . A set of universal rules is postulated which characterize the 'optimal' (most likely) conjunctions of specified features within segments. It is proposed that based upon these rules certain substantive universal properties of the underlying and surface segmental inventories of languages can be captured. [1980:iii (1975)]

Later she adds:

> It is argued here that some conjunctions of specified features are more likely to occur than others; if a segment is characterized by a likely set of features then that segment is likely to occur in many languages. As a first approximation, the theory of markedness can be said to be a theory of the most likely intrasegmental conjunctions of specified features. A likely specification of a feature in a segment is termed an UNMARKED specification; an unlikely one is termed a MARKED specification. [ibid.:1]

The goal is to posit a set of universal conventions—marking conventions—that express the most natural relations among features. The notion of naturalness is determined by the distinction between ''probable segmental systems'' and ''improbable ones'' (Kean, 1980:7 [1975]) and by cross-linguistic tendencies that suggest implicational relations between features.

The markedness conventions and principles proposed by Kean, like those of Jakobson, Greenberg, Chomsky and Halle (1968), and others, attempt to explain general properties of language systems that are not accounted for by family membership or areal transmission.[23] All approaches to phonological markedness share in this goal. Kean's approach, which builds on that of Chomsky and Halle, places the marking conventions in the framework of a system of Universal Grammar. Recall that Universal Grammar is a characterization of the human language faculty and can be thought of as a language acquisition device or "an innate component of the human mind that yields a particular language through interaction with pre-sented experience" (Chomsky 1986:3). Recall also that Universal Grammar is distinct from the study of language universals as developed by Green-berg—a study concerned with investigating the logical equivalences be-tween typologies of linguistic features, on the one hand, and implicational universals and cross-linguistic generalizations, on the other (cf. Greenberg 1978a, Comrie 1981).[24]

It was also pointed out in chapter 2, and reemphasized in this chapter, that there is a much closer relation between universal hierarchies and language-particular values in phonological structure than in syntax and se-mantics. In the latter domains there is often tension between general laws (universals) of markedness and the functional value of a category within a particular language. Consider the situation that arises when the evaluation of oppositions in a particular language is at odds with general laws of markedness, for example, the dominance of objective case pronouns in En-glish, where language-internal facts show that objective pronouns are un-marked. As I have noted, most treatments of markedness assume that nominative is cross-linguistically the most natural or unmarked case. So what is the status of the objective case in English? From the cross-linguistic point of view, it might be said that English has a 'marked' case system.[25] Another example is the opposition between stranded prepositions and non-stranded ones, illustrated by the sentences *Who were you talking to?* versus *To whom were you talking?* In colloquial English, stranding is the unmarked option both stylistically and distributionally. Yet it has been suggested that nonstranding of prepositions is the unmarked option cross-linguistically (cf. van Riemsdijk 1978).

This tension between universal and language-particular values under-scores the fact that universal markedness and language-particular marked-ness can differ. It has been suggested that universal hierarchies determine much of the structure of language by providing a set of ranked feature choices and feature values in language development. However, markedness values within a language are determined by the structure of that language. The facts of a particular language sometimes force an evaluation relation that is unnatural cross-linguistically but perfectly natural for that particular language, as with the nominative/objective case distinction in English.

Despite this tension, both universal and language-particular marked-ness ought to be of great interest to linguists, though each occasions a different research agenda. Investigating the a priori cross-linguistic markedness values involves the challenge of constructing a universal system (in either the Chomskyan or Greenbergian sense). Substantive markedness can also include the study of shared aspects of culture, discourse, experience, and perception that determine universal patterns of evaluation in language development.[26] The study of a posteriori markedness patterns determined by language-particular function, on the other hand, involves the explication of a language, the examination of relations between expression and meaning, and the distribution of units and contexts. As suggested in the last chapter, this approach examines the coherence of linguistic oppositions as an artifact or work of art. In this regard, it should be reemphasized that there is nothing compulsory about the arrangement of markedness values into patterns of assimilation and complementarity. Markedness patterns exist as signs in which expression and content or units and contexts are correlated, but there is no guarantee that all the facts of language will form such signs or that the signs found in different languages are not greatly different. It seems plausible, for example, that agglutinative languages might show iconic relations in morphology whereas English shows relations of complementarity. It may also be that some languages for historical reasons have more or fewer coherent patterns than others. The patterns of value in a language can be likened to the clothes a person wears. In some instances, one's dress forms a coherent ensemble producing a unified effect; other times, clothes are just clothes.

Concluding Remarks on Markedness Patterns

This now brings us to a final question. How do functional markedness patterns relate to linguistic theory? With regard to phonology and morphology, for example, the grammar of English includes syllable structure templates that specify permissible syllable structures and exclude impermissible ones; it includes word formation rules indicating productive morphological processes and rules of word formation; and it includes rules generating phonetic forms from underlying phonemic ones.

The markedness values and patterns of markedness alignment and complementarity are best considered as outside this formal grammar. Rather they are a set of interpretive constructs that supplement grammar. Markedness values and the patterns they form do not determine (or generate) the synchronic facts of grammar and do not always correlate with substantive universals. The interest in markedness patterns lies rather in their role as a superstructure common to various levels of language. The markedness values of elements provide a vehicle with which the overall coherence of systems can be formulated and investigated.

The study of markedness patterns is therefore not intended to replace linguistic theory in any of its forms: descriptive generative grammar, the study of Universal Grammar, or universals research. Generative grammars provide an explanation for the facts of language by deriving them from general rules; Universal Grammar is a metalevel of generative grammar that aims at characterizing language development as a logical problem; universals research describes recurring inventories, structures, and implications. Studies of language-particular markedness, on the other hand, look at the values of forms and meanings, hoping to provide an explication and understanding of grammatical facts and rules.

Language-particular markedness interacts with grammar in the creation of diagrams of markedness values.[27] The rules and conventions of formal grammar will be more or less valued to the extent that they contribute to the diagrammatic superstructure. At the synchronic level markedness molds patterns from expression and meaning. At the diachronic level these patterns are signs that contribute to the drift and change of grammar. It is to this topic that I turn now.

5

Markedness and Language Change

Markedness in Theories of Language Change

At any point in its history the grammar of a language is made up of features and rules organized into a system of elements, contexts, and processes. Over time the structural relations, inventories, and rules of a living language change and grow, and the possible changes that can occur take various forms. Phonemes are lost or added; novel pronunciations arise for existing words or sounds; inflectional paradigms are leveled or extended; syntactic patterns are broadened or curtailed; words are borrowed; meanings are shifted. But in spite of the variety of changes possible and in spite of the diversity of approaches, two questions underlie historical linguistic research: How does language change? and Why does language change? The first question is concerned with the description of the mechanisms of change. It asks how the synchronic grammars of different historical periods are related. The second question asks what causes change. This question can be further divided into the question of the *actuation* of change and the *spread* of change. The former has to do with the start of a change—its introduction into the language—while the latter focuses on the factors that cause a change to take hold. Both of these subquestions have resisted fully satisfying answers, and the failure of change to be initiated and to spread under precisely definable conditions has sometimes sparked doubt about the study of change itself. Leonard Bloomfield, for example, remarks that "the causes of sound change are unknown" (1933:385). And Paul Postal suggests:

> There is no more reason for languages to change than there is for automobiles to add fins one year and remove them the next, for jackets to have three buttons one year and two the next, etc. That is, it seems evident within the framework of sound change as grammar change that the "causes" of sound changes without language contact lie in the general tendency of human cultural products to undergo "nonfunctional" stylistic change. [1968:283]

Nevertheless interest in the question of why language changes has not completely succumbed to skepticism. From the point of view of markedness, the two general approaches we have observed—the universalist and the language-particular—may again be distinguished. Some studies have connected the question of why language changes to the general laws of linguistic systems, drawing on implicational universals as constraints on the notion of possible change and as predictors of likely developments. Research on universal markedness relates to this aspect of historical linguistics by providing a notion of possible human language and thus of possible linguistic change.[1]

Other markedness-based approaches to language change view the drift of language as based in the structure of a particular language itself: according to this view the markedness values (and markedness diagrams) of a language may contribute to the understanding of the actuation and spread of change, through, for example, general principles affecting marked and unmarked categories and through the establishment of diagrams in the language. This view sees language change as involving the establishment and extension of evaluative patterns in the norms of speakers. Competing rules and forms are more coherent or less coherent (with the overall sign structure of the language) to the extent that they fit into or optimize the diagrams inherent in the language. Historical linguistics may be taken to include the explication of changes in a particular language on the basis of the signs that are immanent in the structure of the language. According to this view, a language can have a long-range teleology—the development of an overall diagrammatic coherence—that exists on top of grammar and apart from universal laws. Linguistic variation—the competition among forms within a language community—will be predicted to resolve itself in favor of the coherence of the evaluative system as well as in the adherence to universal laws. The facts of language change thus provide an important testing ground for language-particular markedness relations and diagrams. The empirical content of language-particular markedness assignments can be tested in cases where it helps to explain historical developments that are anomalous or underexplained from other points of view.

Laws of Synchrony and Diachrony

The first proposal to be discussed arose from Jakobson's study of typological universals, the results of which were synthesized in *Child Language, Aphasia, and Phonological Universals,* in which he specifies a hierarchy of phonological oppositions and posits a diachronic role for this hierarchy:

> As we have said, the analysis of the most varied languages reveals general synchronic laws of solidarity. According to these laws, a sec-

ondary value cannot exist in a linguistic system without the corresponding primary value. From this fact two consequences emerge for
the evolution of any given linguistic system as well: without the primary value, the corresponding secondary value cannot arise in a linguistic system, and without the secondary value [being lost], the
corresponding primary value cannot be eliminated. Thus, the laws of
solidarity turn out to be panchronic. They retain their validity at every
stage and in the course of every change of all of the languages of the
world. [1968:59 (1941)]

The universal and panchronic validity, as well as the inner logic, of
the observed hierarchical sequence of phonological oppositions permits us to assume the same sequence for glottogeny. Many earlier
assumptions about the origin of language are, in this way, refuted,
while others, on the contrary are confirmed: *e.g.*, Trombetti's view
that stop sounds are more original than fricative sounds, or van Ginneken's brilliant hypothesis, which attributes an original priority to
the first consonantal oppositions in contrast to the vocalic oppositions. Both the ontogeny and, probably, the phylogeny of language are
based on the same underlying principle, which governs the whole
realm of language. . . . This principle is simple to the point of being
trivial: one cannot erect the superstructure without having provided
the foundation nor can one remove the foundation without having removed the superstructure. [ibid.:93]

In these remarks Jakobson is referring not only to featural markedness
but also to the overall ranking of oppositions. His proposal places a substantive constraint on the set of possible historical changes. It entails, for
example, that a change like the merger of Old English rounded front vowels
with unrounded front vowels is a possible change (since unrounded front
vowels are unmarked in contrast to rounded front vowels), but that a merger
of front unrounded vowels with rounded ones should be impossible. Likewise, the development of voiced fricative phonemes in Middle English
exemplifies the emergence of a marked series of phonemes from the unmarked series; the converse situation, a language having only voiced fricatives and developing voiceless ones, should be precluded.
    There are two possible ways that this foundation principle, as I will
call it, can be interpreted. On the one hand, it can be treated as a strict
constraint on actuation of sound changes such that no changes are possible
that yield marked segments if their unmarked counterparts are not in the
language. On the other hand, the foundation principle could instead be
treated as a long-term desideratum of the spread of changes, though not as
an absolute requirement. Treating the principle as an absolute constraint

would require us to maintain that there can never be changes that neutralize unmarked sounds to marked ones or any additions of marked sounds to a language without the presence of their unmarked counterparts in that language.[2] But this assertion appears to be too strong, since it excludes, for example, such developments as the first part of Grimm's law, in which voiceless stops were converted to voiceless fricatives. Since fricatives are marked as opposed to stops, the first part of Grimm's law would be precluded, apparently incorrectly.[3] Rejecting the absolute view as too extreme, we can then entertain the weaker view that the foundation principle is a means of keeping order in a phonological system: systems can exist in violation of the foundation principle but in the long run the principle will be maintained. On this view, the conversion of voiced stops to voiceless ones in Grimm's law is understandable as a consequence of the (still unexplained) change of voiceless stops to fricatives.

While the remarks of Jakobson cited above imply the absolute view, others have advocated this weaker position. Consider, for example, Greenberg's remarks about Grimm's law:

> Of these [dynamic diachronic factors] the chief would be the tendency for a more complex (marked) item to lose its mark whenever it no longer contrasts with the corresponding unmarked item. Thus in the presumed course of events embodied in Grimm's first law, once unvoiced stops had become fricatives, we would have been left with such sets as b^h, b, f. The b with its marked feature of voicing having no partner p, was free to lose its mark and become p. Now given b^h, p, f, in similar fashion the b^h having no partner b could lose its marked feature of aspiration, although it became a voiced fricative rather than a voiced stop in most environments. [1966:63]

Greenberg also notes that sound changes can not all be viewed as unmarkings, pointing out that phonetic assimilation may induce marked feature values in sounds. He concludes that two major classes of regular sound changes can be established:

> The first includes unconditioned changes, particularly mergers, and those conditioned changes in which the specific class of environing sounds is irrelevant, e.g., changes in word final [position]. *In these which may be assigned to the paradigmatic aspect of language the overall tendency is for the marked or phonetically complex series to give way to the unmarked or simpler.* . . . The other class of changes which may be considered syntagmatic consists of the mass of assimilatory conditioned changes which often give rise to marked features.

Thus the answer to the objection that 'ease' of articulation, an expression which is avoided here, but which can be given objective content, should produce constantly simpler phonologic systems in the evolution of language is that there are two kinds of 'ease', paradigmatic which favors simplification by loss of additional articulatory features regardless of context and syntagmatic which favors the genesis of new assimilatory modifications. [ibid.:64]

The hypothesis that the inherent laws that organize the sound structure of language are a component of historical change has been applied and developed in various ways. In part this is due to the introduction of sequential and syllable context into markedness theory. It is also due in part to the identification of unmarkedness with phonological naturalness not just of oppositions, but also of phonological inventories (paradigms of sounds), syllable structure, the phonological form of lexical items, and the expression of phonological rules and processes (syntagmatic processes). Inventories, lexical items, constructions, and rules can be evaluated as more or less 'marked' according to their naturalness.[4]

Chapter 9 of Chomsky and Halle (1968) provides a convenient point of departure for further discussion of one approach to universal markedness conventions. Chomsky and Halle observe that an account of phonological features and simplicity solely in terms of plus and minus feature specifications has the defect of allowing unnatural and implausible rules and phonological inventories to be as highly valued as ones that are "more to be expected in a grammar" and that are "observed in many languages."[5] To address this defect the authors propose a set of marking conventions that give the natural values of features in a variety of segmental and sequential contexts and that, with certain supplementary principles, provide a tentative definition of phonological complexity both in segment inventory, in the sound shapes of lexical items, and in the application of phonological rules.

The notion of complexity found in Chomsky and Halle (1968) and in Kean (1980 [1975]) is, like Greenberg's and Jakobson's definitions of phonological markedness, based on typology and cross-linguistic optimality, though it differs in that the grammar as a whole can be said to have an overall complexity value ('markedness') determined in part by the markedness conventions. Chomsky and Halle connect the notion of complexity defined by the marking conventions with an implied theory of change when they note that "obviously these matters are significant not only for synchronic description but also for historical linguistics"(p. 402)[6]

While Chomsky and Halle do not make any specific proposals in *The Sound Pattern of English* as to how their marking conventions could fit into a theory of change, it was not long before others suggested ways that marking conventions would be used to gauge the complexity of rules and grammars and to evaluate changes as leading to greater or lesser overall complexity. The thesis of such approaches is that less complex phonological systems will be favored over more complex ones, where complexity is defined by the marking conventions.[7]

As was the case with the absolute interpretation of the foundation principle, it would be incorrect to preclude changes that increase the segmental complexity of a system or that increase the complexity of the lexicon or the phonological rules of a language. Rather we must allow for the possibility that the complexity of a phonological system can increase (motivated, for example, by borrowing, language contact, assimilation, or syntactic pressure such as contraction). Clarification of markedness increases and decreases in phonological change may ultimately come from a classification of phonological rules and phonological changes. One such classification that might prove useful is given by Andersen (1973), though it is not in the Chomsky and Halle framework.[8] Andersen contrasts the functions of phonological rules from several perspectives, and he makes an important distinction between adaptive rules and implementation rules. The former are rules that speakers follow in adapting their speech to the changing norms of their speech community. The latter are rules that implement phonetically the existing phonological relations of the system and that lack direct reference to extralinguistic reality. Adaptive rules will have the stylistic or social function of matching the received norms while staying within the phonological system of the language.

New implementation rules yield other types of changes: *neutralization* changes, which neutralize phonological oppositions in some environment, and variation changes, which change the distribution of feature values in different contexts. According to Andersen, variation changes obey markedness assimilation in that "the more marked value appears in marked contexts, and the less marked value in unmarked contexts" (1973:85). Andersen (1972) also suggests that neutralization changes obey markedness assimilation.[9] The goal of such a classification is to distinguish changes that are amenable to explication in terms of markedness from those that are not. We might expect that markedness will be less relevant to adaptive changes, which Andersen defines as "change[s] not explainable without reference to factors outside the linguistic system in question," but more pertinent to evolutive changes involving neutralization and variation, which Andersen describes as "entirely explainable in terms of the linguistic system."

In addition to the classification of rules and changes, other factors impinge on the role of universal markedness conventions as a characterization of phonological naturalness (or 'markedness') and change. One potential problem is that universal marking conventions are not sensitive to the weighting among features, a weighting that interacts with markedness in determining the naturalness of a system. As noted in the last chapter, not all phonological features count equally. Some marked distinctive features are more marked—less expected—than others. It is, for example, less usual for vowels to be distinctively voiceless than for consonants to be, or for a language to have voiceless versus glottalized stops rather than voiceless versus voiced ones. But the simple view of all marked features as being equally complex fails to capture this fact.[10] In addition, marking conventions need to take into account how much markedness is natural in a sound inventory (cf. Kean 1980 [1975] for some suggestions). If markedness is viewed only in terms of the number of Ms in a segment inventory, then the maximally unmarked sound system would be one consisting solely of the vowel /a/. Certainly this is a conclusion to be avoided. To constitute a real theory of naturalness, the markedness values of features will have to be sensitive to the fact that a certain number of marked features are expected in any natural sound system.

Besides the weighting of features in the universal hierarchy, the language-particular phonological hierarchy or ranking of features must also be considered. As we have seen in earlier chapters, not all features are used distinctively in every language, and the markedness value of a feature in some language may depend on whether it functions distinctively or redundantly in that language. Its markedness value may also depend on its rank in the hierarchy of features that determines the phonological structure: whether it is subordinate to a feature that conditions a reversal or is superordinate to that feature.[11]

Since a feature value may be marked in one language but unmarked in another, such language-particular ranking and reversals attenuate the status of universals as compulsory laws of language change. The language-particular component of markedness and ranking requires that a markedness-based approach to change attend to language-internal structure as well as universals. In the analysis of a given language, language-particular markedness relations will supercede predictions arising from universals. A simple analogy that brings this out is the case of left- and right-handedness. As a universal, the unmarked value for handedness is, of course, right-handedness. But this obvious statistical law does not mean that particular individuals should be predicted to favor their right hands regardless of past handedness behavior. If I am left-handed, left is unmarked for me, and any person investigating my handedness behavior will quickly learn to expect me to behave in a left-handed way, according to my particular internal makeup, not according to the general laws of statistical populations.

Syntactic Naturalness as Complexity

Thus far in this chapter, we have focused entirely on the diachronic consequences of implicational universals and of Chomsky and Halle's notion of phonological complexity as some degree of 'markedness'. Before moving on to some exemplification of language-particular markedness values and iconic diagrams of markedness values, I offer a brief illustration of the application of these approaches in syntax. I should point out, of course, that the same potential difficulties arise with these ideas in syntax that arose in phonology. The identification of 'markedness' with complexity, for example, raises the problem of relevance (whether 'markedness' is relevant for every type of grammar change), weighting (whether all marked categories or rules are of equal weight), and overgenerality (whether universal values are valid for a particular system). In addition, when we consider syntax, the balance of complexity at different levels must be taken into account. Sometimes morphological and phonological simplifications result in complication of grammar: this seems to occur, for example, in the development of the modal auxiliaries in reaction to the loss of subjunctive inflection in English (cf. Steele, et al. 1981).

To give a sense of proposals concerning syntactic 'markedness', I will briefly highlight two approaches—those of Elizabeth Traugott (1973) and of David Lightfoot (1979). (See also the references in note 2 of this chapter.)[12] While these two proposals differ considerably in focus, it is significant, I think, that neither tries to maintain the strong view that all changes lead to less complex systems. As in phonology, it must be recognized that changes in the direction of increased syntactic markedness are not ruled out.

Traugott (1973) identifies unmarkedness in syntax with natural syntactic categories and types that can be determined by implicational relationships. Traugott suggests that a language can develop marked categories because "children innately have the capacity to reach down further, so to speak, into the implicational hierarchies, and give surface expression to" marked categories, given the right conditions in their language (1973:318). She also suggests that if a language already has many marked categories, some may be lost because "children do not reach that far down into the implicational hierarchy; it will then appear that the language has, to that extent, been simplified." Traugott remarks that unmarking seems to be the more typical situation, but she emphasizes that an increase in marked categories is possible: "It is usually said that changes in the histories of languages go from marked to unmarked; they obviously also go vice versa, since marked forms that are lost at one stage are often renewed at a later one" (ibid.:317). In sum, Traugott's view has three aspects: she adopts the foundation principle (since she defines markedness via implicational universals), sees the loss of marked categories as a likely reaction to complexity, and sees the gain of marked categories as possible in some circumstances.

Lightfoot's is a more recent approach that, although not entirely dissimilar from Traugott's approach, defines markedness not in terms of implicational universals but in Chomsky's core grammar sense (see chapter 2). The complexity of a particular grammar is thus its distance from one of the core grammars defined by Universal Grammar. In Lightfoot's view change sometimes results

> in a steady complication of a grammar, rendering it as a whole more marked, less highly valued. In the examples discussed, these piecemeal changes are followed by a catastrophe in roughly the sense of Thom (1972, 1973), a major re-analysis of the grammar eliminating the markedness and complexity which had been gradually accumulating. [1979:78]

Lightfoot sees grammars as experiencing increases in markedness (complexity) but views such increases as ultimately leading to a radical restructuring of the grammar in which marked constructions are reanalyzed as new unmarked (core) constructions. In its simplest terms, his theory is one of gradual increases in 'markedness' followed by sudden decreases.

Phonotactic Change as Unmarking

In this section I exemplify the role of markedness in the historical development of English consonant clusters. Recall from chapter 4 that onsets and codas in English are unmarked if they are simple and marked if they are complex (CC or CCC). The overall trend of the language has been for the conversion of complex clusters to simplex ones, that is, toward unmarking of complex syllable structures. In Old English, for example, we find clusters of /h/ plus a following resonant: /hn/, /hl/, /hr/, as in *hnutu*, *hlavord*, *hraven*. In Middle English, these clusters are simplified to /n/, /l/, and /r/, yielding ultimately *nut*, *lord*, and *raven*. Another simplification involves the Old English cluster /ŋg/, which becomes a simple velar nasal /ŋ/ in Middle English (though, of course, the orthography reflects the earlier structure).

Some Middle English onset and coda clusters also become simplified in the Modern English period. The coda cluster /mb/, as in *comb, womb, climb, tomb, bomb, lamb,* and *limb* loses its final voiced stop. The coda clusters /lk/ and /lm/ are simplified to /k/ and /m/ in words such as *folk, yolk, talk, walk, balk, balm, alm, psalm, almond,* and *salmon*.[13] And the onset clusters /kn/ and /gn/ lose their initial velar obstruent: *know, knee, knight, gnaw, gnat, gnome, gnostic.*

These cluster simplifications are summarized below, where # indicates a word boundary:

(1)   (a)   #hl, #hr, #hn   >   #l, #r, #n
               (b)   ŋg#   >   ŋ#
               (c)   mb#   >   m#
               (d)   #kn, #gn   >   #n
               (e)   lm#   >   m#
               (f)   lk#   >   k#

While the change from marked to unmarked syllable structure is prosaically evident in terms of the complex/simple opposition, this is not the extent of the role of markedness in cluster simplification. I wish to argue that in each instance it is the marked member of the cluster that is eliminated. Markedness thus will enable us to understand not only the fact of simplification, but also its details.

The determination of which consonant is the marked member of the cluster can be made on the basis of the usual typological considerations (taking into account sequential and syllable context), and reinforced by such language-particular phonological factors as the other clusters present in the languages. In principle any CC cluster in the language should admit to an analysis as C(unmarked)C(marked) or C(marked)C(unmarked).[14] The markedness value of a consonant in isolation will, of course, be relevant to its markedness value in a cluster, but this is not the only factor, as we saw in the last chapter. The position of the consonant in the cluster and the features of the adjacent consonant will also play a role in the markedness value of consonants in a cluster.

Let us consider each cluster in turn. The clusters in (1a) follow the general pattern #fricative plus stop. In such clusters the stop position is the unmarked one and the fricative position the marked one. (Cairns and Feinstein (1982) posit this evaluation on typological grounds. It is also suggested by the relative unmarkedness of stops over fricatives.) Within the class of fricatives, /h/ is highly marked, and compact fricatives are otherwise excluded from complex onsets in English. A situation of double marking therefore obtains with respect to cluster-initial compact fricatives: they are marked as fricatives with respect to stops, and they are marked as compact segments versus noncompact ones. Given this double marking, the simplification of such clusters and the loss of /h/ rather than /l/, /r/, or /n/ fits into a general pattern of unmarking.[15]

In (1b) and (c) we find changes in which final voiced obstruents are lost following a nasal. I posit here that in a nasal plus stop# coda the features abrupt and consonantal undergo a markedness reversal in both the nasal and the following stop. This reversal is parallel to that obtaining in other stop plus stop sequences mentioned in the last chapter. After the reversal the markedness values of the nasal and the stop will be as below:

(2)

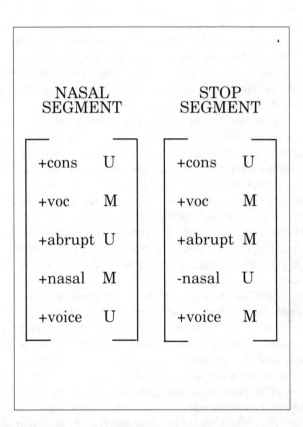

NASAL SEGMENT		STOP SEGMENT	
+cons	U	+cons	U
+voc	M	+voc	M
+abrupt	U	+abrupt	M
+nasal	M	-nasal	U
+voice	U	+voice	M

If this reversal of the values of the features abrupt and consonantal is correct, the markedness value of the final voiced stop will be greater than that of the nasal segment.[16] Hence we can view the loss of /b/ rather than /m/ and the loss of /g/ rather than /ŋ/ as unmarkings.

In case (1d), onset clusters of a velar obstruent followed by a nasal lose their initial segment: /kn/ and /gn/ become /n/. Aside from the fact that both voiced and voiceless stops are lost, this situation is exactly like the one just discussed except in onset rather than coda position. As Cairns and Feinstein (1982) have pointed out, the unmarked obstruent plus nasal onset clusters are prenasalized stops; other onset clusters of stop plus nasal are marked. In the #velar stop plus nasal sequences under discussion, we can again analyze the markedness values as due to a reversal of the features consonantal and abrupt. There is further language-internal evidence for analyzing the nasals as unmarked with respect to the velars in such onset clusters. Note that in other consonant plus nasal onsets (sn, sm), the syllable position of the nasal is the unmarked position usually occupied by a true stop, while the preceding /s/ has the marked position. This is to say that /sn/ and /sm/ pattern just like /sl/, /sp/, /st/, and /sk/, where the /s/ is in the marked position and the following stop segment is in the unmarked position.[17] The clusters /kn/ and /gn/ are thus parallel in value to /sn/ and /sm/, with the nasal segment evaluated as the unmarked cluster member and the nonnasal as the marked member. Given this ranking, the loss of the velars rather than the nasals is consistent.

Next consider the loss of /l/ in /lm/ and /lk/ clusters. Contrasted to the loss of /b/ after /m/ and the loss of /g/ after /ŋ/, this seems to be an unexpected development, since the liquid is lost and the obstruent remains. Instead, liquids are often the marked segments in coda clusters.[18] This result is suggested further by the relative ordering of nasals and liquids in /lm#/ codas: the nasal follows the liquid. There are no /ml#/ codas. Nasals, in this regard, pattern like the unmarked obstruent stops (/lb/, /lp/, /ld/, etc.). So I assume that since the reversal suggested for the feature nasal does not apply to liquids and since liquids instead retain their usual more marked value in clusters, we can analyze the loss of /l/ from /lm/ and /lk/ clusters as an unmarking.

One further observation can be made about why deletion occurs with /lk/ and /lm/ clusters rather with clusters of /l/ plus some other consonant. Both /lk/ and /lm/ are, in terms of the phonotactic pattern of English, marked clusters. Among voiceless obstruents /k/ is marked for compactness whereas /p/ and /t/ are unmarked. In addition, the voiced counterpart of /k/ does not occur after /l/, giving further narrowness to the combination of /l/ plus a compact consonant. Similarly, among the sonorant consonants that occur after /l/, /m/ is the most marked. The combinations /lr/ and /lŋ/, which would be more marked, do not occur at all. The simplification of /lm/ clusters leaves /ln/ as the only /l/ plus sonorant combination.

The pattern is thus complete. The cluster simplifications considered can be analyzed as a long-term pattern of unmarking, adding a diachronic perspective to our earlier discussion of synchronic phonotactics: the markedness assignments developed in the previous chapter, based on both universal and language-particular factors, are confirmed and extended by historical means. While an exhaustive analysis of marked and unmarked categories in the English sound system and their role in change has not been presented, it is hoped that the present discussion has shown how such an analysis might proceed.

The Tendency Not to Accumulate Marks

In the discussion of sound change so far, I have introduced the idea that certain types of sound change involve unmarking, though unmarking is not the only type of sound change possible. In this section, I wish to shift the focus somewhat to consider the consequences of the "principle of compensation" for language change. This is a claim about the way in which features combine to make up systems of elements. Recall that Jakobson, following Brøndal, describes unmarked categories as (tending to be) more differentiated than marked categories. A typical example is the fact that in Russian (and many other languages) the unmarked singular nouns distinguish categories of person (that is, they accumulate marks for those features), whereas the marked plural nouns syncretize person categories. Jakobson remarks that "the 'principle of compensation', established by Brøndal for morphology and limiting accumulation, has remarkable analogies in the structure of phonological systems" (1984: 158). Waugh expands on the role of the principle in phonological structure:

> Another commonly recognized phenomenon I will call "the tendency not to accumulate marks—or the tendency to combine markedness with non-markedness." This correlates with the observation that certain phonological sub-systems tend to be more differentiated than others. For example, since in the consonantal system, nasality is a mark, there is a general tendency not to elaborate the nasal consonants more than or even equally to the oral consonants. In other words, the nasal mark is generally not combined with other marks. . . . [1979:158]

The synchronic interpretation of the principle of compensation is that unmarked superordinate categories in feature hierarchies should be more elaborated or subclassified than marked ones, and this often is the case in phonology and grammar. Compare the number of consonant sounds with alveolar articulations (/l/, /n/, /t/, /d/, /s/, /z/, /θ/, /ð/) to the number of consonants at any other place of articulation. Or compare the number of morphological distinctions made in the present tense with the number in the past tense. The diachronic interpretation of the principle of compensation concerns the addition and loss of subordinate features from categories. In the case of addition of a new feature, the expectation would be that the new features will first be imposed on unmarked categories and only later on marked categories. In the case of loss, the prediction would be that subordinate categories will be lost first from marked categories. Elaborations of one opposition by another will proceed as in (3) below, if the principle of compensation is relevant:

(3)   Addition of a subordinate feature value

Stage 1:

feature +A (U)   feature −A (M)

Stage 2:

feature +A (U)   feature −A (M)
feature +B

Similarly, loss of a feature would be as in (4):

(4)   Loss of a subordinate feature value

Stage 1:

feature +A (U)   feature −A (M)
feature +B   feature −B

Stage 2:

feature +A (U)   feature −A (M)
feature +B

The foundation principle interacts with the principle of compensation in the following way. The foundation principle predicts that when just one feature value is added to a language that feature value will be the unmarked one; conversely if only one feature value is lost it should be the marked feature value. Thus, [+B] in (3) and (4) should be unmarked and [−B] should be marked. Note too that the interaction of the principle of compensation and the foundation principle is a form of markedness assimilation in the addition of new features.

The principle of compensation has a certain plausibility as a principle of lexical change, since the marked lexical item is usually the more specific of a pair of opposed items and since it might be natural to think that new uses of a word will occur by projecting complexity (new feature specifications) onto the general categories rather than onto the specific ones.[19]

Natural though this reasoning seems, this is not the only way to think about lexical change, and it is equally logical and plausible that change might occur in the opposite way, with complexity projected onto complexity. This view is particularly compelling when we consider that the unmarked element often subsumes the meaning of its marked counterpart. Given this, the marked term might be used for new senses precisely because its standard sense can be also carried by the unmarked term. The point of this discussion is not to resolve the issue in favor of either of these dispositions but to show that each is a plausible scenario of change and hence that a narrow view of lexical change has no a priori basis. Neither approach to lexical change—the projection of complexity onto simplicity or the projection of complexity onto complexity—can be said to be any more natural and logical than the other in terms of our commonsense (pretheoretic) notions of how change is likely to proceed.

So while it may be that the principle of compensation is valid for the development of phonological and grammatical categories, for the lexicon a more reasonable idea might be to think of differentiation and simplification as competing processes.[20] For example, with respect to the loss of features there are three logical possibilities: (a) for marked categories to lose features first; (b) for marked and unmarked categories to lose features simultaneously; (c) for unmarked categories to lose features first.[21] The principle of compensation will predict that changes of type (c), loss of a feature in the unmarked category first, should be a less likely type of change than (a) or (b). With respect to the addition of features, there are also three possibilities: (d) for unmarked categories to gain new features first; (e) for both categories to gain features simultaneously; (f) for marked categories to gain features first.

An interesting example of type (d) can be found in the use conventions for the pronoun forms *he* and *she* in recent years. If masculine is taken as the unmarked feature of the masculine/feminine gender opposition, these pronouns, prior to the woman's movement, had the following feature analysis:

(5)   he (U) : she (M) :: nonfeminine (U) : feminine (M)

The assumption that *he* is the nonsignalization of the feature feminine leads to the expectation that *he* may refer either to males or to referents of unspecified sex:

(6)   a. When a boy turns 18, he becomes a man.
           b. When a girl turns 18, she becomes a woman.
           c. When someone turns 18, he is legally an adult.

Such usages as (6c), however, implicitly exclude females, since the pronoun's specific meaning cannot be separated from its general one.[22] As objections came to be raised about the generic use of *he* in contexts where a referent of either sex was actually intended, the use of the pronouns *he* and *she* and the use of the compound *he or she*, took on an added semantic distinction. Use of *she* or *he or she* or *they* to refer to either sex adds a feature we could call [feminist], where [feminist] indicates overt affiliation with the woman's movement. So, expressions like

(7)   a. When someone turns 18, he or she is legally an adult.
           b. When someone turns 18, she is legally an adult.
           c. When someone turns 18, they are legally an adult.

make a certain political statement. The use of *she* (or *he or she*) in generic contexts is semantically marked as [feminist]. (The use of *they* in (7c) is more difficult to characterize since, in addition to being marked as [feminist], it signals nonprescriptive grammar as well.) Contrast the expressions in (7) with (6c). Unlike the pronouns in (7a) and (7b), the pronoun in (6c) does not necessarily indicate an overt political affiliation to those who use it.[23] This is because the pronoun *he* has the unmarked value of an opposition [feminist]/[nonfeminist] that is superimposed on the gender distinction. The feature [nonfeminist] (and thus the use of *he*) does not necessarily indicate antipathy to the woman's movement—it might, but it might simply indicate a strong adherence to the rules of prescriptive grammar or an unwillingness to make a statement or ignorance of the issue of sexist language.

In the situation just sketched, we find that both marked and unmarked pronominal features (feminine and masculine) are affected by the new opposition ([feminist]/[nonfeminist]). This illustrates a case in which there is no special priority in lexical change for the elaboration of unmarked categories to precede elaboration of marked categories. Rather we have a case in which the attempt to avoid the clash between the specific and general interpretations of the unmarked pronoun precipitates an elaboration of the marked term and a concomitant elaboration of the unmarked term. The result is a new opposition superimposed on the old. Notice too that this has the character of a markedness assimilation: the marked feature [feminist] is assigned to the marked categories of feminine and compound pronouns, and, as a consequence, the unmarked feature [nonfeminist] is assigned to the unmarked category of masculine pronouns.

(8)   he : she :: nonfeminine (U) : feminine (M) ::
           nonfeminist (U) : feminist (M)

(9)   he : he or she :: simple (U) : compound (M) ::
           nonfeminist (U) : feminist (M)

I end this section with a comment on the possible future development of these pronoun forms. If proponents of nonsexist usage are successful and *he* is replaced as the generic singular pronoun, then the markedness values of [feminist] and [nonfeminist] in pronouns will have reversed. The unmarked usage will be *they* or *he or she,* while the marked usage in generic contexts will be to use *he.* Correspondingly, the unmarked social attitude will be affiliation with the goals of the woman's movement and the marked social attitude will be disassociation from it.

Markedness Diagrams as a Goal of Change

We now turn our attention more closely to markedness within specific linguistic systems, focusing on the evaluative structure of English and its role in change. We have already discussed at length the iconism and reversed iconism found in the synchronic analysis of language. Here I wish to show that coherent patterns of markedness values also may be viewed as a goal of language change. As Shapiro emphasizes,

> covert patterns of correspondence determine tendencies of development, so that the drift of a language can be explicated as a gradual actualization in its surface forms of virtual patterns, patterns that are established over time as a part of the linguistic competence of speakers. It is these patterns that constitute the functional system or the productive center of language . . . and which determine which deviations from the received grammar will be accepted, which rejected. The dynamics of language follow a trajectory of maximizing the patterns of diagrammatization and minimizing or ultimately eliminating those that are devoid of such semeiotic basis.[1983:18–19]

The dynamics of language change constitute a test of the reality of synchronic markedness patterns. If evaluative diagrams are a true component of language, then it ought to be the case that the formation and optimization of markedness patterns should be a result of language change. The long-term drift of language, should reveal a patterning of expressions and meanings and of units and contexts. To the extent that it does, the circle of reasoning that establishes synchronic patterns of markedness will be confirmed diachronically. We turn then to some exemplification of iconic sign patterning as a principle in historical analysis, looking once again at the domain of grammar. Two examples will be considered below: the periphrastic *do* forms and the second person pronouns.

We will look first at the development of periphrastic *do,* summarizing here a point made in Battistella (1985, 1985a). As is well-known, periphrastic *do* arose as an optional tense carrier in affirmative declarative sentences and spread to interrogative and negative sentences.[24] The *do* forms of interrogatives and negatives coexisted with earlier (non-*do*) forms of interrogation and negation until the non-*do* forms were dropped from the language. Below I give some examples from the language of Shakespeare, which is a midpoint in the interplay between the *do* and non-*do* forms:

(10)   *Negative*
            I do not sue to stand. [Richard II 5.3.129]
            Or if there were, it not belongs to you. [2 Henry IV 4.1.98]

(11)   *Interrogative*
            And did you leave him in this contemplation? [As You Like It
            2.1.64]
            What do you see? [Midsummer 3.1.120]
            What sayde he? [As You Like It 3.2.221]
            Sent he to Macduffe? [Macbeth 3.6.39]

(12)   *Negative Interrogative*
            Do not you love me? [Much Ado 5.4.74]
            Came he not home to night? [Romeo and Juliet 2.4.2]

The use of *do* in affirmative declarative sentences could be either nonemphatic or emphatic, as the following examples show:

(13)   *Nonemphatic*
            The Serpent that did sting thy Fathers life,
            Now weares his Crowne. [Hamlet 1.5.39–40]

(14)   *Emphatic*
            V. Thou art a merry fellow and car'st for nothing.
            C. Not so, sir, I *do* care for something, but . . .
            I *do* not care for you. [Twelfth Night 3.1.32]

    In the course of the development of the *do* forms, the nonemphatic use of *do* was eliminated in affirmative declarative sentences. Thus in present-day English, periphrastic *do* serves in the three functions shown below: it is the tense carrier in interrogative and in negative sentences, and is a signal of emphasis in sentences that lack an aspectual or modal auxiliary:

(15)   a. Did anyone tell you what happened?
            b. I didn't get a chance to speak with her.
            c. But I *do* want to go!

None of the periphrastic uses of *do* are attested in Old English (cf. Ellegård 1953, Hausmann 1974, Traugott 1972), though *do* was used as a substitute verb in coordinate structures. The earliest periphrastic uses of *do* seem to be from the early Middle English period. Robert Hausmann suggests that nonemphatic *do* began around 1300, though F. Th. Visser (1969) suggests that it already existed in preconquest times but was not used in writing until nonliterative verse came into vogue in the thirteenth century. Visser dates the appearance of nonemphatic *do* in prose as slightly later, but before the fourteenth century, and he says that "proliferation rapidly set in, and by the fifteenth century the periphrastic construction ultimately became almost as common in prose as it was in poetry" (p. 1498). The use of nonemphatic *do* peaked in the sixteenth century but began to decline in the seventeenth century and was lost completely by about 1850.

The *Oxford English Dictionary* dates emphatic *do* at 1581, though Visser (p. 1511) has noted that there is a great divergence of scholarly opinion on this dating, ranging from about 1300 to the sixteenth century. He argues that it is futile to try to pinpoint an earliest instance, and suggests treating emphatic *do* as arising from the assignment of emphasis to the nonemphatic form.

The use of *do* in interrogatives began about 1385 as an option that coexisted with question formation by inversion of the main verb. The *do* pattern increased consistently, and, by about 1700, it had supplanted main verb inversion in interrogative sentences. The earliest attestation of *do* in negative sentences is from about 1400, and this use arose, according to Visser, "almost simultaneously" (p. 1529) with its use in positive sentences. The *do* forms coexisted with examples such as *I went not* until about 1900, after which forms with the negative after the main verb become restricted to fixed phrases such as *She loves me not*.[25]

The question of *how* these changes were implemented in the grammar can be approached in several ways (cf. Hausmann 1974, Lightfoot 1979, Steele et al. 1981, Roberts 1985). For present purposes, it is sufficient to view the changes in terms of surface grammatical patterns. In Old English, interrogatives were formed by inversion of the tensed verb, and negatives were formed by positioning *not* after the tensed verb:

(16)   Old English

                Interrogative: V S O
                Negative: S V *not* O

In late Middle and early Modern English, the development of auxiliary verbs allowed questions to be formed by inversion of the tensed verb or auxiliary. It also permitted negative patterns in which *not* followed the tensed auxiliary. The inclusion of *do* in the set of auxiliaries was the mechanism for the development of optional *do* patterns for negatives and questions: the use of *do* in questions and negatives follows directly from its use as an auxiliary. The late Middle and early Modern English sentence patterns were as follows, where *Aux* indicates a modal, perfective, or progressive auxiliary:

(17)   Late Middle English and Early Modern English

      Interrogative: Aux S V O
                     do S V O   or   V S O
      Negative: S Aux *not* V O
                     S *do not* V O or   S V *not* O
      Emphatic: S *dó* V O   or   S V́ O
      Nonemphatic: S *do* V O   or   S V O

The pattern in present-day English is a subset of the above:

(18)   Present-day English

      Interrogative: Aux S V O
                     S *do* V O
      Negative: S Aux *not* V O
                     S *do not* V O
      Emphatic: S *dó* V O   or   S V́ O
      Nonemphatic: S V O

Two questions stand out: Why was nonemphatic *do* lost in affirmative declarative sentences? and Why is it the *do* forms rather than the non-*do* forms that survive in interrogatives and negatives? This presents a real puzzle, since the apparent drift of the language favored the *do* forms in some cases but not in others. As a piece to this puzzle, I suggest that the development of the *do* forms reflects the greater alignment of markedness values and that these changes are motivated by the overall iconic sign structure of the language.

In pursuing this line of reasoning we must first clarify the formal and semantic oppositions that play roles in the sign structure. At the semantic level, we are concerned with the oppositions between negative and affirmative, between interrogative and declarative, and between emphatic and nonemphatic. In each case the first-mentioned categories—negative, interrogative, and emphatic—represent the specification of some semantic feature. The opposite categories—affirmative, declarative, and nonemphatic—are the nonspecification of the features in question and are more broadly defined and therefore unmarked. It will be useful in what follows to think of the markedness of various types of sentences as composite values, with affirmative declarative sentences being treated as maximally unmarked and each of the semantic categories negative, interrogative, and emphatic adding a marked feature to the sentential markedness value.

There are four oppositions of expression that figure in the pattern: *do* versus the absence of *do, not* versus the absence of *not,* simple main verbs versus auxiliary-plus-main-verb sequence, and inverted versus noninverted word order. As we have seen in chapter 3, it is often the case in syntax that the absence of a sign is the unmarked member of an opposition and the overt sign is the marked member. This is borne out in the distributions of *do* and *not.* These elements occur in a fairly restricted set of environments and hence meet the distributional criterion for marked categories (auxiliary *do,* for example, can only occur in tensed clauses and is precluded before *be* and *have; not* is precluded from derived nominals, complements of perception verbs, and from contexts that already have a negative adverb).

Next we consider the opposition between simple main verbs and auxiliary-plus-main-verb sequences. The narrowness of distribution and the morphological syncretization of the auxiliaries suggests that they are, as a class, marked verbs, as does their association with marked semantic categories such as aspect and modality. Main verbs, by contrast, are unmarked verb types.

Finally, consider the opposition between inverted and noninverted word order. Here the noninverted (declarative) orders is clearly the more broadly defined one (since, for example, overt inversions do not occur in subordinate interrogative clauses and need not occur even in simple questions like *Who left?* and *You're moving to Alaska?*). Noninverted word order will be unmarked; inverted word order will be marked. The following table summarizes the markedness values of semantic and syntactic categories:

(19)   *Marked Expression*   *Unmarked Expression*

              do   Ø
              not   Ø
              auxiliary + main verb   main verb
              inversion   noninversion

              Marked Meaning   *Unmarked Meaning*

              negative   affirmative
              interrogative   declarative
              emphatic   nonemphatic

We may now analyze the pattern of changes as markedness diagrams. Consider first the relation between formal and semantic markedness when periphrastic *do* became an option in nonemphatic affirmative declarative sentences. This pattern shows a misalignment of markedness values:

(20)   *do* : nonemphatic, affirmative, declarative ::
             M syntax : U semantics

The introduction of auxiliary *do,* a marked formal element, into the maximally unmarked semantic structure yields a complementary pattern of form and meaning values. The preferred pattern of values in English syntax, however, appears to be one in which the markedness values are strictly iconic:

(21)   *do* : Marked semantic feature :: M syntax : M semantics

For example, counterposed to the complementary pattern of values in (20) are the patterns that arise when *do* is used in the marked semantic contexts of interrogation and negation:

(22)   *do* : interrogative sentence :: M syntax : M semantics

(23)   *do* : negative sentence :: M syntax : M semantics

The fact that *do* forms have ultimately supplanted the non-*do* forms in interrogative and negative sentences can be treated as a change in which a more iconic diagram of expression and meaning was established.

It is worth digressing briefly to consider the syntactic analysis of this change. The loss of the non-*do* forms of the interrogative and negative can be given a unified syntactic analysis in terms of the realization of tense in a clause. In standard accounts of English syntax, tensed clauses have an underlying structure in which a tense operator exists separately from the verbal stems (auxiliaries and main verbs) of the clause. In affirmative declarative sentences in Modern English, the tense operator is attached to the main verb by a tense-lowering rule, giving sentences like *They left.* Both question formation and negation are processes affecting the tense operator of a clause that prevent the operator from lowering onto the main verb. In question formation, lowering is blocked because the tense operator and the subject invert; as a result supportive *do* is inserted, giving patterns like *Did Mary take the exam?* or *Who did John visit?* Similarly, negation involves the placement of *not* after the tense operator, blocking lowering and resulting in examples like *They didn't leave*. The behavior of auxiliary verbs and the copula in Modern English differs from that of main verbs. Auxiliaries and the copula are raised from their position in the verb phrase and attached to the left of the tense operator. As a result, they invert with the operator in questions, and they occur before the negative element in negative clauses (cf. *Is Mary taking the exam?* or *Aren't they leaving?*).

Now consider the behavior of main verbs in Middle English. At this stage of the language, main verbs have the option of patterning like auxiliary verbs. In questions, for example, Middle English main verbs can invert with the subject; and in negative clauses, the main verb can precede the negative element. The patterning of Middle English main verbs can be accounted for straightforwardly if we assume that main verbs as well as auxiliaries were able to undergo verb raising in Middle English (cf. Roberts 1985). This simultaneously accounts for their ability to invert with the subject in questions and for the positioning of *not* after the main verb. Of course, it was not obligatory for main verbs to undergo verb raising; in cases where raising of main verbs did not occur, question and negative patterns with *do* were also an option. As Roberts (1985) has argued, the change from the Middle English to the Modern English patterns can be analyzed as the loss of the verb fronting option for main verbs. As a result, the only patterns of negation and question formation to remain were those involving *do*. (Auxiliaries and the copula in Modern English continue to allow verb fronting.)

Notice that while this is an essentially syntactic account of the loss of the non-*do* forms, the resulting patterns are consistent with the overall evaluative structure of the language: marked semantic categories are implemented by marked syntactic categories. In Middle English the marked categories of negation and interrogation were implemented by the addition of *do* or by verb fronting. In Modern English they continue to be implemented by the marked syntax of *do* support.[26]

The existence of a pattern in which the marked syntax corresponds to marked semantics also makes sense of the loss of the nonemphatic use of *do* in affirmative declaratives. Since nonemphatic affirmative declaratives are semantically unmarked, the use of *do* would have become progressively less consistent as the more general expression and meaning diagrams became established.[27] The inconsistency in the use of nonemphatic *do* was remedied by changes in usage that preclude supportive *do* in the unmarked sentence type, affirmative declarative sentences.

The loss of nonemphatic *do* is especially important because it suggests that we are dealing with diagrams of values rather than a straightforward generalization of *do* forms. If generalization of *do* forms were the only proposed explanation for the spread of *do* in interrogative and negative sentences, then the loss of *do* in nonemphatic constructions would be anomalous. But by providing an example of unmarking in the semantically unmarked sentence type, the loss of nonemphatic *do* shows the replacement of a complementary diagram by an iconic one. The loss of nonemphatic *do* is thus the exception that tests the rule.

The Shifting of Second Person Pronoun Forms

We turn now to the second person pronoun forms in English and to discussion of the use of pronouns to signal features of social distance. This discussion aims at illustrating the use of markedness to analyze the dynamics of language and culture in lexical change. The process to be discussed is the extension and shift of meaning that ended in the loss of the pronouns *thou/thee/thy* in most dialects of Modern English.

I suggest that the social use of English forms *ye/you/your* and *thou/ thee/thy* (hereafter the Y and TH forms, respectively) in Middle English involved elaboration of the singular/plural number distinction with a secondary opposition, which I will call *deferential/nondeferential*. The development of these new pronoun meanings in Middle English was due to the use of Y forms in the singular to indicate social deference. I suggest that the unmarked value of the opposition deferential/nondeferential first occurred in the TH forms and in the plural use of Y forms, and that the opposition deferential/nondeferential underwent a semantic weakening that resulted in a reevaluation of the markedness values of the opposition. This reevaluation in turn eventually led to a double marking of the TH forms, consistent with their loss.

Before discussing the development of TH and Y forms in English, let us examine second person pronouns from a broader perspective. The development of TH and Y forms is part of a quite general tendency in the European (and other) languages in which second person plural pronouns come to be used in reference to social superiors. Brown and Gilman describe this phenomenon, which they call the power semantic (they use the abbreviation T to stand generally for the category second person singular and V to stand for the category second person plural):

> the superior says T and receives V. . . . The character of the power semantic can be made clear with a set of examples from various languages. In his letters, Pope Gregory I (590–604) used T to his subordinates in the ecclesiastical hierarchy and they invariably said V to him. In medieval Europe, generally, the nobility said T to the common poeple and received V; the master of a household said T to his

slave, his servant, his squire, and received V. Within the family, of whatever social level, parents gave T to children and were given V. In Italy in the fifteenth century penitents said V to the priest and were told T. In Froissart (late fourteenth century) God says T to His angels and they say V; all celestial beings say T to man and receive V. In French of the twelfth and thirteenth century man says T to the animals. In fifteenth century Italian literature Christians say T to Turks and Jews and receive V. In the plays of Corneille and Racine and Shakespeare, the noble principals say T to their subordinates and are given V in return. [1960:255–56]

The use in English of TH and Y forms to indicate social distinctions is a part of this general trend.[28] In pre-Norman England, the distinction between TH and Y forms was a simple number distinction. In the late thirteenth and fourteenth centuries (see Kennedy 1915 and Stidson 1917 for evidence from literary texts of the period), the plural forms came to be used in addressing superiors, due to the influence of French use of *tu* and *vous*.

How can we interpret this change? First, the plural pronouns underwent a further differentiation, being used in Norman England as both plural pronouns and as formal singular ones. Here we see the semantic breadth of the unmarked term—its ability to subsume both poles of the singular/plural opposition. The development of the formal singular Y forms is noteworthy too in that it illustrates that unmarked features need not exhibit their double semantic value at all stages of the language; rather it may be that semantic unmarkedness exists in the potential to have a double value, a potential lacked by the marked opposite.

Second, the "power semantic" that arose in the pronoun system, like other semantic differences, is defined by a semantic opposition. We can characterize the new meanings of the TH and Y forms as a secondary semantic opposition subordinate to the number oposition that existed in pre-Norman English. This subordinate opposition we can label as deference opposed to nondeference. The posited feature [deferential] will indicate a 'reverential' (extremely polite) posture by the speaker. [Deferential] is the feature value that would occur in the singular or plural use of the Y forms to address social superiors. The corresponding feature [nondeferential] would occur in the TH forms and could also occur in Y forms used as plurals. Since the TH forms and Y forms used in the plural were unspecified for 'reverential' posture, the use of these forms could have been taken as either giving no indication of deference or as indicating a purposeful nondeference. The feature value [nondeferential] would have therefore been the unmarked feature value.

The situation in pre-Norman English before the new opposition arose can be illustrated thus:

(24)   Pre-Norman English

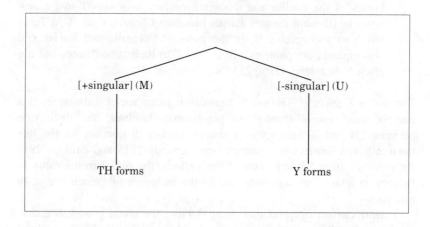

The feature hierarchy after the opposition deferential/nondeferential arose is illustrated below:

(25)   Post-Norman English

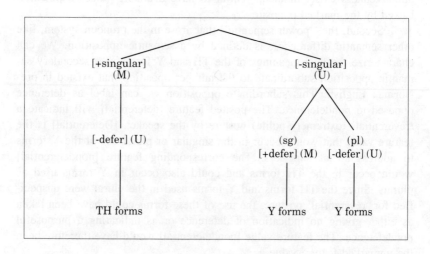

Note that in (25) the Y forms have both a singular and a plural use. The labels (sg) and (pl) are used here to indicate that the feature [deferential] was associated with the singular use of the Y forms and that the feature [nondeferential] was associated with the plural use of these forms. The elaboration of the [-singular] feature follows the principle of compensation: the unmarked feature is more differentiated than the marked feature is. Shortly after the Y forms took on their deferential sense, the TH forms came to signal close family relationships, intimacy, and shared values, and, in some cases, contempt as well. This development signals, I believe, a shift and reevaluation of the opposition between [deferential] and [nondeferential]. After the use of Y forms to indicate extreme politeness to social superiors became established, the conditions on its use would naturally become less restrictive. In this way, the social meaning of the usage would weaken to indicate simple politeness rather than social superiority. The weakening of the meaning of the Y forms can be seen as similar to the bleaching of meaning of intensifiers that occurs in words like *great, fanastic, incredible,* and *excellent.* As these forms are used hyperbolically to indicate rather ordinary things, their literal meanings are weakened until they are no longer truly intensive.

The shift of [deferential] to mean 'polite' rather than 'reverential' would have caused a parallel shift of the meaning of the feature [nondeferential], since one term of an opposition cannot be changed without changing the other as well. The new meaning of [nondeferential] would have been the opposite of politely neutral address, namely a familiarity either construed as intimacy or as rudeness, depending on the context. The meaning of the opposition thus shifts from (26a) to (26b):[29]

(26)   [deferential]   [nondeferential]

a. specification of reverence (M)   /nonspecification of reverence (U)
b. nonspecification of familiarity (U) /specification of familiarity (M)

Along with the change in the meaning of the features [deferential] and [nondeferential] there is also a change in their markedness relation, as indicated in (26). As the Y forms came to be the general pronouns for neutral address, the feature value characterizing this usage would have become the unmarked feature value. And since the TH forms adopted a narrowed and specialized meaning, the feature value characterizing them would now be marked. The semantic weakening of the feature meanings thus yielded changes in use that entailed a reversal of markedness values in the (redefined) features: at first [nondeferential] was the unmarked feature; after the semantic shift, [deferential] was unmarked.

The feature hierarchy after the redefinition of the features and the markedness reversal can be illustrated thus:

(27)

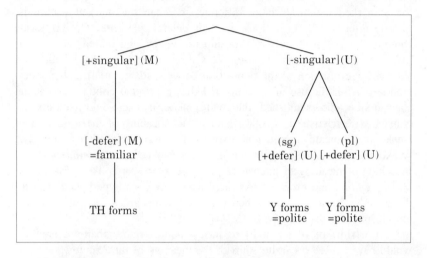

Notice that the feature value associated with the plural use of Y forms has been changed from [−defer] to [+defer]. This is because the plural use of Y forms remains socially neutral throughout the process of change. But as the meaning and markedness value of the feature shifts, the feature value that characterizes the neutral use of the Y forms also changes to remain consistent with the fact that use of the Y forms in the plural does not necessarily signal anything about the speaker's attitude toward the hearer. Notice also that since the value [+defer] is assigned to both the singular and plural uses of the Y forms, we can simplify the illustration in (27) to one with a single occurrence of the feature [deferential].

The TH forms became quite rare even in upper-class speech by the sixteenth century and were completely lost in the eighteenth century. In social terms, this loss may have been connected to connotations of excessive familiarity and implied inequality of the TH forms, especially in the face of increasing social egalitarianism (cf. Brown and Gilman 1960). As a lexical process, the loss straightforwardly involves the elimination of the branch of the hierarchy in which the (doubly) marked forms appear. The loss of the TH forms again changes the relationship between features. Since there are no longer marked [nondeferential] pronouns, the feature value [deferential] does no work in the pronoun system and can be eliminated. Moreover, since there are no longer distinct [singular] forms, the contrast between singular and plural in the second person can also be collapsed to the unmarked value.

(28)

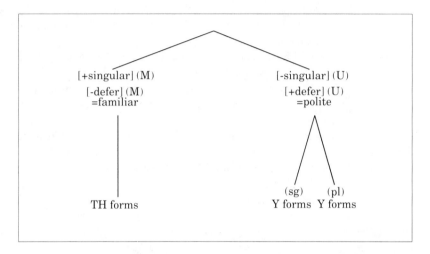

The scenario I have just sketched also helps us to understand a further turn in the development of the pronominal forms. Brown and Gilman make an interesting point about the norms of address used between individuals of roughly equal power status. These norms reflected social class distinctions in that equals of the lower social class used the second person singular (TH) forms while equals of the upper social classes used the plural (Y) forms:

> Since the nonreciprocal power semantic only prescribes usage between superior and inferior, it calls for a social structure in which there are unique power ranks for every individual. Medieval European societies were not so finely structured as that, and so the power semantic was never the only rule for the use of T and V. There were also norms of address for persons of roughly equivalent power, that is, for members of a common class. Between equals, pronominal address was reciprocal; an individual gave and received the same form. During the medieval period, and for varying times beyond, equals of the upper classes exchanged the mutual V and equals of the lower classes exchanged T. [1960:256]

A way of understanding this pattern of usage can be found in the structural analysis sketched above. Observe that the feature analysis reflected by (25) and (27) would have coexisted as (27) developed from (25). Suppose that the form used in reciprocal address—that is, in address among social equals—was the unmarked pronoun form. If the change from (25) to (27) occurred first among upper-class speakers and later among the lower classes, there would have been a period in which the upper-class usage was guided by the system in (27) while lower-class usage was still guided by (25). Speakers of the lower classes would have had a system in which the Y forms were still marked for extreme politeness, so the natural form of reciprocal address would have been the unmarked TH forms. Speakers of the upper classes, having already adopted the system in which the Y forms were unmarked and the TH forms marked for familiarity, would have used those forms as the natural form of reciprocal address.

A markedness-based approach to the TH and Y forms allows us to devise a system of description consistent with the known facts and to draw them into a broader explanatory framework of lexical analysis and change. Theory and history come together in a mutual consistency that gives texture and depth to both: the development of the pronouns can be seen as reflecting a broader asymmetry of language, while the theory of markedness can be more closely connected to the facts of language as revealed in linguistic change.

The Direction of Change

I have suggested in this chapter that language change can be grounded both in language-particular and in universal markedness relations. From one perspective markedness relations inherent in the facts of a particular language exist as a system of linguistic values that are felt in the patterns and norms of succeeding generations. From the other perspective, markedness exists as a language-independent system that constrains possible changes and evaluates the cross-linguistic naturalness of a system. From both perspectives, however, the quest for the essence of language lies in an evaluative superstructure going beyond an arbitrary pairing of expression and meaning.

From one point of view, the study of language as a system of language-particular signs is central. Linguistic entities are viewed as signs, each made up of a sign vehicle (or expression), an object (or meaning), and a markedness value that relates the vehicle and object and that situates them with respect to other signs. The roots of the language-particular view in the theory of the sign might prompt us to call it a semiotic approach. If so, the essence of semiosis will be the way in which generations of speakers unconsciously read diagrams of these sign values and use their tacit understanding of them to guide their preferences and norms.

From the other point of view, universals of language are central. Languages are systems of rules, representations, features, and inventories in which biological and cultural laws obtain. While these laws can be attenuated and even broken by the situation in a particular language, the foundation of language is held firm by cross-linguistic markedness values that provide a pressure that restores the balance of disruptive changes and generally favors certain types of developments. Universal markedness guides grammars toward recurring asymmetries, implications, and correlations.

6

Retrospective and Prospectus

A Look Back

Throughout this book language has been examined in terms of properties that underlie linguistic structures and their organization into nonequivalences. From the Prague School perspective, we have looked at language as a structured hierarchy in which certain conceptual and perceptual categories are more dominant than others. According to this view, markedness is a relation between the grammatical, lexical, phonological, and stylistic categories of a language. We have also discussed markedness values as language universals, identifying two different approaches: the Universal Grammar approach of Noam Chomsky and the language universals approach of Joseph Greenberg.

We have looked at the ways in which markedness relations can be established and at some problems that arise. I have suggested that values in a language can be determined by a set of diagnostics that include indeterminateness, distributional breadth, prototypicality, optimality, syncretization, and simplicity, and I have emphasized that these diagnostics are best viewed as heuristics rather than as a hard-and-fast algorithm.

The role of language-particular markedness in the overall sign structure of language has also been considered at length. Since the marked/unmarked relation ranges over all levels of linguistic structure, it applies globally to the bundling of phonological features into phonemes, syntactic features into grammatical categories, semantic features into conceptual categories, and pragmatic features into categories of language use. The globality of markedness is also evident in the way in which markedness relations can organize expression and meaning in feature hierarchies and in the combination of features in contexts. Markedness is thus relevant at both the paradigmatic and syntagmatic axes of language. The overall globality of markedness can be schematized as follows:

(1)

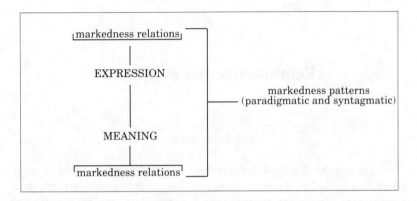

Reduced to its essentials, this book has been about four things: its two major themes have been diagrams of values and hierarchy of structure; its secondary themes have been typology and change.

Diagrammaticity has been one major theme of this work. From the observation that markedness values form patterns of alignment and complementarity has developed the thesis that markedness relations might be systematically implemented in iconic and reverse iconic diagrams of markedness values. Such diagrams, which may obtain both between forms and meanings and between units and contexts, have been illustrated in chapters 3 through 5 with examples from the areas of grammar, sound structure, and morphology.

The central theme of this book has, of course, been the notion of hierarchy. The Jakobsonian emphasis on the asymmetry of feature values has grown into a view of markedness in which all functional properties of language—whether structurally focal ones such as nasality, consonantality, and singularity or more ad hoc properties—distinguish two nonequivalent terms. At the level of meaning, the asymmetry can usually be conceived of in terms of the signalization of the property (by the marked term) versus either the nonsignalization of the property or the signalization of the opposite (by the unmarked term). At the level of expression, asymmetry is reflected in the relation between forms: the marked element is more narrowly defined, while the unmarked is less narrow.

Hierarchy is also central to the application of markedness to language universals research, though in a somewhat different way. The hierarchical relation between marked and unmarked elements relevant to universals research is an implicational relation between typologically less natural elements and typologically more natural ones.

Typology has thus been a recurrent subtheme in the preceding chapters. One thing that linguists agree on is that the relations defining linguistic systems and subsystems do not include just any possible relationship, but choose from a menu of linguistically and culturally possible ones. Modern linguistics has a strong interest in universal asymmetries and hence in universals of markedness. Since the focus of the present book has been English, cross-linguistic markedness relations have been subordinated to language-particular ones. However, markedness theory might ultimately reconcile language-particular and universal markedness, unifying cross-linguistic naturalness and language-particular dominance.

A second subtheme has been the role of markedness as a component of the historical analysis of language. Markedness relations act as a superstructure against which potential changes in the structure of the language are evaluated. Both language-particular markedness relations and universal markedness relations appear to have roles in change. While the strong view that all change results in unmarking must be rejected as too simplistic, markedness-based universals can serve to define a general notion of natural change, and, in addition, language-particular relations and relational diagrams serve as a goal and mechanism of change.

In this book I have tried to distinguish the main applications of markedness in linguistics, to exemplify how markedness values can be established at various levels in English, and to show how markedness may be applied to the synchronic and diachronic study of language. Needless to say, work remains to be done in all aspects of markedness theory: the theory of markedness diagrams must be further elaborated (both synchronically and diachronically), and a suitably constrained and predictive theory of markedness diagrams should be a future goal. In addition, the theory of universal markedness will benefit from clarification of the notion of natural system and a better understanding of the relation between language-particular markedness and universal conventions.

This rather full agenda will carry on the legacy of the Prague School of linguistics which both pioneered the concept of markedness and also provided the impetus for typological studies of phonology and grammar. And this agenda also reflects other interests of Roman Jakobson, the most influential member of the Prague School, in its concern with the motivatedness of the sound/meaning correlation via markedness. Attention to both the universal and the language-particular aspects of markedness, and to the diachronic as well as the synchronic planes of language places both approaches to markedness theory firmly in the Prague School and Jakobsonian traditions.

There are, of course, connections to be pursued between markedness theory and other interpretive traditions. For one thing, the definition of markedness as the value of an opposition may find an analogue in

C. S. Peirce's theory of signs. Shapiro (1983) has attempted to bring together the Jakobsonian and Peircean traditions, arguing that markedness is a species of interpretant and that linguistic structures and changes are informed by abductive reasoning (cf. also Andersen 1972). Connections arise also between markedness and poststructuralist literary-critical theory. Schleifer argues that the deconstructionism of Jacques Derrida has as its basis the denial of neutralization between marked and unmarked terms—and a displacement of the usual evaluative hierarchy of signs by its reverse "in such a way that it resists and disorganizes the [usual] hierarchy" (1987:388).

In this book, I have tried to show how markedness theory can be applied to the explication of grammatical and phonological structure and linguistic change. Needless to say, the discussion given in the preceding chapters does not exhaust the range of linguistic topics that may be analyzed in terms of markedness. Language-particular analyses can be extended to questions of aesthetics and language style. It is possible to examine narrative and poetic techniques and the conventions that underlie metaphor and other figures in terms of marked and unmarked techniques and the patterning of such stylistic oppositions. More prosaic aspects of discourse and text organization might also be studied. For example, the question of how grammatical and lexical oppositions function to define various linguistic registers or genres of text ought to be of considerable interest. Moreover, markedness analysis might play a role in developing a taxonomy of the discourse options available for the expression of different categories of meaning. (Work on narrative structure, literary language and conversation includes Bailey 1981, Chvany 1985, Denny 1985, Fox 1987, McCardle and Haupt 1983, Scotton 1983, Shapiro 1976, 1983, and Longman 1987).

Applied linguistics is another area in which markedness can provide new insights to familiar problems. Over the last decade Fred Eckman and others have investigated second language acquisition in light of universal markedness hierarchies and have had success in predicting both the difficulties of nonnative speakers and the order in which nonnative speakers acquire certain constructions.[1] It ought to be equally possible to apply markedness to the problems of teaching writing to native speakers. In fact, it would seem that both the language-particular and the universalist approaches would be valuable in composition research, the former for analyzing the relationships among competing patterns and norms, and the latter for examining the development of writing skills.

Wider Horizons

This book has been primarily about language, since that is the domain within which markedness has been most extensively studied as well as my own particular area of interest. But now it may be appropriate to consider the application of markedness to other systems of relations. Jakobson's remarks to Trubetzkoy, cited at the beginning of this book, are worth repeating now:

> I am coming increasingly to the conviction that your thought about correlation as a constant mutual connection between a marked and unmarked type is one of your most remarkable and fruitful ideas. It seems to me that it has significance not only for linguistics but also for ethnology and the history of culture, and that such historico-cultural correlations as life~death, liberty~non-liberty, sin~virtue, holidays~working days, etc., are always confined to relations a~non-a, and that it is important to find out for any epoch, group, nation, etc., what the marked element is. For instance, Majakovskij viewed life as a marked element realizable only when motivated; for him not death but life required a motivation. Cf. the way the relation of life and death differs for the two heroes of Tolstoy's "Master and Worker". Another example: the *Checkists* said that everyone is a man of the White Guard, and if not, it must be proved in every separate case. Here the Soviet allegiance is a marked element. At present in Soviet print there has emerged a slogan; they used to say "all those who are not against us are with us", but now they say "all those who are not with us are against us". . . . I'm convinced that many ethnographic phenomena, ideologies, etc. which at first glance seem to be identical, often differ only in the fact that what for one system is a marked term may be evaluated by the other precisely as the absence of a mark. [Trubetzkoy 1975:162ff.]

Structuralism in anthropology, literature, and art—as in linguistics— is based on the doctrine that the elements of a system (a social system, a literary genre, a particular text, a language) are organized into relations that underlie the complex phenomena of the system. The relations define inventories of categories—social, literary, artistic, linguistic. Among anthropologists, Claude Lévi-Strauss is particularly well known for adopting the principles and aims of structural linguistics (principally Prague School phonology, see chap. 1, n. 8), though the analysis of societies in terms of a general theory of relations is common to both Lévi-Strauss's approach and the symbolic anthropology of others such as E. E. Evans-Pritchard, Edmund Leach, Rodney Needham, and James Fox. What structural anthropology shares with structural linguistics is its search for a "general theory of relationships" in which it may be possible "to analyze societies in terms of differential features characteristic of the systems of relationships which define them" (Lévi-Strauss 1958:95–96).

Application of the theory of markedness to structural anthropology
seems to me to be worth detailed investigation in the future. Though Jakobson's influence on Lévi-Strauss was substantial, the notion of marked and
unmarked poles of an opposition does not seem to figure in Lévi-Strauss's
work. Lévi-Strauss of course recognized the nonequivalence of some oppositions and the organization of these values into homologies (see in particular his "Do Dual Organizations Exist?" chapter 8 of *Structural
Anthropology*), but he seems to treat oppositions as mutually exclusive relations rather than relations between the presence and absence of a property. It is possible that the reexamination of his studies of kinship, myth,
and social organization incorporating the logic of markedness might result
in a new understanding of the relational structure of such systems.[2] Such a
project, of course, is neither possible nor desirable in this chapter. I will
instead briefly illustrate the application of markedness to one particular
domain of cultural organization: the oppositions between right and left and
its correlation with other oppositions.

Right and Left in Symbol Classification

The aim of this section is to explore how the principles of markedness
organization are reflected in systems of cultural symbols, thereby broaden-
ing the scope of our investigations to include the sign structure of culture as
well as that of language. This section will concern the correlation of symbol values associated with the distinction between right-sidedness and left-
sidedness, an area first studied in detail by the French sociologist Robert
Hertz (1973 [1909]) and the subject of an interesting collection of essays
entitled *Right and Left: Essays on Dual Symbol Classification* (Needham
1973; see also Fritsch 1968).

The asymmetry of right- and left-handedness is of course in part biological, the usual superiority of the right hand being linked to factors of
hemispheric dominance. But there is also a considerable social and conventional component to the dominance of the right side that can be found both
in familiar European cultures and in more unfamiliar ones as well. According to Hertz, "the left hand is repressed and kept inactive, its development
methodically thwarted" (1973:5). In some cultures this is done by material
bonds, in others by less obvious means.

In our own society, the right hand is "the good hand." It is the hand
used in shaking hands, in saluting, in pledging allegiance to the flag, and in
giving legal testimony. The right hands are the ones joined together in mar-
riage ceremonies.[3] A special significance is also imputed to the right hand
in Judeo-Christian religious symbolism: Psalm 118 states, for example,
"The right hand of the Lord hath the preeminence"(v.16) And, as Hertz

remarks, "It is not by chance that in pictures of the Last Judgment it is the Lord's raised right hand that indicates to the elect their sublime abode, while his lowered left hand shows the damned the gaping jaws of Hell ready to swallow them." (1973:13[1909])

In other cultures, and in our own when we examine it closely, an iconic relationship can be established between the values of the right/left opposition and the values of other culturally relevant oppositions. Hertz, Evans-Pritchard, Needham, and others have analyzed cultural material that suggests the near universality of certain correlations among oppositions. These analyses show a parallelism of values in the implicit symbol systems that underlie myth, ritual, and social convention and also in the explicit association of right and left with certain functions and ideas. The sketches in Needham (1973) present a wide range of oppositions in relation to the right/left opposition, but for now I focus on the ones that appear to be most widespread:

(2)   Unmarked   Marked

           right   :   left
           male   :   female
           life   :   death
           auspicious :   inauspicious

Hertz himself ascribes this parallelism of symbols to the opposition between the sacred and the profane that he sees as "dominat[ing] the spiritual world of primitive men" (1973: 7), and according to which all things are classified and evaluated. Hertz is undoubtably correct that the parallelism is connected to universal principles of classification, though in the framework of this book we might ascribe the universality to the idea that there can be no conceptualization (no sign formation) without a simultaneous evaluation of concepts. However, my goal in the present discussion is more modest than that of accounting for the origin of this parallelism; it is rather to show that the correlations between symbol categories exhibit the same kind of diagrammatic patterning as linguistic values.

Let us consider then some of the ways in which the correlations between right/left, male/female/, life/death, and auspicious/inauspicious are manifest in three sample cultures, those of the ancient Greeks, the Kaguru of Tanzania, and the Nyoro of Uganda.

The Greeks

As Lloyd (1973) shows, the symbolic associations of right and left figure importantly in the theories and explanations of the Greek philosophers of the fifth and fourth centuries BC. In the *Iliad* and the *Odyssey,* for example, omens of the right side are considered auspicious, and omens of the left side are considered inauspicious; the right hand is used for greetings, for libations and for pledges. Moreover, in the Table of Opposites given by Aristotle, the concepts right, male, and light are arranged on the side of good, while left, female, and darkness are arranged on the side of bad. These symbolic associations are played out in various ways: they are seen in the myth that the souls of the just travel to the right and upward at death while the souls of the unjust travel to the left and downward;[4] they are also manifest in Parmenides' theory that a child's sex is determined by its position on the left side of the womb if it is a female and the right side if it is a male; in Anaxagorias' theory that a child's sex is determined by the side of the body that the father's sperm comes from (left for females, right for males); and in Aristotle's theory that right, above and front are the *archai* of dimensions and of locomotion, growth, and sensation, a theory that played an important role in his biological explanations.

The Kaguru

Now consider a widely different culture, that of the Kaguru, a Bantu-speaking people of Tanzania whose classification system is discussed by Beidelman:

> The Kaguru conceive of certain rights and obligations, social group attributes, and directions in opposite terms. These terms form a dualistic symbolic classification which is best considered under the categories of either 'male' and 'female' or 'right' and 'left'. [1973:132]

Beidelman notes that the Kaguru consider the right hand to be clean and to have strength and to be associated with masculine qualities; the left hand is unclean, weak, and associated with feminine qualities:

> When I asked the Kaguru why some said that male (*mugosi* or *ume*) creatures are always physically stronger than females (*mwanamuke* or *-ike*) and that likewise the right hand is stronger than the left. Others said that this was due to the way persons were fashioned in the womb; they said that a person was made of two joined sides, the right half derived from the father, the left from the mother. [ibid.:132]

The significance of right and left also arises in Kaguru omens. If a person on a journey hears a touraco cry out on the right side, the belief is that something important will soon happen to his paternal kin; if a touraco cry is heard on the left side something important will happen to his maternal kin. Beidelman also comments on the associations of right and left in everyday Kaguru practices:

Kaguru encourage all children to use the right hand. A child who grows to favor his left hand is in no way punished, but people may sometimes jokingly comment on this and, if it is a left-handed boy, they may sometimes say he is "like a wife" (*kame muke*) in this respect. Kaguru eat with the right hand; they use it for greeting persons and for shaking hands. None of these acts would be performed politely with the left. [ibid.:135]

The Nyoro

Among the Nyoro, a Bantu people of Uganda, Needham observes that "in the crucial events of life, and the major institutions of the society, the right is pre-eminent and auspicious while the left is inferior and inauspicious" (1973:301 [1967]). Needham's exemplification includes the following observations. When a child is born, the afterbirth is buried to the left of the door if the child is female and to the right if the child is male. In certain types of augury the throat of a fowl is cut and the flow of blood is observed; if the blood runs more freely from the left artery than from the right artery then the omen is bad; if the blood flows equally or if it flows more freely from the right artery then it is a good omen. In Nyoro burial customs, the body of a man is buried on its right side and that of a woman is buried on its left side. And in making blood pacts, men sit opposite one another, make several incisions near their navel, and catch a few drops of blood in the right hand, then rub a coffee bean in the blood and give the bean to their partner with the right hand. Needham notes that "the very awkwardness of these movements emphasizes the importance which is attached to using the right" (p. 303). Needham sums up his survey of Nyoro symbol classification by remarking that according to context right is associated with "the king, chiefs, landowners, men, masculine tasks, civil behavior, and good omens" and left with "the queen, subjects, interlopers, women, feminine tasks, sexual activity, and bad omens"(p. 305).

These ethnographic notes give just a sample of the evidence concerning the distinction of right- and left-sidedness and the widespread preeminence of the right. The reader is directed to the articles and references in Needham (1973) for more detailed treatments of the above examples and for discussion of symbol classification and asymmetry among peoples as diverse as the Rotinese of Indonesia, the Mapuche of Chile, and the Osage Indians of Missouri and Kansas. As Needham notes,

The issue can be studied in such varied fields as the Homeric poems, alchemy, and thirteenth century religious art, in Hindu iconography, classical Chinese state ceremonies, emblem books and bestiaries, as well as Maori ritual, Bornean divination, and the myths of the most disparate cultures. [1973:110(1960)]

Markedness Assimilation in Symbol Classification

The alignment of symbol values sketched in the preceding sections can be considered as instances of markedness assimilation in which cultural categories that have like values in those systems are symbolically or functionally connected in the rituals of the culture. This conjecture seems well founded in light of the use and distribution of these symbols in the examples discussed.[5]

It is possible to find evidence of similar value assimilation in our own culture. I have already discussed the generally unmarked status of masculine gender in language. The same markedness relation that holds between grammatical gender obtains between the masculine and feminine sex roles. While context impinges on the markedness evaluation of the opposition male/female, it is the masculine role that remains the more broadly defined in American culture. This is demonstrated by the fact that traditionally male attributes and occupations can be adopted by females with fewer symbolic constraints than traditionally female attributes and occupations can be adopted by males. So, for example, if a woman is a college professor, dentist, police officer, Supreme Court Justice or presidential candidate there is less of a clash between sex and the sex role associated with the occupation than if a male is engaged in a traditionally female occupation such as nursing. A similar situation exists with regard to dress. In the United States today, men's clothing is unmarked and can be worn (except in marked formal occasions in which the maximal contrast is maintained) by either sex: witness the popularity of the business suit among professional women and the conventional unisex attire of college students. Women's clothing, on the other hand, is marked. For a male to wear women's clothing, except in a masquerade situation, is proscribed behavior.

The unmarkedness of the male social role is manifest in other sociolinguistic data as well. We find it in the often-discussed naming and referring conventions, in which the term referring to the male is syntactically prior to the term referring to the female: *Mr. and Mrs., boys and girls, husband and wife* (and the older *man and wife*),[6] even in the order of pronouns in the putatively nonsexist *his/her*.[7] We find it in the formation of married names, where the man's surname conventionally subsumes that of the woman.

Consider next the status of the concepts right and left. As Linda Waugh (1982) has emphasized, our society is oriented toward the right hand in ways almost too numerous to mention. Automobile ignitions, most elevator buttons, classroom desks, cooking and serving utensils, scissors and tools, manual pencil sharpeners, three-ring binders, telephone cords, and wall switches are all designed with right-handed users in mind. And the terminology of sidedness reflects this dominance as well. A left-handed ball glove is specifically named as such (cf. the question *Does anybody have a glove I can borrow?* vs. *Does anybody have a left-handed glove I can borrow?*). Similarly, a boxer who leads with the right hand (and thus reserves his or her stronger left hand for crosses and uppercuts) is referred to as a *southpaw*, though one who leads with his or her left is not a *northpaw*.

Not only is our culture organized according to the view that its members are right-handed, but the unmarkedness of the right side is also reflected in the relative stability of its forms in the Indo-European languages:

The diferent way in which the collective consciousness envisages and values the right and left appears clearly in language. There is a striking contrast in the words which in most Indo-European languages designate the two sides.

While there is a single term for "right" which extends over a very wide area and shows great stability, the idea of "left" is expressed by a number of distinct terms, which are less widely spread and seem destined constantly to disappear in the face of new words. Some of these words are obvious euphemisms, others are of extremely obscure origin. "It seems," says Meillet, "that when speaking of the left side one avoided pronouncing the proper word and tended to replace it by different ones which were constantly being renewed." [Hertz 1973:11 (1909)]

Following Meillet, Hertz proposes to account for the stability of terms for right and the instability of terms for left by suggesting a tendency toward pejoration in which terms for left become associated with undesirable ideas and come to be replaced by euphemisms. The association of the right and left with concepts traditionally representing "good" and "bad" is of course quite well known. Terms associated with cognate words for left include *sinister* and *gauche*, while terms etymologically associated with the right include *dextrous, correct* (and *right* itself used with this sense), *rectitude*, and *adroit*.

In our society, the opposition life/death is also evaluated such that life is the unmarked term of the opposition and death the marked term.[8] As I have noted, Jakobson pointed out that it is the choice of death, not the choice of life, that requires some conscious motivation. That is to say, people generally assume that life will continue and is worth continuing, and it is only in special cases—such as deep depression or in the context of a philosophical or literary existentialism that this relation is reversed and life requires continued motivation. The unmarkedness of the concept of life as opposed to death may be in part reflected in attitudes toward such issues as euthanasia, abortion, and capital punishment.

The above examples are meant to be suggestive rather than exhaustive.[9] What is to be emphasized is that cultural symbols, roles, and concepts are amenable to a revealing classification into oppositions between a more broadly defined, dominant concept and a more narrowly defined, marked one.[10] And these values may form patterns of alignment in which symbols of like value function in parallel to signal the likeness of concepts in a culture's symbols and rituals. The "language" of cultural symbols, roles, and concepts may turn out to show the same diagrammaticity that is found in grammatical and phonological structure.

Inversions

So far I have talked only about markedness assimilation in cultural signs. Now, however, I want to consider markedness complementarity in cultural signs, to complete the parallel with linguistic semiotics. As is the case in grammar and phonology, there seem to be specific subpatterns in which the markedness values of signs combine in a complementary fashion.

To exemplify this, let us return briefly to the Nyoro cultural system. Needham, who has paid considerable attention to the study of complementaries in classificatory systems, has noted that the general dominance of the right side and its associated categories is sometimes reversed. In special cases involving birth, death, and the milking of cows, the left side assumes preeminence:

> the Nyoro in certain circumstances conventionally resort to symbolic reversal. The customs in question are of the same type, thus defined, but they can be distinguished secondarily as relating to either (a) situation, or (b) social status; one kind of reversal is relative and temporary, the other is absolute and permanent. [1973:306 (1967)]

Needham notes, for example, that while cows are normally milked from the right side, a special cow is milked from the left side when the king dies (the milk is then poured into the corpse's mouth). Here the inversion can be understood as an assimilation of the markedness of death with the markedness of the left side. Since left is the marked term, it is natural for the left to be used in the ritual associated with the marked pole of the life/death opposition. As further support for this reversal Needham points out that when an ordinary Nyoro is buried, the children of the deceased sprinkle earth on the grave, first brushing in a little with their elbow, "men using the left elbow, women using their right" (ibid.). He also remarks:

The use of normally inappropriate sides of the body, when pushing the earth into the grave with the elbows, is also an instance of situational reversal, but rather more complex. In this situation the participants do not adopt in common a ritual which has generally inauspicious or mortuary connotations, for while the men use the left (just as they might occupy the left side in milking the funeral cow), the women, who are already associated with the left, have recourse instead to the right. In doing so, the sexes first align themselves, as it were, with their respective "sides" of the symbolic classification, men with the right and women with the left, and then they override the distinctive meanings of the symbolism in favour of a relational definition of the situation. It is no longer the specificity of the opposed connotations of right and left that counts, but the very relation of opposition which, more fundamentally, is manipulated in order to express the reversal. This also is easily recognized as a common symbolic process, for there are many reports from other societies of the belief that the state of death is in various particulars a continuation of life under an opposite sign. [ibid.:307]

The reversal here can be schematized as follows:

(3)

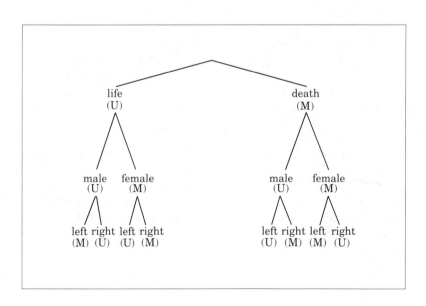

Needham also describes cases in which an evaluation associated with social status is the reverse of what might otherwise be appropriate to the occupant of that status. An interesting case concerns the Nyoro princess, who is treated symbolically as an unmarried male. For example, after a princess is born the placenta is buried on the right side of the house (whereas that of other females is buried on the left). And after she dies the princess is buried with her hands under the right side of her head (again unlike other females, who are buried on their left side). Needham reports that

> Roscoe tells us expressly, in connection with the burial of the placenta, that "a princess was always considered and spoken of as a prince and treated as a boy" (158). Moreover, in the general treatment of children "no difference was made between princes and princesses: they were both called prince and received the same honour from the people" (161). . . . Princesses are forbidden to marry, and although they may have sexual liaisons with their half-brothers they may not become pregnant; if they do so, the birth is concealed from the king and normally the child is killed (171). They are "really encouraged to live promiscuously with their half-brothers," but intercourse with a commoner is punished with great severity, and to bear the child of a commoner would entail being put to death (171–72).

> It is because princesses are treated like princes . . . that when they die their hands are placed under the right side of their head. In this they stand opposed to the queen, who of all princesses is the only one to be allowed to marry; she is fully feminine in this regard, and accordingly is buried with her hands under the left side of her head. [ibid.:308–9]

Needham regards this as a symbol reversal that permanently marks social status. In our terms, it can be analyzed as a syncretization of the opposition between male and female within the doubly marked category of royal offspring. As a result, both prince and princess assume the generally unmarked symbol value (that of male), and therefore the values for the subordinate left/right opposition are as for the king and for nonroyal males. The structure of oppositions in this system might be something like:

(4)

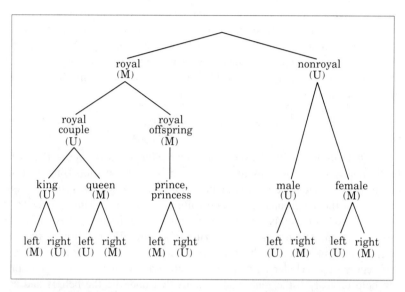

Since the category 'queen' is not in the domain of the syncretization, the values of left and right 'queen' are parallel to left and right for the category of nonroyal women.

Other cases of reversed or complementary markedness values are not difficult to find. For example, Needham notes that Nyoro diviners conventionally use the left hand to cast cowrie shells, a practice "which is by far the commonest technique resorted to whenever Nyoro are in trouble" (p. 301). And James Fox (1973) notes a nice example concerning the burial practices of the Rotinese of Indonesia. The Rotinese distinguish between good deaths and bad deaths, the latter including death in childbirth, being gored by a water buffalo, being hit by lightning, being killed by another person, being bitten by a crocodile, being carried away by a flood, or being drowned by the sea. According to Fox (1973:358 ff.), the burial of those who have suffered such a bad death entails a reversal of the symbolism associated with a good death.

The purpose of this section has been to extend the notion of evaluative superstructure to the domain of cultural oppositions, symbols, categories. The emphasis has been on the evaluative asymmetry of cultural signs. It has been suggested that some cultural oppositions exhibit a contrast between narrowly defined and broadly defined terms that parallels the marked/unmarked opposition in language. In addition, I have shown that markedness values in culture pattern according to the same principles of assimilation and complementation that are found in the structure of language. The realization that like principles inform both language and culture is, of course, a starting point not a conclusion, and markedness assimilation and complementarity may be a promising way of mapping out culture sign systems, their function, and teleology. And conversely, the application of markedness beyond language will help us to better understand the principle and its limits.

A Few Final Examples

One purely practical aspect of a markedness-based approach to cultural sign systems concerns the way in which an opposition (linguistic or cultural) may have different markedness values not only cross-culturally but also within the subgroups of a single culture. As a consequence, a category may be used differently by different groups and mean widely different things to them. The practice of referring to a cultural opposition as fixed is convenient, but obscures the likelihood that semantic relations differ for different groups. Understanding the differential evaluation of oppositions can help to analyze the relational systems that underlie the beliefs and actions of various sociocultural groups.

To make matters more concrete, consider the example of written versus spoken language. Among linguists, the unmarked medium is the spoken language and the marked medium is written language. Speech is the more broadly defined subsuming concept, as Waugh (1982) points out: spoken language is universal whereas literacy and writing are not; spoken language is learned prior to spelling, reading, and the conventions of rhetoric; spoken language is historically prior to written language. Nevertheless, it is quite common among nonlinguists to reverse the evaluative relations between speech and writing and to treat writing as basic and speech as an informal deviation. This is the basis for the common response that one hears when introduced as an English teacher, namely, *I guess I'd better watch how I speak.* The implication of the comment is of course that people should speak more as they write (or as they should write). If we were to translate the markedness relation into semantic features we can see the value reversal even more clearly. For linguists (in their professional mode), the opposition between spoken and written language is characterized as [language] versus [written language]. As Waugh points out, this relation is reflected in the common use of the term *language* to refer either to speech alone or to language in general (*What language is that written in?*) and also in the use of the compound term *written language* to refer to writing. Among nonlinguists, including popular grammarians and many English teachers, the markedness values are reversed. *Language* refers to language in general or to the written language; spoken language is referred to as *the way we talk, colloquial language,* or simply *speech.* For such speakers, the opposition is characterized as [language] versus [spoken language].

A similar evaluation holds for the term *grammar.* For linguists the unmarked sense of grammar is, theoretical distinctions aside, a complete description of the usages of native speakers (equivalently, an abstract mental model accounting for native speakers' intuitions). The marked sense of grammar is expressed in the compounds *good grammar, formal grammar,* or *prescriptive grammar* and refers to the normative adjudication of the gaps and variations found in descriptive grammar. Among nonlinguists, however, the values and definitions are reversed. The unmarked sense of grammar is prescriptive grammar and the marked sense of grammar is descriptive.[11]

The study of cultural categories in terms of the evaluation of the oppositions that define them should be useful also in better understanding the use of other abstract terms such as *science, the humanities, medicine,* among others, since it provides a framework for representing different hierarchizations and conceptualizations of meaning. The oppositional relations that exist in any culture, text, or discourse can be organized in a hierarchical evaluative relationship, and an understanding of the role of markedness in creating and maintaining this relationship will give us a clearer picture of the conceptual systems that these relations comprise. And, since markedness may provide clues about a speaker's expectations, intentions, or hidden assumptions, markedness analysis may prove to be useful as well in explicating the dynamics of discourse between individuals or groups operating with different value systems.

Our conceptual systems are frameworks that we use so automatically that we are normally unaware of their structure and organization. Yet these systems determine many of our everyday perceptions and opinions and affect the way we make decisions and interact with others. Determining the asymmetries that inhere in our cultural systems is certain to shed light on the patterns that underlie conventional wisdom and reasoning. It might also provide us with an understanding of unargued cultural assumptions that we take as background information. As a result it might allow us to better characterize ways in which such asymmetries can result in misunderstandings, confusions, and fallacies of reasoning.[12] And we might also compare the value an opposition has for different groups or individuals—for speaker versus hearer, author versus reader, female versus male, liberal versus conservative, working class versus middle class, enfranchised versus disenfranchised, and so on.[13]

I want to point out in closing a type of puzzle that can arise when we consider the possibility that different individuals (or groups) vary in what they take to be unmarked behavior. This problem is illustrated by the following observation made by Deborah Tannen in a review of Mary Catherine Bateson's *With a Daughter's Eye*:

> Chap. 6 'One white glove and the sound of one hand clapping', contrasts [Margaret Mead's and Gregory Bateson's] personal and intellectual styles. It begins with an anecdote of a late encounter in which MM is trying to convince GB to put on socks before going on stage. [Mary Catherine Bateson] asks why MM thought it important to wear socks, while GB did not (though one might ask if he thought it important not to wear socks, since wearing them is the unmarked case). [1986:202]

When an individual engages in marked behavior of some kind, how is this to be interpreted? Marked behavior may be a conscious decision—a stylistic option, or a challenge or subversion of the existing superstructure. It may also be an unconscious decision determined by a system of markedness values that is the reverse of that generally held. In the first case one intends one's behavior to be marked; in the second case one believes one's behavior to be unmarked, though from the point of view of general values (of, for example, the hearer, the audience, the reader, society in general) it is marked.[14]

In the case just described, Tannen's question is apt, since it is hard to imagine a system of Western dress in which not wearing socks on stage would be unmarked (rock concerts aside). But things are not always so obvious. To raise one final example, consider the matter of appropriate dress for male college faculty members. Is casual dress marked in opposition to the unmarked business suit of other white-collar work? Or is academic dress a separate cultural domain in which different markedness values obtain, casual dress being unmarked and the business suit marked? While the answer would take us far beyond the scope of this book into a detailed description of the oppositions underlying dress codes and an analysis of "informants' " intuitions about dress, I believe that such puzzles can be solved as the structure of cultural codes is worked out.[15] But these are puzzles for another time.

Notes

Chapter 1

1. The terminology "general" versus "specific" follows Jakobson (1984 [1957]), though elsewhere he uses these terms in other ways. The definition of semantic markedness as signalization of A versus nonsignalization of A/signalization of not A follows that given in Jakobson's article "The Structure of the Russian Verb" (1984 [1932]). In that article, he equates the unmarked also with the idea of semantic "zero categories." This idea, developed further in "Zero Sign" (1984 [1939]), sometimes results in the marked category thought of as having the "plus interpretation" while the unmarked category has the "zero interpretation" along with the "minus interpretation" (cf. Waugh 1982). In Prague School phonology the marked category is sometimes referred to as the positive pole of the opposition and the unmarked category as the negative pole. These locutions refer however to their hierarchical relation not necessarily to their plus/minus label, which is a function of the name selected for the opposition. Compare note 9 below.

In connection with Jakobson's definition of semantic markedness as signalization of A versus nonsignalization of A/signalization of not A, it is worth pointing out the basis of markedness in the scope of logical negation. If a positive feature value is the specification of some property A, the negation of [specification of A] could be either [not [specification of A]] or [specification of [not A]].

2. Greenberg says, for example:

> Viewed psychologically there is perhaps justification for seeing a similarity between the implied, fundamental characteristic, that is the unmarked member, whether in phonology, grammar, or semantics, and the Gestalt notion of ground, the frequent, the taken-for-granted, whereas the marked character would answer to figure in the familiar dichotomy. [1966:60]

Waugh also remarks that

> the logical relationship between the unmarked and marked terms of any grammatical opposition . . . may be metaphorically characterized as a subset-set relationship where the marked category is the subset and the unmarked category is the set, or alternatively as a figure-ground relationship where the marked pole is the figure and the unmarked pole is the ground. [1982:302]

See also Holenstein (1976:123–124) and Chvany (1985). It is important to emphasize the metaphorical nature of this characterization, since the figure/ground relationship always crucially depends on such matters as the construal of a scene
(Langacker 1987) or a speaker's point of view (Comrie 1986).

3. The following remarks are illustrative:

It has become increasingly clear, however, that the nature of markedness has
been misunderstood by linguists and other semioticians alike. [Waugh
1982:299]

[I]t is not easy to find an articulate formulation of a theory or program for
markedness in any school of linguistic description. [Brakel 1984:12]

Although probably all versions of markedness theory follow the classic version in making claims about correlations within and across the three domains
of distribution, syntagmatic complexity, and paradigmatic complexity, they
also differ widely in the more specific content of their hypotheses [Moravcsik
and Wirth 1983:3]

Compare also Cairns (1986:14), Comrie (1986:85), van Langendonck (1986), and
Andrews (1984:chap. 2).

4. Actually, there are several versions of markedness with a universalist perspective. See chapter 2 for further elaboration.

5. The principle of markedness assimilation, was originally put forward by
Henning Andersen (1968:175; 1972:44–45).

6. Many of the biographical details reported here are derived from the excellent obituary articles by Kučera (1983) and Frank (1984).

7. For some discussion of Prague School linguistics, see Lepschy (1970),
Jakobson (1971: 711–22), and Anderson (1985).

8. Trubetzkoy, who lived from 1890 to 1938, was something of a child
prodigy who published articles on the folklore of the Finns, Voguls, Ostyaks,
and Votyaks while he was only fifteen. After receiving the degree of *Kandidat*
(equivalent to a doctorate) in linguistics from Moscow University and teaching
there briefly, Trubetzkoy, who was a Russian nobleman, was forced to flee
Moscow in 1917. He taught at the University of Sofia in Bulgaria from 1920 to
1922 and then settled in Vienna, where he occupied a chair in Slavic philology and
where he remained throughout his life. See the "Autobiographical Notes on N. S.
Trubetzkoy as related by Roman Jakobson" in Trubetzkoy (1968:309–23),
Jakobson (1971:501–16 [1939]), and Anderson (1985:85ff.) for more details
on Trubetzkoy's life. The correspondence from Trubetzkoy to Jakobson, which
continued from the 1920s until Trubetzkoy's death, has been published as Trubetzkoy (1975).

9. For an account of Jakobson's influence on Lévi-Strauss, see Lévi-Strauss's preface to Jakobson's *Six Lectures on Sound and Meaning*.

10. In the standard French of France, there is no lax [I] pronunciation, though one does occur in Canadian French, as an allophone of [i]. (I am indebted to Margaret Winters for pointing this out to me.)

11. A feature can be thought of as some conceptual or perceptual property. As such, it defines two values: categories that have the property and categories that do not. In the context of privative oppositions (oppositions between A and not A), the presence of the feature is considered to be its positive value and the absence of the feature is its negative value. In this way, the property selected to define the feature is connected to the evaluation of the opposition. In the Prague School framework, the marked/unmarked relation is intrinsically connected to privative oppositions and the positive pole of the opposition (A) is the marked term. The negative pole (not A) is the unmarked term. Note that this means that on a strict Praguean approach, reversal of the evaluation of an opposition requires a redefinition of the property defining the opposition. The opposition in (i) differs in value from that in (ii):

(i)	[nonnasal] (U)	vs.	[nasal] (M)
	negative value		positive value
(ii)	[oral] (U)	vs.	[nonoral] (M)
	positive value		

The terminological connection of positive and negative value with marked and unmarked sometimes causes confusion with respect to the use of plus and minus features in post-Praguean frameworks such as that of Chomsky and Halle's *Sound Pattern of English*. There features are treated as names of properties and plus/minus values are just names of the poles of an opposition. There is no association of plus with marked and minus with unmarked. Thus (iii) and (iv) would be equivalent ways to state that nasality is the marked feature value:

(iii)	[−nasal] (U)	vs.	[+nasal] (M)
	minus feature		plus feature
(iv)	[+oral] (U)	vs.	[−oral] (M)
	plus feature		minus feature

12. It can even be that languages have the same features and features inventories yet different systems of relations among their phonemes. Consider the situation in which the two phonemes X and Y are defined by the features A and B. In one language it may be feature A that differentiates X and Y and feature B is redundant; in the other it may be that feature B is the distinctive one and feature A is redundant. So, for example, consider voiced, lax obstruents (/b/, /d/, /g/) as opposed to voiceless, tense ones (/p/, /t/, /k/). In some languages, the voiced/voiceless oppo-

sition may be distinctive and the tense/lax opposition redundant; in others, tense/lax might be distinctive and voiced/voiceless redundant. Languages might have the same inventories, but different structures.

13. For an interesting discussion of the differences between Jakobson's and Trubetzkoy's approaches to feature analysis, see Chvany (1984).

14. Compare Trubetzkoy (1969:66–77 [1939]):

In the case of *bilateral* oppositions the basis for comparison, that is the sum of the properties common to both opposition members, is common to these two opposition members alone. . . . The basis for comparison in multilateral opposition, on the other hand, is not limited exclusively to the two respective opposition members. [p. 68]

An opposition is proportional if the relation between its members is identical with the relation between the members of another opposition or several oppositions of the same system. For example the opposition *p−b* in German is proportional because the relation between *p* and *b* is identical with that between *t* and *d* or between *k* and *g*. the opposition *p−š*, on the other hand, is isolated because the German phonemic system does not have any other pair of phonemes whose members would be related to each other in the same way as *p* is related to *š*. [p. 70]

15. In his later work, Jakobson referred to this opposition as compact versus noncompact.

16. See also Holenstein (1976:122–30) and Waugh (1976:63–67). For discussion of Jakobson's motivation for binarism see the references just given and also Jakobson (1962:642ff., 315, 499ff.), Halle (1957), and Anderson (1985:120).

17. Lyons (1977:308) relates semantic markedness to a form of self-hyponymy in which a lexical item has two distinct senses, one of which is subordinate to the other.

18. The ranking of oppositions and feature values has also been related to the development of phonological distinctions in language acquisition and to the loss of distinctions due to neurological deficits. In *Child Language, Aphasia, and Phonological Universals* (1968 [1941]) and in *Preliminaries to Speech Analysis* (1971 [1956]), Jakobson and (in the latter work) Halle maintain that the first sounds to appear in children's language are an *a*-like sound and a *p*-like sound. Next is an *m*, followed by a *t*. The vowel system develops from *a* to *i* and then to *u* (or in some cases *e*), and the consonant system develops by further differentiating a *k*-like sound. Jakobson and Halle (1971 [1956]) have illustrated this by the triple-triangle diagram below (1971:53 [1956]) in which the sounds acquired earliest are found on the points of the external triangle and the sounds that follow in the acquisition sequence are on the points of the internal triangles (the nasal *m* is for some reason excluded from their diagram).

(i)

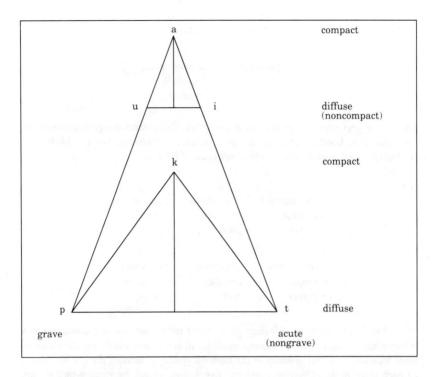

Jakobson and Halle's claims imply a hierarchy of distinctive features and feature values. For sounds in general, the first opposition to arise is between a compact vowel sound *a* and a noncompact consonantal *p*. At this point only the feature values [+compact] and [−compact] are needed to differentiate *a* from *p*; the other phonological properties defining these sounds are redundant (nondistinctive). The feature matrices for *a* and *p* would be as below, with redundant features enclosed in parentheses:

(ii)   *p*   *a*
              −compact   +compact
           (+consonantal)   (−consonantal)
           (+grave)   (−grave)

The phonological system is elaborated as nondistinctive features acquire distinctive value, thus enabling successively more and more phonemes to be defined. The next distinctive opposition to arise is between consonantal and nonconsonantal, leading to a four-phoneme system consisting of compact and noncompact vowels and consonants. The phonological system at this point would be:

(iii)   *k*   *p*
                      +consonantal   +consonantal
                      +compact   −compact
                      (+grave)   (+grave)

                          a   *i*
                      −consonantal   −consonantal
                      +compact   −compact
                      (−grave)   (−grave)

The feature grave remains redundant at this point. Consonants are grave, vowels are nongrave. It is, however, the next feature to acquire a distinctive value, allowing *t to be distinguished from p* and *u* to be distinguished from *i*.

(iv)   *k*   *p*   *t*
              +consonantal   +consonantal   +consonantal
              +compact   −compact   −compact
              (+grave)   +grave   −grave

                  a   *u*   *i*
              −consonantal   −consonantal   −consonantal
              +compact   −compact   −compact
              (−grave)   +grave   −grave

The hierarchization of features is revealed in the way that the distinctiveness between the values of certain features precedes distinctiveness between the values of other features. It is also revealed in the inherent system governing the feature values. At each stage of development, nondistinctive feature values are present that are not needed to differentiate the sounds. The redundant feature values may be viewed as the default values of the features in question, the hierarchically dominant, unmarked values that are revealed by the value of a phonological property before it is put to work in the phonemic system as a distinctive opposition. Conversely, the hierarchy is revealed by the dissolution of oppositions due to language deficit.

Since the role of hierarchy and markedness in language acquisition and language decay is part of the study of implicational universals and since our focus is primarily on language-particular markedness relations, I will not consider order of acquisition or decay as criteria of markedness values. Though acquisition and loss of categories are sometimes proposed as ways of determining marked and unmarked, such criteria play little role in most accounts, and I believe that they raise more problems—both methodological and empirical—than they solve. As Jakobson (1968 [1941]) first noted, the correlation between acquisition and typological optimality is not always perfect. For some discussion of Jakobsonian feature theory in connection with phonological acquisition, see Ferguson and Farwell (1975), who confirm many of Jakobson's predictions but who note some problems as well (such as children's preference for voiced labial and alveolar stops over voiceless velar stops). Ferguson and Farwell also correctly point out that concern with generalizations about acquisition order ignores individual differences in development that may be due to different input conditions and to different acquisition strategies and preferences. See also Ingram (1988), who points out certain methodological problems that arise in determining when a child has acquired a phonological opposition, and Menn, who notes that a good many children do not start with "anything even close" to the optimal consonant vowel opposition and who argues that "the data demand that any markedness theory be considered a theory of probability, as a theory of odds, not as an absolute" (1986:252–53).

It should be pointed out as well that the order of acquisition for English consonants does not fully conform to the predictions of Jakobson's theory. Cf. the order of acquisition for English consonants adopted by Salus and Salus (1974:155), which is consistent in some, but not all, respects with the positions of Jakobson (1968 [1941]) and Jakobson and Halle (1971 [1956]).

19. Book-length studies of Jakobson's linguistics include Waugh (1976), Sangster (1982), and Holenstein (1976). Two new important books, which have become available only after the final version of this study was completed, are Andrews (1990) and Tomić (1989).

Chapter 2

1. Following Jakobson (1968 [1941]) it is sometimes assumed that markedness is correlated to language change, acquisition, and aphasic loss. As Waugh (1979) points out, the early learning of a given feature does not constitute "absolute evidence" for its unmarkedness. While there does seem to be a correlation between markedness and both acquisition and aphasia, it is usually very easy to find counterexamples to such correlations. In developing a set of criteria for determining markedness values, I shall rely mainly on criteria having to do with the synchronic structure of language. The point of this strategy is not to put aside correlations with such factors as language acquisition and language loss, but rather to define markedness values independently of them so that possible correlations might be tested rather than assumed.

Similarly, I focus on diagnostics having to do with synchronic linguistic structure rather than with language change. From the point of view of investigating the role of markedness in change, treating the unmarked as the target of linguistic change by definition makes the study of markedness in change an exercise in justification. After all, if our assumption is that markedness defines change, then that cannot be our hypothesis as well.

2. Optimality is sometimes construed as the frequency of a particular category cross-linguistically (cf. Greenberg 1966, Chomsky and Halle 1968, Gamkrelidze 1975, Zwicky 1978). For some further discussion, see chapter 5 and also Lass (1975).

3. Determinate verbs indicate motion in a specific direction or action with a goal in mind. Iterative verbs are those of repeated action. Injunctive refers to events imposed upon the participant.

4. *Invariant* should not necessarily be equated with *universal*. Sangster defines it thus: "The invariant semantic common denominator of a form is that property or set of properties which remains constant throughout all the specific contextual applications of the form" (1980:52–53). Sangster also emphasizes that there are levels of invariance, and that the concept applies both language-particularly and cross-linguistically: "once the intercategorial invariants have been established for a particular language, we are ready to move to the ultimate level of invariance in language, that of interlingual invariance, or universals" (p. 79). It is worth pointing out that some Slavists in the Jakobsonian tradition have proposed treating markedness in terms of a system of universal semantic features based on those Jakobson used to define the Russian case system. See in particular van Schooneveld (1978), Sangster (1982), and Andrews (1984, 1990).

5. The analysis of the case system presented here follows Jakobson's earlier six case analysis [1936] rather than his later eight case analysis [1958]. See Chvany (1984, 1986) for some discussion of the differences between the two.

6. Andrews makes such a proposal: "It has been the tradition in Jakobsonian analysis to establish properties of meaning based solely on paradigmatic relations [i.e., on contrastive distribution] (1984:58–59)." Given the connection between semantic analysis into features and markedness, semantic analysis should suffice to determine markedness relations, and there should be no need for distribution as a factor, since distribution is "a syntagmatic phenomenom involving variants as well as invariants." There is also some debate over whether the correct interpretation of semantic markedness relations involves substitutability of the unmarked for the marked or inclusion of the meaning of the marked in the meaning of the unmarked and on whether the markedness relation must be defined in terms of semantic invariants or can be defined in terms of actual contextual meanings as well. See Dokulil (1958), Comrie (1976), Lyons (1977), Kučera (1980), and Andrews (1984:68–72). In this book, I adopt the position that markedness values can be determined by semantic intersection of contextual meanings. This position is flexible enough to allow markedness to be applied to a wide variety of semantic categories and seems to be consistent with Jakobson's own practical application of markedness theory (cf. 1984 [1932], [1939], [1957]).

7. Greenberg (1966) proposes criteria to characterize syntactic markedness, adapted from Jakobson (1984 [1939]), Hjelmslev (1969), Trnka (1958), and Trubetzkoy (1969 [1939]). His criteria include:

universal implicational statements
zero expression
par excellence expression
facultative expression

syncretization
contextual neutralization
degree of morphological variation
defectivization
dominance
text frequency

Zero expression refers to zero versus overt formal marking. Par excellence refers to the generic use of the unmarked; facultative expression indicates optionality of the overt expression of a category (par excellence from the point of view of the speaker, according to Greenberg 1966:29); dominance is the use of the unmarked category to refer to a heteronomous collection, as when a compound noun phrase consisting of masculine and feminine gender conjuncts takes one or the other gender for purposes of agreement. Syncretization has been discussed in the text. Defectivization, defined as a lack of certain categories within the marked term, is considered as a variety of syncretization (Greenberg 1966:29). Degree of morphological variation refers to the claim that greater morphological alternation and irregularity exist in the unmarked category. I will treat syncretization, defectivization, and morphological variety as a single criterion in this book, and I also treat zero expression, par excellence expression, and dominance as part of semantic breadth.

Greenberg's approach differs from Jakobson's in that Greenberg seems to view markedness as a property defined by the correlation of these criteria, whereas for Jakobson markedness is defined axiomatically and the criteria are diagnostics. Greenberg (1966:28) equates the criterion of facultative expression to the definition of markedness given by Jakobson (1984 [1939]).

As Schwartz has argued, certain logical relations among these criteria can be set up. She notes that text frequency is a

> consequence of deductions based on the range of distribution-determining factors of neutralization, dominance, and *par excellence* expression in conjunction with other hypotheses about the general nature of human communication, while zero expression, syncretization, and degree of morphological variation can be deduced from relative frequency in conjunction with general principles of human cognition and communicative efficiency. [1980:332]

For apparent counter examples to Greenberg's criteria, see Andrews (1984:68).

Mayerthaler, who defines markedness as universal "naturalness," suggests that it be ascertained by a conjunction of heuristics, which he divides into external and internal:

(a) external sources: 1) children's language, 2) nurse talk, 3) perception tests, 4) slips of the tongue, 5) speech disturbances.
(b) internal sources: 6) historical grammar, 7) pidgin and creole languages, 8) comparative grammar (typology), 9) frequency (of type or occurrence), 10) analogic development, 11) irregularity, 12) neutralization, 13) morphosyntactic and phonological symbolization, 14) transformational accessibility. [1988:2–4]

See also Dressler and Mayerthaler (1987). Concerning the determination of markedness values Mayerthaler says:

> Heuristically, we proceed as follows in determining markedness values: We try to form a conjunction of revelant heuristic sources, maximum 1) 2) . . . 14). If the conjunction can be formed, i.e., if compatible markedness values emerge for each heuristic source, it can be assumed that the corresponding allocation of markedness is empirically related. It is more difficult to assign markedness values if there are one or more contradictions between 1) – 14). In such cases, we group the contradictions for the time being under the heading "Problem." [1988:4]

However, to apply this procedure seriously would lead to a great number of markedness values in the "problems" category. Elsewhere in his book Mayerthaler defines semantic markedness in terms of prototypical speaker properties (see the section "Prototypes and Best Examples").

8. Such a principle was first proposed by George Zipf. See in particular Zipf (1949:65ff).

9. This example is due to Comrie (1981:219). Linda Waugh has suggested to me that it is possible to view the third person singular form in English as marked in function and the zero forms as unmarked. See also Mayerthaler (1988:39–40 [1981]) for another attempt to explain this misalignment.

10. As is clear from his comments on gender in Russian, Jakobson (1984:185 [1939]) was aware of the "chiasmus" of form and meaning. See also the critical comments in Matthews (1974:150–52).

11. As Margaret Winters has pointed out to me, an asymmetry also arises with respect to the adverb *less*, which seems more natural with the unmarked term than with the marked term. Compare (i) and (ii) below:

(i)   John is less tall than Bill.
(ii)   John is less short than Bill.

12. See also Waugh (1982) and Greenbaum (1976). Kučera (1982), who notes "the apparent impossibility of determining a stable frequency of such grammatical forms as tense and aspect in English," suggests that frequency evidence may provide an indication of the weak points of markedness analysis of grammar (see also Bybee 1985). Greenberg himself (1966b:97) concedes that frequency and unmarkedness in word order need not be correlated when he remarks; "It is not difficult to construct an example in which one of the recessive alternatives is more frequent than the dominant."

13. Trubetzkoy viewed occurrence in positions of neutralization as the best diagnostic of the unmarked term in phonology (cf. Trubetzkoy 1969:81 [1939]).

14. Note also that *host* is the form used as a verb (*When hosting a bridal shower*, versus *When hostessing a bridal shower*) and that *host* takes priority in fixed expressions such as *Your host and hostess are*.

15. For further discussion of this particular example, see Battistella (1986).

16. As pointed out by Moravcsik and Wirth (1986), the greater differentiation of the unmarked category can be considered analogous to the wider distribution of the unmarked. Differentiation involves distribution at the paradigmatic level, while range involves distribution at the syntagmatic level.

17. See also Ross (1972, 1973a, 1973b), Lakoff (1977), Clark and Clark (1978), Bates and MacWhinney (1982), Bybee and Moder (1983), and Hopper and Thompson (1984).

18. Winters notes another sense of salience that can be correlated to prototypicality: for certain categories some features are central (or most salient), and elements that have these features are more prototypical than elements that do not. To take Winters's example, the salient feature of the item *cup* is "being a container". Cups are protoptypically containers; cups that do not function as containers are less prototypical.

19. Mayerthaler suggests a number of markedness assignments based on prototypical speaker attributes, although he gives many of these without further support or argumentation, commenting only on those that "are not immediately understandable" (12). A sample of these assignments of unmarked/marked categories includes the following: speaker/nonspeaker, subject/other, more animate/less animate, first person/non-first person, second person/third person, real world/other worlds, perceptually accessible/less perceptually accessible, indicative/nonindicative, real/unreal, topic/comment, nondiminuation/diminuation, more neutral form/less neutral form, nonpejorative/pejorative, and so forth. See Mayerthaler (1988:10ff. [1981]).

20. Compare Greenberg (1966:chap. 4):

> The possibility of translation for every one of the five characteristics of the unmarked/marked dichotomy in phonology as enumerated earlier into grammatical terminology under fixed rules of translation and with unmarked and marked corresponding to each other in each case is sufficient evidence that the analogy between these concepts in phonology and grammar is not a farfetched one. [p. 60]

Jakobson maintained a difference between phonological and semantic marking in terms of the inherent nature of oppositions at these two levels. Phonological oppositions were between the presence and absence of a phonological features while semantic oppositions were between the signalization of a semantic feature and its nonsignalization.

21. See, for example, Cairns (1968, 1986) and Shapiro (1972, 1980).

22. For further discussion of the criterion of frequency in determining phonological markedness values, see Lass (1975) and Cairns (1986).

23. Gamkrelidze (1975), following Melikishvili (1970, 1972) has suggested using relative text frequency to determine the "functional strength" of phonemes. He suggests for example, that in systems with a voicing opposition, the voiced labial /b/ is functionally stronger than the voiced velar /g/ and that

> the feature of labiality, in the condition of simultaneous combination with the feature of voicing, is unmarked, as opposed to the feature of velarity, which is a marked feature in combination with voicing.

> In the voiceless stops (both simple and glottalized), on the other hand, the velar stop /k/ (and correspondingly /kʰ/ and /k'/), which is the unmarked member of the opposition has greater functional load than the labial stop /p/ (and correspondingly /pʰ/ and /p'/), which is the marked, functionally weaker member. [1975:235]

Gamkrelidze goes on to note that gaps in phoneme systems confirm these correlations of marking. He observes that gaps in the languages with a voicing opposition in the class of stops pattern as follows:

	(i)		(ii)		(iii)
b	—	b	p	b	—
d	t	d	t	d	t
g	k	—	k	—	k

In this case, syncretization and frequency point to the same conclusion, which Gamkrelidze sums up "the features for point of articulation form a definite hierarchical series. Voicing is best combined with labiality, and voicelessness with velarity, while dentality occupies an intermediate position." [1975:236]

24. It should, however, be borne in mind that acoustic and articulatory naturalness may themselves be in conflict: what is a simplification from the point of view of speech production might be a complication from the point of view of speech perception (or vice versa).

25. See Nathan (1986) and Jaeger (1980) for discussion of phonemes as prototypes.

26. Another possible source of evidence for unmarkedness comes from the theory of natural phonology (Stampe 1979 [1972], Donegan 1985 [1978]), which analyzes regular sound substitutions as manifestations of innate limitations of human speech abilities.

27. See Trubetzkoy (1969:146–47 [1939]).

28. See Brakel (1984) and Szemerényi (1973) for discussion of the proposal that voicing is generally the unmarked feature.

29. The term *markedness reversal* must be used with care, as it is defined differently in the literature. Contrast the description of reversal given by Waugh, for example, with those of Andersen (1972), Shapiro (1972), and Andrews (1985).

30. Andersen (1974) and Shapiro (1972, 1974), who treat phonological markedness similarly to Trubetzkoy, consider both phonological universals and language-particular ranking of features.

31. See also Kiparsky (1974:263), van Riemsdijk (1982:261 [1978]), Lightfoot (1979:76), Pustejovsky and Burke (1981) and Belleti et al. (1979). And see especially Hyams (1986:161) for some criticism of proposals that equate the child's initial hypothesis with the unmarked case.

32. As a matter of expository convenience, I will put aside the differences in various proposals for determining language-independent markedness values discussed above and will refer to all of them as "universal markedness" theories.

Within the Universal Grammar approach might also be included the work of Bickerton (1981); Bickerton's notion of naturalness (1981:280) and his interpretation of Universal Grammar as a bioprogram differ from Chomsky's approach in detail, however (cf. Bickerton 1981:297–98). Also included might be the approach of Mayerthaler (1987:31–32), whose Naturalness Theory assumes the existence of a variety of "pre-linguistic" and "quasi-linguistic" universal principles in addition to specifically linguistic ones.

Chapter 3

1. This debate can of course be traced back to arguments in *Cratylus*. See Jakobson (1965) and Robins (1967) for discussion.

2. For further discussion of Peirce's semiotic theories see Savan (1976) and Shapiro (1983).

3. In addition to the work of Jakobson, studies of iconic relations include Andersen (1972, 1973, 1979), Bolinger (1977), Bybee (1985a), Chvany (1984), Comrie (1986), Frishberg (1975), Haiman (1980, 1983, 1985a), Lapointe (1986), Mannheim and Newfield (1982), Mayerthaler (1988 [1981]), Quirk (1970), Robertson (1983), Shapiro (1972, 1974, 1980, 1983, 1986), and Waugh and Newfield (1986). While not strictly concerned with iconism per se, Kuno (1987) and Foley and van Valin (1984) have proposed communicative principles that involve markedness relations between grammar and context.

4. Andersen (1974:n. 15) notes the marked status of *I* relative to *me*. Also Jakobson (1984:71 [1936]) points out that in Basque and the North Caucasian languages, the markedness values of the cases may be reversed from languages like Russian. Otherwise, however, it is generally an unargued assumption that in

nominative/accusative-type languages, nominative is the unmarked case. Compare Greenberg (1966a:95), Jakobson (1966:270), Mayerthaler (1988:21 [1981]).

5. The distinction between formal and colloquial style is paralleled in the opposition between the interrogative and relative pronoun forms *who* and *whom*. In colloquial use, the unmarked form *who* can be used generally and the marked *whom* is required only with an immediately preceding preposition. In formal usage, the unmarked objective case is expressed by the marked pronoun form and the marked nominative case by the unmarked pronoun form.

6. Note also the contrast between the examples in (i) and those in (ii): in (i) the emphasis appears to be on the verbal nouns, while in (ii) emphasis is on the embedded pronouns:

(i)   I dislike their bothering me.
        I resent his running things.

(ii)   I dislike them bothering me.
        I resent him running things.

(I am indebted to Margaret Winters for bringing these examples to my attention.)

7. Silverstein (1976), van Langendonck (1986), Mayerthaler (1988 [1981]), and others have suggested that subject position is unmarked for animate nouns and object position for inanimates. If this is so, and if we treat determiner position as the "subject" of a noun phrase, as suggested by Chomsky (1981), then the animacy restriction can be treated as a neutralization to the unmarked term of the animacy/inanimacy opposition within noun phrases.

8. Note that for the unmarked third person (see below), the base for the reflexive is the objective case form, a fact that provides further evidence for the unmarked status of the objective.

9. On the structural status of determiners, see Baker (1978:341) and Jackendoff (1977:115).

10. It is worth noting that Chomsky (1980:30) treats "exceptional case marking" as the product of a marked (i.e., noncore) rule of grammar.

11. Jakobson (1972:77) defines style in language as "a marked—emotive or poetic—annex to the neutral, purely cognitive information." Adopting this view, we can take styles of language that add particular affective values to be generally marked. Style in language, however, is an area in which real-world context plays an important role. As noted in chapter 1, there can be cultural contexts in which formal style is unmarked (such as a prom or wedding) and cultural context in which informal style is (a trip to the mall). However, the contexts in which different styles are marked and unmarked should not overlap, and it ought to be possible to determine which contexts are marked and which are unmarked according to which contexts are

general and which are narrowly focused. Significantly, these contexts should not be the same ones.

12. We can return for a moment to the zero-nominative pronouns mentioned earlier in Czech and Russian. These zero pronouns differ from the zero nominative of English in that they are licensed by virtue of the rich agreement inflection of those languages. However they also contrast with the zero-objective case of nonfinite constructions in those languages, which is independent of rich inflection. In languages like Czech and Russian, the zero nominative signals the presence of agreement inflections on the tensed verb while the zero objective does not. The opposition between nominative and objective zero pronouns might then be viewed as one of dependence on agreement versus nondependence on agreement. It may then be that nominative zero pronouns are marked cross-linguistically as opposed to objective ones.

13. The emphatic reflexive has a curious distribution in that it is precluded with objective case pronouns, but allowed with nominative pronouns and nouns (cf. McDaniel and Battistella 1986):

He himself left.
John himself came.
I saw the president himself.
?I saw him himself.

14. It is especially telling to compare the discussion in Greenberg. In arguing for the unmarkedness of the singular forms of personal pronouns in Chinese and Korean, Greenberg emphasizes the ability of the singular pronouns to refer both singularly and plurally. With respect to Chinese, he says:

In pronouns, there are instances in which the plural is facultatively expressed, e.g., in the older form of Mandarin, where, in addition the singular has zero expression, e.g., wŏ 'I', or on occasion 'we', plural wŏ men, always 'we'. [1966:34]

The parallel of the function of the English plural pronouns to the function of the Chinese singular ones has not, to my knowledge, been previously noted.

15. Note that various dialects have reestablished the formal opposition between singular and plural with such forms as you all, you uns, and youse. Predictably, these forms are stylistically marked from the viewpoint of the standard language.

16. The markedness values given here follow those of Jakobson (1984 [1932, 1956]) for the person categories of Russian. The arguments and examples for the markedness of person categories follow the very insightful analysis of these categories in English by Waugh (1982). Compare Mayerthaler (1988 [1981]) for a view of the person categories that treats first person as least marked and third person as

most marked. Greenberg (1966) concludes on the basis of text frequency that second person is the most marked person category. Compare Schwartz (1980) for discussion of Greenberg's analysis.

17. In such cases as this, when there is no phonological evidence of a formal marking relation, the globality of markedness as a relation applying to expression and meaning is attenuated. There are two ways of preserving this globality. One is to simply assume that the markedness values of forms in such cases are determined directly by the semantic markedness value of the categories in question. The other is to treat the markedness of a form as determined by phonological regularity within the grammatical subsystem under consideration. I opt for the latter here, defining the zero of imperatives and subjunctives as unmarked by virtue of their regularity. It might be objected that this runs counter to the criterion of syncretization, which should treat the more variable category as unmarked. However, syncretization is a criterion for semantic markedness, not for the markedness of forms, and I will treat less regular forms as indications of markedness at the level of expression. This eliminates the argument that past participle forms are less marked than the present participle forms since they exhibit more variation in their shapes (having, for example, *–en* and *–ed* forms as opposed to the single *–ing* shape of the present participle).

18. With respect to the future forms *will* and *shall*, it seems that *will* would be the unmarked form, for American English, and *shall* the marked form. As with the marked pronouns, the unmarked forms replace the marked in colloquial speech. Note that the prescriptive dictum of using *shall* in the first person corresponds to the use of the marked form in the most marked person, though, of course, actual American English usage largely disregards this dictum.

19. In examples like *I will leave now*, where the future appears to be used with a present meaning, it is rather that the meaning of the adverb *now* (the present tense adverb) is referring to the immediate future.

20. The English perfect, (following the usage of Slavists, cf. Comrie 1976:11ff.) differs from the perfective in the Slavic languages in that the opposition for Slavic is perfective versus imperfective while for English it is perfect versus simple. The contrast between perfective and imperfective plays an important role in the application of markedness theory to Slavic languages. Readers are referred to Kučera (1979, 1981) and to the papers in Flier and Timberlake (1985).

21. The progressive aspect does not correspond exactly to the imperfective aspect of the Slavic languages. Compare Comrie (1976:23ff), who gives the general characterization of imperfectivity as "viewing a situation from within" (i.e., having some kind of internal temporal structure) and who gives "the most typical" classification of aspectual oppositions as follows:

(i)

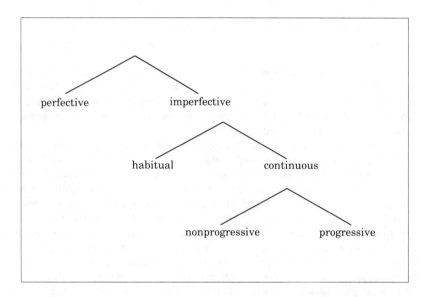

22. See also Bybee (1985a), who suggests that the perfect is often subject to local markedness.

23. In fact, this is the usual approach (cf. Jakobson 1984 and [1932], [1939], [1957]; Shapiro 1980).

24. It is possible that these features also define the progressive aspect and the passive voice, with which the participles are cognate. Such an identification is not, of course, necessary to the analysis here.

25. See Hopper and Thompson (1980), Kalmár (1982), and Chvany (1984) on the correlation of grammatical features with the discourse feature of foregrounding. As Chvany emphasizes, discourse context can play a role in reversing the informativeness of otherwise inherent markedness values. Her distinction between inherent markedness values and contextual ones seems promising as a means to further refine the concepts of local and general markedness.

26. There is some evidence from psychology that passives take longer to process than actives. However, passives with their agents suppressed appear to be easier to process than actives, so it is difficult to draw conclusions about markedness from this evidence.

27. For background, see Greenberg's "Some Universals of Grammar with Particular Reference to the Order of Meaningful Elements" in Greenberg (1966a). In that paper, Greenberg develops a set of forty-five tentative universals of word

order. He remarks, "The vast majority of languages have several variant orders but a single dominant one" (1966a:76). Jakobson explicitly associates this dominant order with unmarked meaning, commenting that "Greenberg's first universal could be restated as follows: In declarative sentences with nominal subject and object the *only or neutral* (*unmarked*) order is almost always one in which the subject precedes the object" (1966:269).

Steele, in a study of work order variation in sixty-three languages, also distinguishes marked and unmarked word orders in terms of variations from a typical ordering. She points out that "All languages have a dominant word order, a surface ordering of subject, object and verb relative to one another that is at least more common that other possible orders" (1978:587).

Steele also gives some useful suggestions for determining the basic word order or orders for a language, noting that highly marked orders can be identified by speakers' intuitions which "identify [a pattern] as a very special word order" (1978:592) and that marked orders are sometimes specifically identified as special in grammars, and often may be distinguished from the basic order by a special morphology or intonation contour. See also Hawkins, who identifies three overlapping criteria in making "basicness" decisions about Adjective Noun doublets: frequency in text samples and in the grammatical systems and the situation where "a special type of grammatical meaning may be associated with one order of Adj and N, but not the other," which he refers to as grammatical markedness (1983:13). Compare also Tomlin, who states that basic word order means "unmarked or prototypical constituent order" (1986:34).

28. See also Shapiro (1972, 1974) for discussions of complementarity in phonological structure.

29. It has sometimes been suggested that the iconism of markedness value is compulsory (cf. Andersen 1972: 44; Jakobson 1971: 357). However, the existence of complementary patterns and of competing principles of organization suggests instead that the iconism of markedness values is just one principle that plays a role in the organization of linguistic forms. See Haiman (1983), Mayerthaler, (1987, 1988 [1981]), and Shapiro (1983). Shapiro links markedness patterns to Peirce's notion of abductive reasoning, a form of reasoning that, according to Peirce (1965–1966: vol. 5, sec. 181) involves acts of insight that are potentially fallible. Shapiro remarks: "The fallibility of abduction means, as far as the theory of grammar is concerned, that there is nothing obligatory, necessary, or inevitable about the coherence of language data *in the short run*" (1983:93).

30. This chapter has also helped to highlight some of the limitations of the Praguean approach to markedness. Given that grounding of the markedness relations in semantic relations within a language aligns markedness theory with interpretive disciplines, attention must be paid to the positing of markedness values. If the explanation of patterns is that they are implementations of markedness relations, then the assignment of markedness values should be independent of the patternings them-

selves. It is probably not always possible to maintain a rigorous division between markedness values and patterns, but the preferred strategy should be to define values with respect to meaning, prototypicality, and distribution rather than on the basis of filling out partial patterns already defined.

Chapter 4

1. The discussion in this chapter is intended to be neutral with respect to particular theoretical frameworks. For background and further discussion of phonological theory, see Anderson (1985), Lass (1984), Lepschy (1970), and Sommerstein (1977).

2. Andersen (1974) has also emphasized that the ranking of features in the hierarchy may vary from language to language and that these differences of hierarchy and function will affect the markedness values in particular cases.

3. To illustrate this more graphically, consider (i) and (ii) below; (i) illustrates markedness values in replication.

(i)   Vocalic Subhierarchy

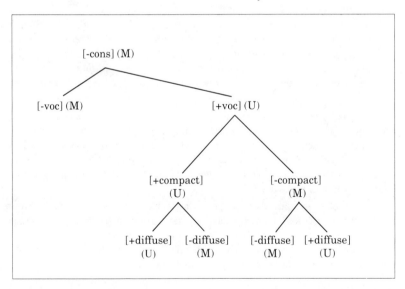

A positive feature under a positive feature has the same markedness value. A negative under a negative has the same value. Features assigned by a pattern of reversal or complementation are illustrated by (ii):

(ii)   Consonantal Subhierarchy

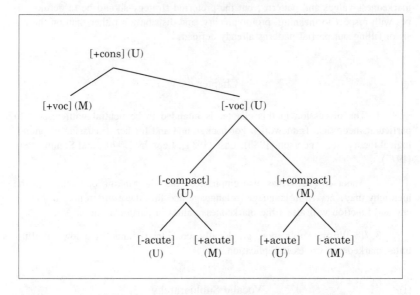

Shapiro's view of markedness reversal is that:

> If a feature is non-distinctive for a segment in which its phonetic analog is
> nonetheless present, then the MARKEDNESS VALUES otherwise assigned
> to the polar terms of that feature WILL BE REVERSED. . . . The reversal of
> markedness values at one point in the hierarchy will, in turn, entail the re-
> versal of values throughout the rest of the hierarchy subordinate to the node
> originally affected. [1972:348]

4. This raises the issue that phonological function (distinctiveness vs. redundancy) may play a role in markedness assignments. On this question Andersen
(1974) takes a somewhat different approach. He argues that redundant features have
their unmarked value in most contexts, though they may undergo phonological
markedness assimilations in marked contexts. He remarks that when an opposition
is not distinctive in a phoneme

> it will be characterized by the properties associated with the unmarked term
> of that opposition; or the properties of both terms of the opposition may be
> assigned in complementary distribution, those of the marked term in a nar-
> rowly defined (simultaneous or sequential) environment, or set of environ-
> ments, those of the unmarked term elsewhere. [1974:893–94]

5. At the level of sequential context, a proposal that runs parallel to Shapiro's is the complement convention of Kean (1980:11 [1975]), which exhaustively
characterizes the markedness values of a feature in the following way:

(iii)   a.   [u F] → [@ F] / X
                         b.   [m F] → [−@ F] / X

c. [u F] → [−@ F] / X̄
d. [m F] → [@ F] / X̄

In prose, this says that if the unmarked value of F is @ ('+' or '−') in context X, then the marked value will be the opposite of @ in X; furthermore, in the complement of context X, X̄, the value @ will be the marked one and its opposite (−@) will be the unmarked value. Notice that if we adapt Kean's principle to treat one of the contexts as marked and the other as unmarked, then the complement convention could serve as a characterization of syntagmatic markedness assimilation.

6. Nasal vowels are, it seems, more marked than nasal consonants. A fully adequate account of segment complexity must take such differences into account, perhaps by ranking nasality differently within the vocalic and consonantal hierarchies or perhaps by treating markedness as scalar rather than binary.

7. As noted earlier, the markedness assignments are those suggested by Jakobson's implicational laws. In the opposition of grave versus nongrave some further refinement may be needed: languages like Hawaiian, which lack acute (nongrave) stops but not grave ones, present a problem for the view that acute consonants are generally unmarked and grave marked. (There seem to be no languages that lack grave stops.)

In connection with the feature grave, it should be pointed out that Gamkrelidze (1975) has argued that the markedness of voiced and voiceless stops interacts with point of articulation. He shows, on the basis of cross-linguistic data, that voicing combines most naturally with labiality and that voicelessness combined most naturally with velarity. If he is correct, it might be that the features compact and noncompact are subordinate to voiced and voiceless while grave and nongrave (acute) are subordinate to compactness:

(i)

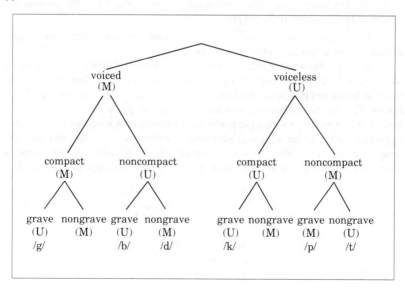

In such a system, the markedness values would be as follows:

(ii) | | Voice | Compact | Grave |
|---|---|---|---|
| voiced labials | +(M) | −(U) | +(U) |
| voiced dentals | +(M) | −(U) | −(M) |
| voiced velars | +(M) | +(M) | +(U) |
| unvoiced labials | +(U) | −(M) | +(M) |
| unvoiced dentals | +(U) | −(M) | −(U) |
| unvoiced velars | +(U) | +(M) | +(U) |

8. It may also be useful to discuss in more detail the interrelation of the features of voicing and tenseness. The most common situation is for a language to have *voiced and lax* or *voiceless and tense* stops. The markedness values are as in (i):

(i)   p, t, k   M tense, U voice
                    b, d, g   U tense, M voice

where both sets of segments have an equal composite markedness value. In general where phonemic *p*, *t*, and *k* are opposed to *b*, *d* and *g*, these sounds are opposed as either tense versus lax or as voiced versus voiceless, with the other pair of features (voiced/voiceless and tense/lax respectively) being redundant. Taking context into account, we must treat the markedness values in (ii) and (iii) (on following page) as holding when these features are phonemic and the markedness values in (iv) and (v) (on following page) as relevant when the oppositions are subordinate to one another.

In (iv) voicing is distinctive and tenseness is redundant, so the unmarked value of tenseness is for voiced consonants to be lax and voiceless ones tense. In (v), where tenseness is distinctive, the unmarked value of voicing is for tensed consonants to be voiceless and lax ones voiced.

9. The opposition diffuse/nondiffuse is not relevant for the consonants. Compare Jakobson and Halle (1971).

10. In minimal three-vowel systems with a basic height contrast, the feature diffuse will be redundant rather than distinctive.

It is also known that minimal vowel systems like (ii) below are possible in which the contrast is vertical (strictly in terms of height) rather than triangular (in terms of height and backness). Andersen (1974:895) suggests that the ranking of features will permit the optimal system of vowels to be either a triangular one or a vertical one. If the compact/noncompact opposition is expanded with a tonality (acute/grave) opposition, a triangular system is obtained; if compactness is expanded with the opposition diffuse/nondiffuse, the rarer vertical type is obtained. And, of course, a language can have both oppositions, as in the typical five-vowel system shown in (iii):

```
     (i)   i    u            (ii)      e
           a                           a
        (Arabic)                   (Adyghe)


          (iii)  i    u
                 e    o
                    a
```

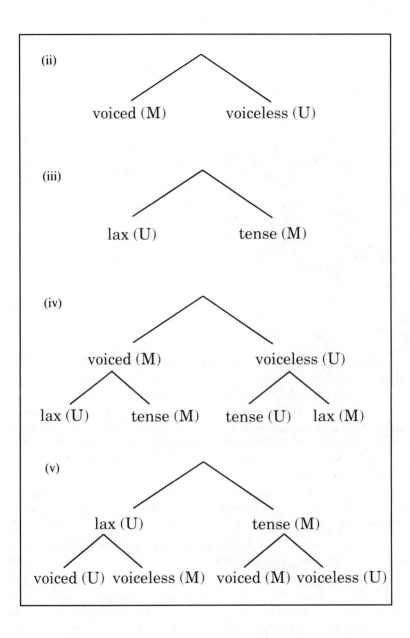

(ii)

voiced (M)   voiceless (U)

(iii)

lax (U)   tense (M)

(iv)

voiced (M)   voiceless (U)

lax (U)   tense (M)   tense (U)   lax (M)

(v)

lax (U)   tense (M)

voiced (U) voiceless (M)   voiced (M) voiceless (U)

11. The suggestion in diagram (11) is, to some degree, dictated by our work-ing assumption that features are organized in binary hierarchies with a single feature at each branch point. If this assumption is relaxed to allow for representations in

which the features flat and grave receive markedness values as a pair (cf. Waugh 1979), then the mutual dependency of values might be represented as below:

(i)

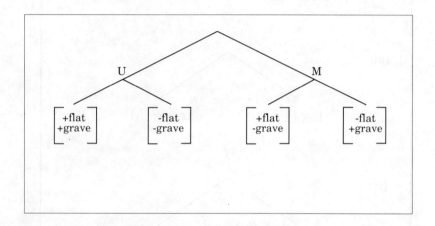

12. Andersen (1974) takes tenseness as unmarked for vowels. Kean (1980 [1975]) does not discuss the feature. For discussion of the opposition between long and short vowels, see Greenberg (1978a).

13. I will be concerned primarily with feature values in English. Proposals regarding the contextual markedness of features from a universalist viewpoint can be found in Bailey (1973, 1977, 1977a, 1978), Brasington (1982), Cairns (1969, 1986, 1988), Cairns and Feinstein (1982), Chomsky and Halle (1968), Greenberg (1965, 1978), and Kean (1980 [1975]).

14. I assume that all three conditions must be met for reversal to obtain in this case—that is, a pair of segments must both have the features [−compact, +acute, −abrupt] for their markedness values to be reversed.

15. The exclusion of /tl/ and /dl/ onsets seems to be quite general cross-linguistically. Compare Vennemann (1988:19).

16. The markedness reversal posited is similar in spirit to the idea of *bloc neutralization* in Shapiro (1972:349; 1972a) in which "multiply marked" consonants are deleted. In bloc neutralization the syncopated cluster stands as the unmarked counterpart to the unsyncopated one. For discussion of marked/unmarked combinations in diphthongs, see Andersen (1972).

17. It is worth mentioning that the stops in the unmarked place of articulation, /t/, /d/, and /n/, are extremely malleable. Consider the following examples of alveolar stops in coda position:

foo[p]ball
Ba[k]cave
sig[m]post
ha[č]check
ca[p]box
Ru[k]gers
fa[f]farm

I am indebted to Margaret Winters and Geoff Nathan for pointing this out to me.

18. Mayerthaler (1987, 1988 [1981]), in his theory of natural morphology, proposes a principle of constructional iconicity/diagrammaticity, which maintains that "with much more than chance frequency there is a featureless encoding" of the unmarked categories. (1987:48) According to Mayerthaler, constructional iconicity is only one of the factors in the evaluation of morphological encodings, others being a *principle of uniform encoding* (or Humboldt's universal, which asserts that 'one form—one meaning' is the preferred encoding), a *principle of transparency* (that optimal encodings are compositional and that morpheme boundaries coincide with syllable boundaries). Mayerthaler extends the term markedness to refer to morphological encodings that optimize these three principles.

The theory of morphological naturalness, though it defines markedness as a universal, also allows for a level of language-particular naturalness (cf. Mayerthaler 1987:26; Dressler and Mayerthaler 1987:10). The theory also recognizes that constructional iconicity is not a compulsory characteristic of language and sets up a hierarchy of principles to define morphological naturalness and natural morphological change: system-congruity > class-stability > uniformity/transparency > constructional iconicity > phonetic iconicity.

19. Note that some words have singular/plural doublets: *dwarf, handkerchief, hoof, scarf, wharf.*

I should point out also that for some words the stem alternation is extended to the noun/verb pairs (e.g., *hou[s]e* vs. *hou[z]e, life* vs. *live, bath* vs. *bathe*), an observation that could suggest that verbs are marked with respect to the nouns that are related to them by zero derivation. For some remarks on markedness relations between words related by zero derivation, see Odlin (1986) and Shapiro (1989).

20. The examples in (24) through (28) are from Aronoff (1976).

21. For further discussion of haplology, see Menn and MacWhinney (1984) and Stemberger (1981).

22. Shapiro (1980, 1983) has given examples of complementarity in morphophonemics in Japanese and Russian. He describes his view of complementarity thus:

The cornerstone of a general understanding of word structure, specifically of morphophonemics, is what I have called the *principle of markedness complementarity.* Grossly considered, this principle states that oppositely marked stems and desinences attract, identically marked stems and desinences repel. [1983:146]

23. Following Chomsky and Halle (1968), Kean develops a set of markedness conventions that assign values to segments and that allow a segment's inherent complexity to be given as the total number of marked features. She also develops a set of formalized conditions that express generalizations about the relations among marked and unmarked features in segment systems. Another feature of the marking conventions approach of generative phonology is that the conventions are used as part of the apparatus of generative phonology itself. In terms of the simplicity or evaluation metric that applies to grammars, marking conventions play two roles. Unmarked lexical specifications do not count in the evaluation of the complexity of a lexical form. In addition, marking conventions may be used as linking conventions, which allows secondary feature changes on the output of a rule to be omitted from the rule formalism if the result is the unmarked value. The idea is to incorporate markedness into a larger evaluation metric by treating unmarked features as not counting in the determination of rule complexity.

24. The relation between Universal Grammar and language universals may be thought of in this way: Universal Grammar is an abstract theory concerned with language acquisition as a logical problem and involves typology and universals primarily as they serve as evidence for better formulations of Universal Grammar. On this view, absolute universals might be thought of as those principles and structures that follow directly and immutably from Universal Grammar, while nonabsolute universals and family universals might be viewed as more flexible parameters of Universal Grammar that are fixed by experience.

25. I use the single quotes here to indicate the use of the terms markedness and marked to mean that a language or some rule or subsystem of it is cross-linguistically unnatural—that it is not highly valued cross-linguistically. Note that this makes 'markedness' a complexity metric comparing ideal systems and actual ones rather than an evaluative relation between terms of an opposition within a system.

In a situation such as that described in the text another possibility is that universal markedness conventions are sensitive enough to predict the language-particular evaluation of objective and nominative based on other features of English. The English case system would be an 'unmarked' situation (in the sense described above) and the cross-linguistic evaluation of nominative as the unmarked case feature would be attenuated such that nominative would sometimes be unmarked and sometimes marked, with typological factors determining the dominance for a particular language. I have no convincing argument for one analysis over the other, and in our present state of knowledge such a unification of language-particular and universal markedness is still a promissory note. However, the possibility does exist of resolving the conflict between universal and particular markedness values.

26. This has been particularly emphasized by Mayerthaler (1988 [1981]) and Dressler et al. (1987). Though Mayerthaler (1987) categorizes his universal marked-

ness approach as Universal Grammar, he uses the term with a slightly different sense than Chomsky does.

27. Of course, in many instances we might expect a parallel between structures that are marginal and excluded by the formal grammar of a language and structures that are highly marked. So, for example, consider the reversal described in (14) above. While (14) is not intended here as a rule of English phonology or of Universal Grammar, but rather as an interpretive rule (an evaluation of the possible feature combinations reflecting the patterns that inhere in the data of the language), the syllable structure conditions of English grammar (cf. Selkirk 1986) will exclude these combinations. I shall leave open the extent of these parallels and how they might be characterized.

Chapter 5

1. We cannot hope to survey every approach to this question. For more discussion of phonological change, see Jakobson, (1968, 1962), Andersen (1972, 1974), Hopper (1973, 1977), Gamkrelidze (1975), Greenberg 1978b, Vennemann (1972, 1988); for markedness in syntax, see Lightfoot (1979), Hawkins (1979), Joseph (1980), Traugott (1973), Vennemann (1975), Mayerthaler, (1987, 1988 [1981]), and Wurzel (1987).

2. Lass discusses an even stronger view that he associates with the phonological markedness theory of Chomsky and Halle (1968). Commenting on a marking convention proposed by Chomsky and Halle (1968), Lass remarks that

> it should predict for instance that a language without front round vowels is unlikely to gain them, and even more important, if it has them, that they will be unstable, i.e., be lost through merger with unround ones, etc. Thus more changes in the history of the language will be of the type [y] > [i] than the reverse; and probably, ceteris paribus, the functional load on unmarked vowels should be higher than that on unmarked ones. [1975:479]

Discussing a series of changes in the Old English (West Saxon) sound system, he suggests that the change of [ø] to [e] was an unmarking, but that the changes from [iu] to [y] and from [eo] to [ø] resulted in more marked segments. Lass comments: "Of the three changes, two are in the direction of greater markedness, and one even restores a marked vowel that had been lost earlier" (p. 479). Summing up this and other examples, Lass says: "not only do unmarked vowels disappear and marked ones develop, but mergers go in the counterpredicted direction, and in many cases marked vowels have a higher functional load that unmarked ones" (p. 483).

3. The analysis of Grimm's law is an area in which universal marking hierarchies and the constraint that any posited reconstruction must be a typologically possible one have yielded impressive results. As Jakobson (1962:528 [1958a]) observed, the traditional view of the Indo-European stop system as a series of voiceless stops, a series of voiced stops, and a series of voiced aspirated stops is typologically doubtful. Such a reconstruction posits a system with voiced aspirates

(marked segments), but lacking the unvoiced aspirate counterparts. Hopper (1973, 1977) has suggested that the Indo-European plain voiced stops were actually voiceless glottalized stops, which would be marked sounds. In this view, the "traditional" system of Indo-European consonants in (i) is instead analyzed as the more typologically plausible system in (ii) (I omit the labiovelar/uvular and glottal consonants):

(i)	Voiceless	p	t	k
	Voiced aspirate	bh	dh	gh
	Voiced	(b)	d	g
	Fricative	s		
(ii)	Voiceless aspirate	ph	th	kh
	Voiced aspirate	bh	dh	gh
	Glottalized	(p')	t'	k'
	Fricative	s		

4. I am using quotes around the words *markedness* and *marked* in the sense introduced in the last chapter in which 'markedness' indicates system complexity. Since I obviously cannot hope to survey all extant proposals concerning phonological naturalness, I will treat them as a genre. For details of individual proposals see the references cited in note 8 of chapter 4.

5. Specifically, Chomsky and Halle suggest

the need for an extension of the theory [of the *Sound Pattern of English*] to accommodate the effects of the intrinsic content of features, to distinguish "expected" or "natural" cases of rules and symbol configurations from others which are unexpected and unnatural. In the linguistically significant sense of the notion "complexity," a rule that voices vowels should not add to the complexity of a grammar but a rule that unvoices vowels should, whereas in the case of obstruents the opposite decision is called for. Similarly, if a language has a five-vowel system, the rules that determine the configuration [/a/ /e/ /i/ /o/ /u/] should not add to the complexity of the grammar; rather the complexity should increase if these rules, or at least some of them, do *not* appear in the grammar. [1968:402]

6. Chomsky and Halle also remark: "We would expect, naturally, that systems which are simpler, in this sense, will be more generally found among the languages of the world, will be more likely to develop through historical change, etc." (1968:411).

7. An early illustration of sound change from the perspective of Chomsky-Halle marking conventions can be found in the work of Vennemann (1972) and Bailey (1973), which also contains some discussion of the weighting of features.

8. Another proposal of this sort is that of Vennemann (1972), who suggests that a distinction be made between rules that decrease the complexity of affected

segments (which he calls D-rules) and rules that increase the complexity of affected segments (which he calls I-rules). Vennemann asserts, "D-rules, in particular D-rules not leading to merger, must be favored over I-rules by the evaluation metric" (p. 240). He suggests further that D-rules fall into two classes: assimilatory rules and typological adjustment rules, the former motivated by a sequential context and the latter motivated by imbalances in segment systems. Like the proposals of Greenberg and of Andersen, the essential idea is that rules that decrease complexity are made available by the internal hierarchical pressure of language, while rules that increase complexity are not.

9. Andersen says that "one can think of phonetic innovation . . . as universally a phonetic simplification, describable with reference to the distinctive-feature hierarchy of the language in question as a replacement of a marked feature value by a corresponding unmarked feature value." However, he adds to this a principle of 'markedness reversal' or 'markedness dominance' that entails that "in this marked context, the normally marked value for the feature is evaluated as unmarked, while the normally marked value is evaluated as marked—or in other words, that in the marked context, markedness values are reversed" (1972:45). Of course, neutralization of a marked category to its unmarked counterpart supplemented by reversal of markedness values in marked contexts is equivalent to markedness assimilation.

10. Vennemann nicely sums up the problem:

> Whereas segmental complexity in Chapter 9 [of the *Sound Pattern of English*] is simply the *sum* of the marked values of the segment, each M counting *one*, in my analysis it is the total *weight* of the marked values. It seems obvious that a segment marked for Murmur, Affricativization, Glottalization, etc. is less natural than one marked for voice or continuance. In other words naturalness is a feature dependent concept. This concept of "degree of naturalness" or "weight complexity" is in part identical with the hierarchy-of-features idea; in part it goes beyond it in that the weight complexity of a segment is to a great degree determined by its sequential environment and by the entire phonological system in which it functions. [1972:260–1]

11. Andersen (1974a: 44–45) suggests that innovations involving reversals of phonological markedness values are *always* caused by innovations in the ranking of features.

12. An approach to changes in morphological coding is given in Mayerthaler (1987, 1988 [1981]). However, his approach, which attempts to define a notion of natural morphological coding and natural morphological change is similar enough in spirit to the proposals of Traugott and Lightfoot to be considered alongside them. Mayerthaler (1987:51) suggests the following as "theorems of the theory of markedness": (1) Natural change: ("any change from marked to unmarked is a natural change"); (b) Typological pattern: ("the existence of what is more marked implies the existence of what is less marked"); and (c) Developmental pattern: ("violations of the typological pattern imply the application of natural change").

Mayerthaler recognizes the possibility of naturalness conflicts and the attenuation of universals by language-particular norms (cf. Wurzel 1987). Notice also that Mayerthaler admits the possibility of increases in markedness due to change, though such change will be by definition "unnatural."

One thing that is unclear to me is why Mayerthaler asserts principle (c), his Developmental pattern principle. It seems rather that violations of principle (b) (Typological pattern) would arise when *un*natural morphological changes occurred, since these would result in the loss of a unmarked category and the retention of its marked counterpart.

13. Some speakers, of course, pronounce the *l* in words such as *almond,* and *salmon,* though to speakers who omit the *l* such pronunciations are socially marked. The application of markedness to such matters as spelling pronunciations, and the analysis of spelling, punctuation, and writing conventions in general has not received much attention, unfortunately.

14. CCC clusters will be analyzed as C(m) C(u) C(m), assuming that the syllable core is the maximally unmarked segment. For further discussion of preferred syllable structure types, readers are referred to Kaye and Lowenstamm (1981) and Vennemann (1988).

15. Compare Vennemann (1988:15, 21).

16. The simplification of /nd/ clusters in informal speech is also suggestive. When words such as *hand, band, land,* and so on are simplified in rapid speech it is the /d/ that is lost rather than the /n/. Interestingly, this simplification is less noticeable with /nt/ clusters, which suggests that the markedness reversal may be restricted to clusters that agree in voicing as well as other features.

17. In the onset /sl/, of course, the liquid is unmarked since /l/ functions as the core and /s/ as the precore. This cluster is thus parallel to /st/, /sp/, and /sk/ onset clusters.

18. In onsets, however, liquids appear to be less marked than nasals. This is suggested, for example, by the fact that English has onset clusters of /pl/ and /kl/, but not /pn/ and /kn/. Cf. Benson (1986:274). For discussion of /l/ versus /r/ in onset and coda position, see Vennemann (1988:19–20) and Cairns (1986:25–26).

19. Compare, for example, Kuryłowicz's fourth law of analogy, which states that when analogical doublets (like *brothers* and *bretheren*) arise, the older form (*bretheren*) is used for secondary functions while the newly created form receives the primary sense. But as Kiparsky (1974) points out, this law admits of counterexamples like *louses* versus *lice,* and he argues that the analogically derived form generally has the secondary meaning. See also Hock (1986:226–27) and Winters (1987).

20. Changes in the history of English that appear at first glance to be consistent with the principle of compensation include the following: loss of inflections in

the first and second persons of present tense verbs and in the past tense generally, the loss of inflections in the subjunctive, loss of the dual number, loss of the reflexive forms in Old English. In phonology the following might be cited: the loss of length distinctions among low vowels, the reduction of place of articulation distinctions among fricatives, the loss of rounding among front vowels. However, one aspect of English that seems to run counter to the principle is the greater differentiation of inflectional patterns among the reflexes of (marked) strong verbs than among the reflexes of historically weak verbs.

21. I have described types (a) through (c) in terms of the loss of subordinate features from a lexical item or a category. However, we might view the limiting case of feature loss as the collapse of an opposition into one of its terms. In such a case, type (a)—neutralization to the unmarked term—would be the expected change and type (c)—neutralization to the marked term—would be less expected. Conversely, the limiting case of changes of type (d) through (f) would be the addition of new features or oppositions.

22. See McConnell-Ginet (1979) and Frank and Treichler (1989) for further discussion.

23. It may, of course, indicate a covert or an unconscious affiliation. And responding to expressions like (6c) and similar nonfeminist expressions presents difficulties for speakers whose language use is not oriented to traditional male modes. See McConnell-Ginet (1989).

24. For discussion of theories of the ultimate origins of periphrastic *do,* see Ellegård (1953) and Dennison (1985), who view it as a development of causative *do,* and Hausmann (1974), who sees it as a development of an Old English support verb used in ellipsis.

25. Visser (1969:1532) also mentions a negation pattern in which *not* preceded the main verb without *do,* remarking that this pattern was sporadic before 1500 and in decline after 1700.

26. In fact, the loss of verb raising in favor of *do* support increases the overall coherence of English syntax, since the patterns of interrogation and negation in simple sentences become exactly parallel with those of sentences having true auxiliaries like aspectual *have* and *be.* Compare Battistella (1985, 1985a), for an analysis along these lines.

27. If, as Ellegård has suggested, the periphrastic *do* first came into the language as a rhyming technique for poets, then perhaps we can view its introduction as a function of a marked style. It is significant also that the use of *do* in simple nonemphatic sentences never became very frequent (never higher than ten percent of affirmative declarative sentences). The *do* pattern in simple nonemphatic sentences was, in effect, always a marked usage.

28. This use of the second person plural as a mark of respect appears to have originated with the double meaning of Latin *vos* in the fourth century A.D. Williams

(1975:248) speculates that this usage may have originated when the Roman Empire had emperors both in Rome and in Constantinople. In any event, the spread of the form over Europe suggests that plural pronouns may be unmarked in languages other than English.

29. It is retained in certain dialects. See Evans (1969, 1970).

Chapter 6

1. See, for example, Eckman (1977, 1985), Bardovi-Harlig (1987), Benson (1986), Fellbaum (1986), Hyltenstam (1987), and White (1986).

2. See Liszka (1982) and Utaker (1974) for more discussion of Lévi-Strauss's approach to opposition and its contrast with Jakobson's view.

3. Margaret Winters has pointed out to me that in Orthodox Judaism the wedding ring is placed on the bride's right index finger.

4. Compare Lakoff and Johnson (1980:22–24) on the *up/down* opposition in American culture.

5. The existence of such assimilations of cultural categories is also seen in George Lakoff's discussion of the title example of his book *Women, Fire, and Dangerous Things*. Lakoff (pp. 92–104) summarizes the noun classifier system of Dyirbal, an aboriginal language of Australia described by Dixon (1982). The noun classifiers of Dyirbal fall into four categories: there is a classifier for nouns referring to human males and to animals; a classifier for names referring to human females, fire, water, and fighting; one referring to nonflesh food; and one referring to everything else. Lakoff suggests that nouns that share a classifier are generally those connected to the central concept of a classifier category by belief or myth. So, for example, the connection between women, fire, and dangerous things is described as the grammatical extension of an originally mythological association. The moon and the sun are husband and wife in Dyirbal myth. Accordingly, the sun, and by extension fire, are in the same class as human females. Danger is associated with fire, so fighting and other dangerous things have come to be in the women-and-fire category. And water, being fire's opposite, also falls into this category.

6. Mayerthaler and Dressler (1987) suggest that the first term in such "binomial expressions" is the unmarked one. I should mention that hyphenated names, in which the wife's name is augmented by the addition of the husband's surname, are of course marked forms when the husband's name remains unchanged.

7. Apparent counterexamples include the expression *ladies and gentlemen* and the epicene pronoun *s/he*, where orthography plays a role.

8. As Waugh (1982) points out, the unmarkedness of *life* is supported by lexical usage as well as by our intuitions about these concepts. The word *life,* for

example, may include in its reference both life and death. One's *life story* includes one's death, and *the mystery of life* includes the mystery of death. (Cf. also: *life sentence, life cycle, lifeline, lifetime.*) And conversely, the markedness of death is reflected in the many existing euphemisms for death.

9. Waugh (1982) suggests some other aspects of Western culture that might be analyzed in this way:

(i)   barrenness/fertility
        homosexuality/heterosexuality
        black person/white person
        blindness/sight
        deafness/hearing
        living together/married

To these might be added such other value-ladden oppositions as the following:

(ii)   foreign/native
        sexually active/not sexually active
        ethical behavior/unethical behavior
        employed/unemployed
        parent/nonparent
        mother/working mother
        divorced/married
        literate/illiterate
        intellectual/anti-intellectual

10. It is probably not the case that all polar opposites function as binary oppositions in system of cultural values. Consider, for example, the polarity between sacred and profane. Though perhaps functioning as a binary opposition for some cultures, this contrast is better analyzed for mainstream American culture as made up of the oppositions sacred/nonsacred and profane/nonprofane, which define four symbolic categories: sacred and nonprofane, nonsacred and nonprofane, nonsacred and profane, and sacred and profane. It may be fruitful to consider such split oppositions in terms of Lévi-Strauss's claim that oppositions lacking an intermediary term tend to be replaced by oppositions with a mediating third term between the polar opposites (Lévi-Strauss 1963:224).

11. Within linguistics, the unmarked sense of grammar may itself be further subdivided according to whether the term refers to a theory of a language (for example, a generative grammar of language X) as opposed to a theory of grammars in general (for example, Universal Grammar). For some linguists the unmarked sense of grammar is the former, for others the latter.

Similarly, linguists will differentiate the technical notion language. For some language is a mental system (corresponding to Chomsky's (1986) notion of Internalized-language); for others language is a collection of linguistic actions or behaviors (Chomsky's Externalized-language).

12. For example, see Orr (1987) for a discussion of markedness applied to the understanding of adjectives in standardized tests; see also Harris (1973) and French (1979).

13. McCawley (1985) discusses markedness conventions as scientific paradigms in the sense of Thomas Kuhn. And for some discussion of asymmetries in female and male language use, see McConnell-Ginet (1989).

14. These are not mutually exclusive situations. In some instances individuals aim at unmarked behavior within a peer group, but such behavior is marked in relation to the general behavior patterns of other (culturally dominant) groups.

15. For discussion of clothing as a cultural code, see Barthes (1972) and Solomon (1985).

Bibliography

Alexander, Gerda. 1983. *Fortis and Lenis in Germanic*. New York: Peter Lang.

Andersen, Henning. 1968. "IE *s* after *i, u, r, k* in Baltic and Slavic." *Acta Linguistica Hafniensia* 11:171–90.

———. 1969. "A Study in Diachronic Morphophonemics: The Ukrainian Prefixes." *Language* 45:807–30.

———. 1969a. "Lenition in Common Slavic." *Language* 45:553–74.

———. 1972. "Diphthongization." *Language* 48:11–50.

———. 1973. "Abductive and Deductive Change." *Language* 49:765–93.

———. 1974. "Markedness in Vowel Systems." In *Proceedings of the 11th International Congress of Linguists* 2, ed. L. Heilmann, pp. 891–97. Bologna: il Mulino.

———. 1974a. "Towards a Typology of Change: Bifurcating Changes and Binary Relations." In John M. Anderson and Charles Jones, eds., *Historical Linguistics II*. Amsterdam: North-Holland. 17–60.

———. 1975. "Variance and Invariance in Phonological Typology." *Phonologica 1972*. ed. W. Dressler and F. Mares, 67–78, Munich: Fink.

———. 1978. "Vocalic and Consonantal Languages." In *Studia Linguistica A. V. Issatchenko Oblata*, ed. H. Birnbaum, et al., pp. 1–12. Lisse, Netherlands: Peter de Ridder.

———. 1979. "Phonology as Semiotic." In S. Chatman, et al., eds., *A Semiotic Landscape*. The Hague: Mouton, 377–381.

———. 1980. "Morphological Change: Towards a Typology," In J. Fisiak, ed., *Recent Developments in Historical Morphology*. The Hague: Mouton. 1–50.

Anderson, John M., and Charles Jones, eds. 1974. *Historical Linguistics*. (2 vols.) Amsterdam: North-Holland.

Anderson, Stephen R. 1985. *Phonology in the Twentieth Century*. Chicago: University of Chicago Press.

Andrews, Edna. 1984. *A Theoretical Foundation for Markedness: Asymmetry in Language from a Mathematical Perspective* (Ph.D. diss, Indiana University). Ann Arbor: University Microfilms.

————. 1985. "Markedness Reversals in Linguistic Sign Systems." In Gilbert Youmans, ed., *To Honor Roman Jakobson: Papers from the 1984 Mid-America Linguistics Conference*, pp. 169–80. Columbia: University of Missouri.

————. 1986. "A Reevaluation of the Relationship between Grammatical Gender and Declension in Modern Greek and Russian." *International Journal of Slavic Linguistics and Poetics* 34:99–112.

————. 1986a. "Markedness Theory in Morphology and Semantics: The Reconciliation of Contextual versus General Meaning." *SECOL Review* 10:3.

————. 1987. "Jakobsonian Markedness Theory as a Mathematical Principle." In *Language, Poetry, and Poetics*, ed. Krystyna Pomorska, et al. 177–97. Berlin: Mouton.

————. 1990. *Markedness Theory: The Union of Asymmetry and Semiosis in Language*. Durham, N.C.: Duke University Press.

————. (to appear) "Markedness Theory: An Explication of its Theoretical Basis and Applicability on Semantic Analysis." In *Memorial Volume to Honor J. Daniel Armstrong*, ed. Charles Gribble, C. H. van Schooneveld, and Charles Townsend. Columbus, Ohio: Slavica.

Anttila, Raimo. 1972. *An Introduction to Historical and Comparative Linguistics*. New York: Macmillan.

————. 1977. *Analogy*. The Hague: Mouton.

Aronoff, Mark. 1976. *Word Formation in Generative Grammar*. Cambridge: MIT Press.

Bailey, Charles-James N. 1973. *Variation and Linguistic Theory*. Arlington, Va.: Center for Applied Linguistics.

————. 1977. "Linguistic Change, Naturalness, Mixture, and Structural Principles." *Papiere zur Linguistik* 16:6–73.

————. 1977a. "Converging Criteria for Establishing Consonantal Marking Values in Different Positions in the Syllable." *Salzburger Beitrage zur Linguistik* 3:159–78.

————. 1978. *Gradience in English Syllabization and a Revised Concept of Unmarked Syllabization*. Bloomington: Indiana University Linguistics Club.

————. 1981. "Markedness-Reversal and the Pragmatic Principle of 'Reading Between the Lines in the Presence of Marked Usages'," in *Aufsatze zur Englishen Pragmatik*, pp. 2–71. Berlin: Technische University of Berlin.

Baker, C. L. 1978. *Introduction to Generative-Transformational Syntax*. Englewood Cliffs, N.J.: Prentice Hall.

Baltaxe, Christiane A. M. 1978. *Foundations of Distinctive Feature Theory*. Baltimore: University Park Press.

Bardovi-Harlig, Kathleen. 1987. "Markedness and Salience in Second-Language Acquisition." *Language Learning* 37:385–407.

Barthes, Roland. 1967. *Elements of Semiology*. Translated by Annette Lavers and Colin Smith. New York: Hill and Wang.

———. 1972. *Mythologies*. Translated by Annette Lavers. London: J. Cape.

Basbøll, Hans. 1981. "Remarks on Distinctive Features and Markedness in Generative Phonology." In Belletti et al. (1981), pp. 25–64.

Bates, E., and B. MacWhinney. 1982. "Functionalist Approaches to Grammar." In L. Gleitman and E. Wanner, eds., *Language Acquisition: State of the Art*. Cambridge: Cambridge University Press.

Bateson, Gregory. 1972. "Form, Substance, Difference." In *Steps to an Ecology of Mind*, pp. 448–66. New York: Ballantine.

Battistella, Edwin L. 1985. "Markedness Isomorphism as a Goal of Language Change." *Lingua* 65:327–42.

———. 1985a. "Markedness Isomorphism and Auxiliary *do*." In Gilbert Youmans, ed., *To Honor Roman Jakobson: Papers from the 1984 Mid-America Linguistics Conference*, pp. 159–68. Columbia: University of Missouri.

———. 1986. "Formal Versus Semiotic Motivation in Complementizer Allomorphy." In J. Deely, ed., *Semiotics 1985*, New York: Plenum.

———. 1986a. "Marked and Unmarked Pronouns in English." *SECOL Review* 11:66–77.

Beidelman, T. O. 1973. "Kaguru Symbolic Classification." In Needham (1973), pp. 128–166.

Belletti, A. et al., eds. 1981. *Theory of Markedness in Core Grammar*. Pisa: Scuola Normale Superiore di Pisa.

Benson, Bronsen. 1986. "The Markedness Differential Hypothesis: Implications for Vietnamese Speakers of English." In Eckman (1986), pp. 271–89.

Berlin, Brent, and Paul Kay. 1969. *Basic Color Terms: Their Universality and Evolution*. Berkeley and Los Angeles: University of California Press.

Bethin, Christina. 1984. "Local Markedness in Russian Genitive Plurals." *Lingua* 62:319–23.

Bickerton, Derek. 1969. "Prologomena to a Linguistic Theory of Metaphor." *Foundations of Language* 5:34–52.

————. 1981. *Roots of Language*. Ann Arbor: Karoma Publishing.

Bierwisch, Manfred. 1967. "Some Semantic Universals of German Adjectives." *Foundations of Language* 3:1–36.

Birnbaum, Henrik. 1984. Review of *Roman Jakobson and Beyond* by Rodney Sangster. (Berlin: Mouton, 1982). *Language* 60:412–16.

Bloomfield, Leonard. 1933. *Language*. New York: Holt, Rinehart and Winston.

Bodine, Ann. 1975. "Androcentrism in Prescriptive Grammar: Singular 'They,' Sex-Indefinite 'He' and 'He or She,' " *Language in Society* 4:539–50.

Bolinger, Dwight. 1977. *Neutralization, Norm and Bias*. Bloomington: Indiana University Linguistics Club.

————. 1977a. *Meaning and Form*. London: Longmans.

————. 1985. "The Inherent Iconism of Intonation." In Haiman (1985), pp. 97–108.

Brakel, Arthur. 1984. *Phonological Markedness and Distinctive Features*. Bloomington: Indiana University Press.

Brasington, R. W. P. 1982. "Markedness, Strength and Position." In David Crystal, ed., *Linguistic Controversies*. pp. 81–94. London: Edward Arnold.

Brøndal, Viggo. 1943. *Essais de linguistique générale*. Copenhagen: Munksgaard.

Brown, Roger, and Albert Gilman. 1960. "Pronouns of Power and Solidarity." In T. A. Sebeok, ed., *Style in Language*, Cambridge, Mass.: MIT Press. 253–76.

Bybee, Joan. 1985. "Diagrammatic Iconicity in Stem Inflection Relations." In Haiman (1985), pp. 11–47.

————. 1985a. *Morphology: A Study of the Relation between Meaning and Form*. Amsterdam: John Benjamins.

———— , and Carol Moder. 1983. "Morphological Classes as Natural Categories." *Language* 59:251–70.

Cairns, Charles E. 1969. "Markedness, Neutralization, and Universal Redundancy Rules." *Language* 45:863–85.

————. 1986. "Word Structure, Markedness, and Applied Linguistics," In Eckman 1986, pp. 13–38.

————. 1988. "Phonotactics, Markedness, and Lexical Representation." *Phonology* 5:209–36.

———— , and Mark Feinstein. 1982. "Markedness and the Theory of Syllable Structure." *Linguistic Inquiry* 13:193–225.

Chomsky, Noam. 1973. "Conditions on Transformation." In S. R. Anderson and P. Kiparsky, eds., *A Festschrift for Morris Halle.* New York: Holt, Rinehart and Winston.

――――. 1981. *Lectures on Government and Binding.* Dordrecht: Foris.

――――. 1981a. "Markedness and Core Grammar." In Belletti et al. (1981), pp. 123–46.

――――. 1982. *Some Concepts and Consequences of a Theory of Government and Binding Theory.* Cambridge, Mass.: MIT Press.

――――. 1986. *Knowledge of Language: Its Nature, Origin and Use.* New York: Praeger.

――――, and Morris Halle. 1968. *Sound Pattern of English.* New York: Harper and Row.

――――, and Howard Lasnik. 1977. "Filters and Control." *Linguistic Inquiry* 8:425–504.

Christoffersen, Marit. 1980. "Marked and Unmarked Word Order in Old Norse." In Traugott, et al., (1980), pp. 115–21.

Chvany, Catherine V. 1983. "On 'definiteness' in Bulgarian, English and Russian." In M. Flier, ed., *American Contributions to the Ninth International Congress of Slavists* (vol. 1, Linguistics). Columbus, Ohio: Slavica. 75–91.

――――. 1984. "From Jakobson's Cube as *objet d'art* to a New Model of the Grammatical Sign." *International Journal of Slavic Linguistics and Poetics*: 29:43–70.

――――. 1985. "Backgrounded Perfective and Plot Line Imperfectives: Toward a Theory of Grounding in Text." In Flier and Timberlake (1985), pp. 247–73.

――――. 1986. "Jakobson's Fourth and Fifth Dimensions: On Reconciling the Cube Model of Case Meaning with the Two-Dimensional Matrices for Case Form." In R. D. Brecht and J. Levine, eds., *Case in Slavic,* Columbus, Ohio: Slavica. 107–29.

Clark, Eve V. 1985. "The Principle of Contrast: A Constraint on Language Acquisition." In B. MacWhinney, ed., *Mechanisms of Language Acquisition,* Hillsdale, N.J.: Lawrence Erlbaum Associates.

――――, and Herbert H. Clark. 1978. "Universals, Relativity, and Language Processing," In Greenberg (1978), vol. 1, pp. 225–77.

Clark, Herbert H. and Eve V. Clark. 1977. *Psychology and Language: An Introduction to Psycholinguistics.* New York: Harcourt Brace Jovanovich.

Comrie, Bernard. 1976. *Aspect.* London: Cambridge University Press.

————. 1981. *Language Universals and Linguistic Typology.* Chicago: University of Chicago Press.

————. 1981a. "Aspect and Voice: Some Reflections on the Perfect and Passive." In Ph. Tedeschi and A. Zaenen, eds., *Syntax and Semantics 14: Tense and Aspect*, pp. 65–78. NY: Academic.

————. 1985. *Tense.* London: Cambridge University Press.

————. 1986. "Markedness, Grammar, People, and the World." In Eckman (1986), pp. 85–106.

Cook, Albert. 1980. *Myth and Language.* Bloomington: Indiana University Press.

Cooper, William, and John R. Ross. 1975. "World Order." In R. E. Grossman, L. J. San and T. J. Vance, eds., *Papers from the Parasession on Functionalism*, pp. 63–111. Chicago: Chicago Linguistic Society.

Cox, Thomas J. 1986. "Marked Vowel Systems and Distinctive Palatalization." In Eckman (1986), pp. 39–63.

Crothers, John. 1978. "Typology and Universals of Vowel Systems." In Greenberg (1978), vol. 2, pp. 93–152.

Davison, Alice. 1980. "Peculiar Passives." *Language* 56:42–66.

————. 1984. "Syntactic Markedness and the Definition of Sentence Topic." *Language* 60:797–846.

————, and Richard Lutz. 1985. "Measuring Syntactic Complexity Relative to Discourse Context." In David Dowty, et al., eds., *Natural Language Parsing*, London: Cambridge University Press. 26–66.

Dennison, D. 1985. "The origins of Periphrastic *do*: Ellegård and Visser Reconsidered." In R. Eaton, et al., eds., *Papers from the 4th International Conference on English Historical Linguistics.* Amsterdam: John Benjamins, 45–61.

Denny, Rita. 1985. "Marking the Interaction Order: The Social Constitution of Turn Exchange and Speaking." *Language in Society* 14:41–62.

Dixon, R. M. W. 1982. *Where Have All the Adjectives Gone?* Berlin: Walter de Gruyter.

Dokulil, M. 1958. "K Otazce Morfologickych Protikladu." *Slovo a Slovesnost* 19:81–103.

Donegan, Patricia Jane. 1985 [1978]. *On the Natural Phonology of Vowels.* New York and London: Garland.

Dressler, Wolfgang. 1985. "On the Predictiveness of Natural Morphology." *Journal of Linguistics* 21:321–37.

————. 1987. "Word Formation as a Part of Natural Morphology." In W. Dressler, et al., *Leitmotifs in Natural Morphology*. Amsterdam: John Benjamins. 99–126.

————, and Mayerthaler, Willi. 1987. Introduction to W. Dressler, et al., *Leitmotifs in Natural Morphology*. Amsterdam: John Benjamins. 3–22.

————, Willi Mayerthaler, Oswald Panagl, and Wolfgang Wurzel. 1987. *Leitmotifs in Natural Morphology*. Amsterdam: John Benjamins.

————, et al. eds. 1981. *Phonologica 1980*. Innsbruck: Institut für Sprachwissenschaft der Universtität Innsbruck.

DuBois, Jack. 1985. "Competing Motivations." In Haiman (1985), pp. 343–66.

Eckman, Fred R. 1977. "Markedness and the Contrastive Analysis Hypothesis." *Language Learning* 27:315–30.

————. 1985. "Some Theoretical and Pedagogical Implications of the Markedness Differential Hypothesis." *Studies in Second Language Acquisition* 7:289–307.

————, Edith A. Moravcsik, and Jessica R. Wirth, eds., 1986. *Markedness*. New York: Plenum Press.

Ellegård, Alvar. 1953. *The Auxiliary 'do': The Establishment and Regulation of its Use in English*. Stockholm: Almqvist and Wiksell.

Evans, William. 1969. " 'You' and 'Thou' in Northern England." *South Atlantic Bulletin* 29:17–21.

————. 1970. "The Survival of the Second-person Singular in the Southern Counties of England." *South Central Bulletin* 30:182–86.

Evans-Pritchard, E. E. 1953. "Nuer Spear Symbolism." In Needham (1973), pp. 92–108.

Fellbaum, Marie L. 1986. "Markedness and Allophonic Rules." In Eckman (1986), pp. 291–308.

Ferguson, Charles. 1971. "Absence of the Copula and the Notion of Simplicity." In Dell Hymes, ed., *Pidginization and Creolization of Language*. Cambridge: Cambridge University Press.

————, and Carol B. Farwell. 1975. "Words and Sounds in Early Language Acquisition." *Language* 51:419–39.

Fletcher, Charles R. 1984. "Markedness and Topic Continuity in Discourse Processing." *Journal of Verbal Learning and Verbal Behavior* 23:487–93.

————. 1985. "The Functional Role of Markedness in Topic Identification." *Text* 5, 23–37.

Flier, M., and A. Timberlake, eds., 1985. *The Scope of Slavic Aspect*. Columbus, Ohio: Slavica.

Foley, William, and Robert van Valin, Jr. 1984. *Functional Syntax and Universal Grammar*. Cambridge: Cambridge University Press.

Fox, Barbara. 1987. "Morpho-syntactic Markedness and Discourse Structure." *Journal of Pragmatics* 11:359–75.

Fox, James J. 1973. "On Bad Death and the Left Hand: A Study of Rotinese Symbolic Inversions." In Needham (1973), pp. 342–368.

Frank, Francine W., and Treichler, Paula. 1989. *Language, Gender and Professional Writing: Theoretical Approaches and Guidelines for Nonsexist Usage*. New York: Modern Language Association.

Frank, Joseph. 1984. "The Master Linguist." *New York Review of Books*, 12 April 1984, pp. 29–33.

French, P. 1979. "Linguistic Marking, Strategy, and Affect in Syllogistic Reasoning." *Journal of Psycholinguistic Research* 8:425–49.

Friedman, Victor. 1985. "Aspectual Usage in Russian, Macedonian and Bulgarian." In Flier and Timberlake (1985), pp. 234–45.

Frishberg, Nancy. 1975. "Arbitrariness and Iconicity: Historical Change in American Sign Language." *Language* 51:696–719.

Fritsch, Vilma. 1968. *Left and Right in Science and Life*. London: Barrie and Rockliff.

Gamkrelidze, T. V. 1975. "On the Correlation of Stops and Fricatives in a Phonological System." *Lingua* 35:231–61.

Givón, Talmy. 1985. "Iconicity, Isomophism, and Nonarbitrary Coding in Syntax." In Haiman (1985), pp. 187–220.

Granet, Marcel. 1933. "Right and Left in China." In Needham (1973), pp. 43–58.

Greenbaum, Sidney. 1976. "Syntactic Frequency and Acceptability." *Lingua* 40:301–14.

Greenberg, Joseph. 1965. "Some Generalizations Concerning Initial and Final Consonant Clusters." *Linguistics* 18:5–32.

———. 1966. *Language Universals*. The Hague: Mouton.

———. 1966a. "Some Universals of Grammar with Particular Reference to the Order of Meaningful Elements." In J. Greenberg, ed., *Universals of Language* 2nd edition. Cambridge, Mass.: MIT Press.

———. 1966b. "Synchronic and Diachronic Universals in Phonology." *Language* 42:508–17.

————. 1969. "Some Methods of Dynamic Comparison in Linguistics." In *Substance and Structure of Language*, ed. Jaan Puhvel, pp. 147–203. Berkeley and Los Angeles; University of California Press.

————. ed. 1978. *Universals of Language*. Stanford: Stanford University Press.

————. 1978a. "Typology and Cross-linguistic Generalizations." In Greenberg (1978), vol. 1, pp. 33–59.

————. 1978b. "Diachrony, Synchrony and Language Universals," In Greenberg (1978), vol. 1, pp. 61–91.

————. 1979. "Rethinking Linguistics Diachronically." *Language* 55:275–90.

Gundel, Jeanette K., Kathleen Houlihan, and Gerald K. Sanders. 1986. "Markedness and Distribution in Phonology and Syntax." In Eckman (1986), pp. 107–38.

Haiman, John. 1972. "Phonological Targets and Unmarked Structures." *Language* 48:365–77.

————. 1980. "The Iconicity of Grammar." *Language* 56:515–40.

————. 1983. "Iconic and Economic Motivation," *Language* 59:781–819.

———— , ed. 1985. *Iconicity in Syntax*. Amsterdam: John Benjamins.

————. 1985a. "Symmetry." In Haiman (1985), pp. 73–95.

Halle, Morris. 1957. "In Defense of the Number Two." In E. Pulgram, ed., *Studies Presented to Joshua Whatmough on his Sixtieth Birthday*, pp. 65–72. The Hague: Mouton.

————. 1967. "Markedness." In *Proceedings of the Sixth International Congress of Phonetic Sciences*, pp. 61–71. Prague: Academia.

————. 1977. "Roman Jakobson's Contribution to the Modern Study of Speech Sounds." In *Roman Jakobson: Echoes of His Scholarship*, ed. Daniel Armstrong and C. H. van Schooneveld, pp. 123–43. Lisse: Peter de Ridder.

Hamilton, H. W., and J. Deese. 1971. "Does Linguistic Marking Have a Psychological Correlate?" *Journal of Verbal Learning and Verbal Behavior* 10:707–14.

Harbert, Wayne. 1986. "Markedness and Bindability of Subject of NP." In Eckman (1986), pp. 139–54.

Harris, R. J. 1973. "Answering Questions Containing Marked and Unmarked Adjectives." *Journal of Experimental Psychology* 97:399–401.

Harsh, Wayne. 1968. *The Subjunctive Mood in English*. Tuscaloosa: University of Alabama Press.

Hatten, Robert. 1987. "Style, Motivation, and Markedness." In Thomas A. Sebeok and Jean Umiker-Sebeok, eds., *The Semiotic Web 1986.* Berlin: Mouton. 408–429.

———. 1988. "Musical Meaning in Beethoven: Markedness, Correlation, and Interpretation." Manuscript. The Pennsylvania State University.

Hausmann, Robert. 1974. "The Origin and Development of Modern English Periphrastic *do.*" In Anderson and Jones (1974), pp. 159–89.

Hawkins, John W. 1979. "Implicational Universals as Predictors of Word Order Change." *Language* 55:618–48.

———. 1983. *Word Order Universals.* New York: Academic Press.

Hendersen, Michael. 1976. "Redundancy, Markedness, and Simultaneous Constraints in Phonology." *Language* 52:314–25.

Herbert, Robert K. 1986. *Language Universals, Markedness Theory, and Natural Phonetic Processes.* New York: Mouton.

Hertz, Robert [1909] "The Pre-eminence of the Right Hand: A Study in Religious Polarity," In Needham (1973), pp. 3–31.

Hjelmslev, Louis. 1969. *Prolegomena to a Theory of Language.* Translated by Francis J. Whitfield. Madison: University of Wisconsin Press.

Hock, Hans Heinrich. 1986. *Principles of Historical Linguistics.* Berlin: Mouton.

Holenstein, Elmar. 1976. *Roman Jakobson's Approach to Language: Phenomenological Structuralism.* Translated by Catherine and Tarcisius Schelbert. Bloomington: Indiana University Press.

Hopper, Paul. 1973. "Glottalized and Murmured Occlusives in Indo-European." *Glossa* 7:96–134.

———. 1977. "The Typology of the Proto-Indo-European Segmental Inventory." *Journal of Indo-European Studies* 5:41–53.

———, and Sandra Thompson. 1980. "Transitivity in Grammar and Discourse." *Language* 56:251–99.

———, and Sandra Thompson. 1984. "The Discourse Basis for Lexical Categories in Universal Grammar." *Language* 60:703–52.

Hyams, Nina. 1986. *Language Acquisition and the Theory of Parameters.* Dordrecht: D. Reidel.

Hyltenstam, Kenneth. 1987. "Markedness, Language Universals, Language Typology, and Second Language Acquisition." In *First and Second Language Acquisition Processes,* ed. Carol Pfaff, pp. 55–78. Cambridge, Mass.: Newbury.

Ingram, David. 1988. "Jakobson Revisited: Some Evidence from the Acquisition of Polish." *Lingua* 75:55–82.

Jaeger, Jeri. 1980. "Categorization in Phonology: An Experimental Approach." Ph.D. diss, University of California, Berkeley.

Jackendoff, Ray. 1977. *X̄ Syntax: A Study of Phrase Structure.* Cambridge, Mass.: MIT Press.

Jakobson, Roman. 1932. "The Structure of the Russian Verb." In *Russian and Slavic Grammar Studies,* pp. 1–14.

———. 1936. "Contributions to the General Theory of Case: General Meanings of the Russian Cases." In *Russian and Slavic Grammar Studies,* pp. 59–103.

———. 1939. "Zero Sign." In *Russian and Slavic Grammar Studies,* pp. 151–60.

———. 1948. "Russian Conjugation." In *Russian and Slavic Grammar Studies.* pp. 15–26.

———. 1957. "Shifters, Verbal Categories, and the Russian Verb." In *Russian and Slavic Grammar Studies,* pp. 41–58.

———. 1957a. "The Relationship Between Genitive and Plural in the Declension of Russian Nouns." In *Russian and Slavic Grammar Studies,* pp. 135–40.

———. 1958. "Morphological Observations on Slavic Declension (The Structure of Russian Case Forms)." In *Russian and Slavic Grammar Studies,* pp. 105–33.

———. 1958a. "Typological Studies and Their Contribution to Historical Comparative Linguistics." In *Selected Writings* vol. 1, pp. 523–32.

———. 1960. "The Gender Pattern of Russian." In *Russian and Slavic Grammar Studies,* pp. 141–43.

———. 1960a. "Linguistics and Poetics." In *Selected Writings,* vol. 3, pp. 18–51.

———. 1962. *Selected Writings.* Vol. 1, *Phonological Studies.* The Hague: Mouton.

———. 1966. "Implications of Language Universals for Linguistics." in Greenberg (1966a), pp. 263–78.

———. 1968. [1941] *Child Language, Aphasia and Phonological Universals.* The Hague: Mouton.

———. 1971. *Selected Writings.* Vol.2, *Word and Language.* The Hague: Mouton.

———. 1978. *Six Lectures on Sound and Meaning.* Translated by John Mepham. Cambridge, Mass: MIT Press.

———. 1980. *The Framework of Language.* Ann Arbor: Michigan Studies in the Humanities.

————. 1981. "Notes on the Declension of Pronouns." In *Russian and Slavic Grammar Studies*, pp. 145–49.

————. 1981. *Selected Writings*. Vol. 3, *The Poetry of Grammar and the Grammar of Poetry*. Berlin: Mouton.

————. 1984. *Russian and Slavic Grammar Studies 1931–1981*. Edited by Linda R. Waugh and Morris Halle. Berlin: Mouton.

————. 1988. *Selected Writings*. Vol. 8, *Major Works 1976–1980*. The Hague: Mouton.

————, and Morris Halle. 1968. "Phonology in Relation to Phonetics." In *Manual of Phonology*, ed. Bertil Malmberg, pp. 411–49. Amsterdam: North-Holland.

————, and Morris Halle. 1971 [1956]. *Fundamentals of Language*, 2d. ed. rev. The Hague: Mouton.

————, and Linda Waugh. 1979. *The Sound Shape of Language*. Bloomington: Indiana University Press.

Joseph, Brian. 1980. "Linguistic Universals and Syntactic Change." *Language* 56:345–70.

Kalmár, Ivan. 1982. "Transitivity in a Czech Folk Tale." In *Studies in Transitivity*, ed. P. Hopper and S. Thompson, pp. 241–59. New York: Academic Press.

Kaye, Jonathan, and Jean Lowenstamm. 1981. "Syllable Structure and Markedness Theory." In A. Belletti et al. (1981), pp. 287–316.

Kean, Mary-Louise. 1980 [1975]. *The Theory of Markedness in Generative Grammar*. Bloomington: Indiana University Linguistics Club.

————. 1981. "On a Theory of Markedness: Some General Considerations and a Case in Point," In Belletti et al. (1981), pp. 559–604.

Kennedy, Arthur G. 1915. *The Pronoun of Address in English Literature of the Thirteenth Century*. Stanford: Stanford University.

Khlebnikova, Irina. 1973. *Oppositions in Morphology: As Exemplified in the English Tense System*. The Hague: Mouton.

Kiparsky, Paul. 1968. "Tense and Mood in Indo-European Syntax." *Foundations of Language* 4:30–57.

————. 1974. "Remarks on Analogical Change." In *Historical Linguistics*, ed. J. M. Anderson and Charles Jones, vol. 2, pp. 257–75.

Kirsner, Robert. 1985. "Iconicity and Grammatical Meaning." In Haiman (1985), pp. 249–70.

Kiss, Katalin E. 1981. "Focus and Topic: The Marked Constituents of Hungarian Sentence Structure." In Belletti et al. (1981), pp. 347–63.

Kruyt, Albert C. [1941] "Right and Left in Central Celebes." In Needham (1973), pp. 74–91.

Kučera, Henry. 1979. "Some Aspects of Aspect in Czech and English." *Folia Slavica* 2:196–210.

————. 1980. "Markedness in Motion." In Catherine Chvany and Richard Brecht, eds., *Morphosyntax in Slavic.* Columbus, Ohio: Slavica. 15–42.

————. 1981. "Aspect, Markedness, and t₀." In Ph. Tedeschi and A. Zaenen, eds., *Syntax and Semantics 14: Tense and Aspect,* 177–89. N.Y.: Academic Press.

————. 1982. "Markedness and Frequency," In Jan Horecky, ed., *COLING 1982.* Amsterdam: North Holland. 167–73.

————. 1982a. "Roman Jakobson." *Language* 59:871–83.

Kuipers, Aert H. 1970 "Unique Types and Typological Universals." In *Pratidānam,* pp. 68–88. The Hague: Mouton.

————. 1975. "On Symbol, Distinction and Markedness." *Lingua* 36:31–46.

Kuno, Susumu. 1987. *Functional Syntax: Anaphora, Discourse, and Empathy.* Chicago: University of Chicago Press.

Kuryłowicz, Jerzy. 1966. "La Nature des procès dits 'analogique'," In Eric Hamp, et al., eds., *Readings in Linguistics 2,* Chicago: University of Chicago Press, 158–174.

Ladefoged, Peter. 1971. *Preliminaries to Articulatory Phonetics.* Chicago: University of Chicago Press.

La Flesche, Francis. [1916] "Right and Left in Osage Ceremonies." In Needham (1973), pp. 32–42.

Lakoff, George. 1970. *Irregularity in Syntax.* New York: Holt, Rinehart and Winston.

————. 1977. "Linguistic Gestalts." In W. Beach, et al. eds., *Papers from the 13th Regional Meeting of the Chicago Linguistic Society.* Chicago: Chicago Linguistics Society. 236–87.

————. 1987. *Women, Fire, and Dangerous Things.* Chicago: University of Chicago Press.

————, and Mark Johnson. 1980. *Metaphors We Live By.* Chicago: University of Chicago Press.

Langacker, Ronald. 1987. *Foundations of Cognitive Grammar: Theoretical Prerequisites.* Stanford: Stanford University Press.

Lapointe, Steven G. 1986. "Markedness, the Organization of Linguistic Information in Speech Production, and Language Acquisition." In Eckman (1986), pp. 219–39.

Lass, Roger. 1975. "How Intrinsic is Content? Markedness, Sound Change, and 'Family Universals.' " In D. Goyvaerts and G. Pullum, eds., *Essays on the Sound Pattern of English*, Ghent: Story-Scientia. 475–504.

———. 1984. *Phonology: An Introduction to Basic Concepts*. London: Cambridge University Press.

Leach, Edmund, ed. 1967. *The Structural Study of Myth and Totemism*. London: Tavistock Publications.

———. 1982. *Social Anthropology*. New York: Oxford University Press.

Lehrer, Adrienne. 1985. "Markedness and Antonymy." *Journal of Linguistics* 21:397–429.

Lepschy, Giulio C. 1970. *A Survey of Structural Linguistics*. London: Faber and Faber.

Lévi-Strauss, Claude. 1963. *Structural Anthropology*. Translated by Claire Jacobson and Brooke Grundfest Schoepf. New York: Basic Books.

Lightfoot, David. 1979. *Principles of Diachronic Syntax*. Cambridge: Cambridge University Press.

Liszka, James Jakób. 1981. "Peirce and Jakobson: Towards a Structuralist Reconstruction of Peirce." *Transactions of the Charles S. Peirce Society* 17:41–61.

———. 1982. "A Critique of Lévi-Strauss' Theory of Myth and the Elements of a Semiotic Alternative." In Michael Herzfeld and Margo Lenhart, eds., *Semiotics 1981*, New York: Plenum. 297–306.

Ljung, Magnus. 1974. "Some Remarks on Antonymy." *Language* 50:74–88.

Lloyd, Geoffrey. 1973. "Right and Left in Greek Philosophy." In Needham (1973), pp. 167–86.

Longman, Tremper III. 1987. *Literary Approaches to Biblical Interpretation*. Grand Rapids: Zondervan.

Lyons, John. 1977. *Semantics*. 2 vols. Cambridge: Cambridge University Press.

Mannheim, Bruce, and Madeleine Newfield. 1982. "Iconicity in Phonological Change." In A. Ahlqvist, ed., *Papers from the 5th International Conference on Historical Linguistics*. Amsterdam: John Benjamins, 211–22.

Manzini, M. Rita. 1983. "On Control and Control Theory." *Linguistic Inquiry* 14:421–46.

Matthews, Peter H. 1974. *Morphology: An Introduction to the Theory of Word Structure*. New York: Cambridge University Press.

Mayerthaler, Willi. 1987. "System-independent Morphological Naturalness." In *Leitmotifs in Natural Morphology*, ed. W. Dressler, et al., pp. 25–58. Amsterdam: John Benjamins.

———. 1988. [1981] *Morphological Naturalness*. Translated by Janice Seidler. Ann Arbor: Karoma.

McCardle, Peggy, and Edward Haupt. 1983. "Case Order in Sentences: Newer and More Marked." *Language and Style* 16:420–32.

McCawley, James D. 1985. "Kuhnian Paradigms as Systems of Markedness Conventions." In Adam Makkai and Alan Melby, eds., *Linguistics and Philosophy: Studies in Honor of Rulon S. Wells*. Amsterdam: John Benjamins. 23–43.

McConnell-Ginet, Sally. 1979. "Prototypes, Pronouns and Person." In Madeleine Mathiot, ed., *Ethnolinguistics: Boas, Sapir and Whorf Revisited*. The Hague: Mouton. 63–83.

———. 1989. "The Sexual (Re)Production of Meaning: A Discourse-Based Theory." In Francine Frank and Paula Treichler, eds., *Language, Gender, and Professional Writing*, pp. 35–50. New York: Modern Language Association.

Mel'chuk, Igor. 1985. [1977] "Three Main Features, Seven Basic Principles and Eleven Most Important Results of Roman Jakobson's Morphological Research." In Krystyna Pomorska and Stephen Rudy, eds., *Verbal Art, Verbal Sign, Verbal Time*, pp. 178–200. Minneapolis: University of Minnesota Press.

Melikishvili, I. 1970. "Uslovija markirovannosti dlja priznakov, glukhosti, labial-'nosti i veljarnosti." *Matsne* 5:137–58.

———. 1972. "Otnoshjenije markirovannosti v fonologii (uslovija markirovannosti v klassje shumnykh fonjem)." Tbilisi: Avtorjefjerat dissertatsii na soiskanie uchjenoi stjepjeni kandidata filologicheskikh nauk.

Menn, Lise. 1986. "Language Acquisition, Aphasia, and Phonotactic Universals." In Eckman (1986), pp. 241–69.

———, and Brian MacWhinney. 1984. "The Repeated Morph Constraint." *Language* 60:519–41.

Moravcsik, Edith, and Jessica Wirth. 1986. "Markedness—An Overview." In Eckman (1986), pp. 1–11.

Nathan, Geoffrey. 1986. "Phonemes as Mental Categories." In *Proceedings of the 12th Annual Meeting of the Berkeley Linguistic Society*, pp. 212–24. Berkeley: Berkeley Linguistic Society.

Needham, Rodney [1960] "The Left Hand of the Mugwe: An Analytical Note on the Structure of Meru Symbolism." In Needham (1973), pp. 109–27.

―――. 1962. *Structure and Sentiment: A Test Case in Social Anthropology.* Chicago: University of Chicago Press.

―――. [1967] "Right and Left in Nyoro Symbolic Classification." In Needham (1973), pp. 299–341.

―――, ed. 1973. *Right and Left: Essays on Dual Symbolic Classification.* Chicago: University of Chicago Press.

Newfield, Madeleine, and Linda Waugh. 1989. "Invariance and Markedness in Grammatical Categories." In Linda Waugh and J. Reedy, eds., *New Vistas in Grammar: Invariance and Variation.* Philadelphia: John Benjamins.

Nichols, Johanna. 1971. "Diminutive Consonant Symbolism in Western North America." *Language* 47:826–48.

Odlin, Terence. 1986. "Markedness and the Zero-Derived Denominal Verb in English." In Eckman (1986), pp. 155–68.

Orr, Eleanor Wilson. 1987. *Twice as Less.* New York: W. W. Norton.

Panagl, Oswald. 1987. "Productivity and Diachronic Change in Morphology." In *Leitmotifs in Natural Morphology,* ed. W. Dressler, pp. 127–51. Amsterdam: John Benjamins.

Peirce, Charles S. 1965–1966. *Collected Papers of Charles Sanders Peirce.* Edited by Charles Hartshorne and Paul Weiss. Cambridge: Harvard University Press.

Postal, Paul. 1968. *Aspects of Phonological Theory.* New York: Harper and Row.

Pustejovsky, James, and Victoria Burke, eds. 1981. *Markedness and Learnability.* (University of Massachusetts Occasional Papers in Linguistics, vol. 6) Amherst: Graduate Student Linguistics Association Publishers.

Quirk, Randolph. 1970. "Aspect and Variant Inflection in English Verbs." *Language* 46:300–311.

―――, and Sidney Greenbaum 1973. *A Concise Grammar of Contemporary English.* New York: Harcourt Brace Jovanovich.

Reichenbach, Hans. 1947. *Elements of Symbolic Logic.* London: Macmillan.

Rennison, John. 1980. "Singular More Marked than Plural? Some Evidence from Koromfe." *Wiener Linguistische Gazette* 24:61–64.

Roberts, Ian. 1985. "Agreement Parameters and the Development of English Modal Auxiliaries." *Natural Language and Linguistic Theory* 3:21–58.

Robertson, John. 1983. "From Symbol to Icon." *Language* 59:529–40.

Robins, R. H. 1967. *A Short History of Linguistics.* London: Longmans.

Rosch, Eleanor. 1973. "Natural Categories." *Cognitive Psychology* 4:328–50.

——. 1977. "Human Categorization." In *Studies in Cross-cultural Psychology,* ed. N. Warren. pp. 1–49. London: Academic.

——. 1978. "Principles of Categorization." In *Cognition and Categorization,* ed. E. Rosch and B. Lloyd. pp. 27–48. Hillsdale, N.J.: LEA.

Ross, John R. 1972. "The Category Squish: Endstation Hauptwort." In *Papers from the 8th Regional Meeting of the Chicago Linguistic Society,* pp. 316–28. Chicago: Chicago Linguistic Society.

——. 1973. "A Fake NP Squish." In *New Ways of Analyzing Variation in English,* ed. Charles-James Bailey and Roger Shuy, pp. 96–140.

——. 1973a. "Nouniness." In O. Fujimura, ed., *Three Dimensions of Linguistic Theory.* Tokyo: TEC Corp., 137–258.

——. 1987. "Islands and Syntactic Prototypes." In B. Need, et al., eds., *Papers from the 23rd Annual Regional Meeting of the Chicago Linguistic Society* (Part 1: The General Session). Chicago: CLS, 309–20.

Rouveret, A., and J. R. Vergnaud. 1980. "Specifying Reference to Subject." *Linguistic Inquiry* 11:97–202.

Salus, Mary W., and Peter H. Salus. 1978. *Cognition, Opposition and the Lexicon.* Toronto Semiotic Circle Working Papers no. 3.

Salus, Peter H. 1987. Review of Michael Shapiro, *The Sense of Grammar.* The *American Journal of Semiotics* 5:171–77.

—— , and Mary Salus. 1974. "Developmental Neurophysiology and Phonological Acquisition Order." *Language* 50:151–60.

Sangster, Rodney. 1982. *Roman Jakobson and Beyond: Language as a System of Signs.* Berlin: Mouton.

Savan, David. 1976. *An Introduction to C. S. Peirce's Semiotics.* Toronto: Victoria University Press.

Schleifer, Ronald. 1987. "Deconstruction and Linguistic Analysis." *College English* 49:381–95.

Schwartz, Linda. 1980. "Syntactic Markedness and Frequency of Occurrence," In Thomas A. Perry, ed., *Evidence and Argumentation in Linguistics.* New York: de Gruyter. 315–33.

Scotton, Carol Myers. 1983. "The Negotiation of Identities in Conversation: A Theory of Markedness and Code Choice." *International Journal of the Sociology of Language* 44:115–36.

Sebeok, Thomas A. 1976. *Iconicity: The Sign and Its Masters.* Austin: University of Texas Press.

————. 1977. "Roman Jakobson's Teaching in America." In *Roman Jakobson: Echoes of His Scholarship*, ed. Daniel Armstrong and C. H. van Schooneveld, pp. 411–20. Lisse, Netherlands: Peter de Ridder.

Selkirk, Elizabeth. 1986. "The Syllable." In H. van der Hulst and N. Smith, eds., *The Structure of Phonological Representations*, vol. 2, pp. 311–36. Dordrecht: Foris.

Shapiro, Michael. 1969. *Aspects of Russian Morphology*. Cambridge: Slavica.

————. 1972. "Explorations into Markedness." *Language* 48:343–64.

————. 1974. "Markedness and Distinctive Feature Hierarchy." *Proceedings of the Eleventh International Congress of Linguists*, ed. L. Heilmann, vol. 2, 775–81, Bologna: il Mulino.

————. 1976. *Asymmetry: An Inquiry into the Linguistic Structure of Poetry*. Amsterdam: North Holland.

————. 1980. "Russian Conjugation." *Language* 56:67–93.

————. 1983. *The Sense of Grammar*. Bloomington: Indiana University Press.

————. 1985. "Teleology, Semeiosis, and Linguistic Change." *Diachronica* 1:1–34.

————. 1986. "The Russian System of Stress." *Russian Linguistics* 10:183–204.

————. 1989. "On a Universal Criterion of Rule Coherence." Manuscript.

Shaumyan, Sebastian. 1986. "The Semiotic Theory of Ergativity and Markedness." In Eckman, (1986), pp. 169–217.

Silverstein, Michael. 1976. "Hierarchy of Features and Ergativity." In *Grammatical Categories of Australian Languages*, ed. R. M. W. Dixon, pp. 112–71. Canberra: Australian Institute of Aboriginal Studies.

Smith, Neil. 1973. *The Acquisition of Phonology*. Cambridge: Cambridge University Press.

Solomon, M., ed. 1985. *The Psychology of Fashion*. Lexington, Mass.: Lexington Books.

Sommerstein, Alan. 1977. *Modern Phonology*. Baltimore: University Park Press.

Stampe, David. 1979. [1973] *A Dissertation on Natural Phonology*. New York: Garland.

Steele, Susan. 1978. "Word Order Variation: A Typological Study." In Greenberg (1978), vol. 3, pp. 585–623.

———— et al. 1981. *Encyclopedia of Aux*. Cambridge, Mass.: MIT Press.

Stemberger, Joseph. 1981. "Morphological Haplology." *Language* 57:791–817.

Stidston, Russell O. 1917. *The Use of Ye in the Function of Thou.* Stanford: Stanford University.

Szemerényi, O. 1973. "Marked-Unmarked and a Problem of Latin Diachrony." *Transactions of the Philological Society* (1973): 55–74.

Tai, James. 1985. "Temporal Sequence and Chinese Word Order." In Haiman (1985), pp. 49–72.

Tannen, Deborah. 1986. Review of Mary Catherine Bateson, *With a Daughter's Eye: A Memoir of Margaret Mead and Gregory Bateson. Language* 62:198–204.

Thom, R. 1972. *Stabilité structurelle et morphogenèse.* New York: John Benjamins.

———. 1973. "Sur la typologie des langues naturelles: essai d'interpretation psycholinguistique." In M. Gross, et al., eds., *The Formal Analysis of Natural Languages.* The Hague: Mouton.

Tiersma, Peter. 1982. "Local and General Markedness." *Language* 58:832–49.

Timberlake, Alan. 1986. "Hierarchies in the Genitive of Negation." In R. D. Brecht and James S. Levin, eds., *Case in Slavic.* Columbus, Ohio: Slavica, 338–60.

Tomíc, Olga M., ed. 1989. *Markedness in Synchrony and Diachrony.* New York: Mouton.

Tomlin, Russell. 1986. *Basic Word Order: Functional Principles.* London: Croom Helm.

Townsend, Charles. 1985. "Can Aspect Stand Prosperity?" In Flier and Timberlake (1985), pp. 286–95.

Traugott, Elizabeth C. 1972. *A History of English Syntax.* New York: Holt, Rinehart and Winston.

———. 1973. "Some Thoughts on Natural Syntactic Processes." In Charles James Bailey and Roger Shuy, eds., *New Ways of Analyzing Variation in English.* Washington: Georgetown University Press, 313–22.

———. 1974. Review of *Irregularity in Syntax* by George Lakoff (1970). *Language* 50:161–69.

———, et al. 1980. *Papers from the 4th International Conference on Historical Linguistics.* Amsterdam: John Benjamins.

Trnka, Bohumil. 1958. "On Some Problems of Neutralization." In *Omagiu lui Jorgu Iordan,* pp. 861–66. Bucharest: Academia Republicii Populare Romine.

Trubetzkoy, Nikolai. 1968. *Introduction to the Principles of Phonological Description*. Translated by L. A. Muny. The Hague: Martinus Nijhoff.

———. 1969. [1939] *Principles of Phonology*. Translated by Christiane A. M. Baltaxe. Berkeley and Los Angeles: University of California Press.

———. 1975. *Letters and Notes*. Edited by Roman Jakobson. The Hague: Mouton.

Tversky, Amos, and Itamar Gati. 1978. "Studies of Similarity." In Eleanor Rosch and Barbara Lloyd, eds., *Cognition and Categorization*. Hillsdale, N.J.: LEA, 79–98.

Utaker, Arild. 1974. "On the Binary Opposition." *Linguistics* 134:73–93.

van Langendonck, W. 1979. "Definiteness as an Unmarked Category." *Linguistische Berichte* 63:33–55.

———. 1984. "Markedness, Prototypes and Language Acquisition." Preprint van het Departement Linguistiek, Katholieke Universitiet Leuven, no. 91.

———. 1986. "Markedness, Prototypes and Language Acquisition." *Cahiers de' l'institut de linguistique de Louvain* 12:39–76.

van Oosten, Jeanne. 1986. *The Nature of Subjects, Topics and Agents: A Cognitive Explanation*. Bloomington, In.: Indiana University Linguistics Club.

van Riemsdijk, Henk. 1982. *A Case Study in Syntactic Markedness*. Dordrecht: Foris.

van Schooneveld, Cornelius H. 1977. "By Way of Introduction: Roman Jakobson's Tenets and Their Potential." *Roman Jakobson: Echoes of His Scholarships*, ed. Daniel Armstrong and C. H. van Schooneveld, pp. 1–11. Lisse, Netherlands: Peter de Ridder.

———. 1978. *Semantic Transmutations*. Bloomington, Ind.: Physsardt.

Vendler, Zeno. 1967. "Verbs and Times." In Z. Vendler, ed., *Linguistics in Philosophy*, pp. 97–121. Ithaca: Cornell University Press.

Vennemann, Theo. 1972. "Sound Change and Markedness Theory: On the History of the German Consonant System." In R. P. Stockwell and Ronald Macauley, eds., *Linguistic Change and Generative Theory*. Bloomington: Indiana University Press. 230–74.

———. 1975. "An Explanation of Drift." In *Word Order and Word Order Change*, ed. C. Li, pp. 271–305. Austin: University of Texas Press.

———. 1988. *Preference Laws for Syllable Structure*. Berlin: Mouton.

Visser, F. Th. 1969. *An Historical Syntax of the English Language* (Part 3). Leiden: Brill.

Waugh, Linda. 1976. *Roman Jakobson's Science of Language*. Lisse, Netherlands: Peter de Ridder.

———. 1976. *A Semantic Analysis of Word Order*. Leiden: Brill.

———. 1979. "Markedness and Phonological Systems." In *The Fifth LACUS Forum*, ed. W. Wolck and Paul Garvin, pp. 155–65. Columbia, S.C.: Hornbeam Press.

———. 1979a. "Remarks on Markedness." In D, Dinnsen, ed., *Current Approaches to Phonological Theory*. Bloomington: Indiana University Press. 310–315.

———. 1982. "Marked and Unmarked: A Choice between Unequals in Semiotic Structure." *Semiotica* 38:299–318.

———, and Madeleine Newfield. 1986. "Iconicity and the Morpheme: Toward a Model of the Lexicon." To appear in *Lingua*.

Weyl, Hermann. 1952. *Symmetry*. Princeton: Princeton University Press.

White, Lydia. 1982. *Grammatical Theory and Language Acquisition*. Dordrecht: Foris.

———. 1986. "Markedness and Parameter Setting: Some Implications for a Theory of Adult Second Language Acquisition." In Eckman (1986), pp. 309–27.

Wieschhoff, Heinz. 1938. "Concepts of Right and Left in African Cultures." In Needham (1973), 59–73.

Williams, Edwin. 1981. "Language Acquisition, Markedness, and Phrase Structure." In S. Tavakolian, ed., *Language Acquisition and Linguistic Theory*. Cambridge, Mass.: MIT Press. pp. 8–34.

Williams, Joseph. 1975. *Origins of the English Language*. New York: Free Press.

Winters, Margaret. 1987. "Cognitive Grammar and Kuryłowicz's Laws of Analogy." Paper presented at the 8th International Conference on Historical Linguistics, Lille.

———. 1990. "Toward a Theory of Syntactic Prototypes." In S. L. Tsohatzidis. ed., *Meanings and Prototypes: Studies in Linguistic Categorization*. London: Routledge. 285–307.

———. 1988. "Transparency as a Feature of Prototypical Morphemes." Manuscript, Southern Illinois University, Carbondale.

Witkowski, Stanley R., and Cecil H. Brown. 1983. "Marking Reversal and Cultural Importance." *Language* 59:569–82.

Woisetschlaeger, Erich F. 1976. *A Semantic Theory of the English Auxiliary System*. Bloomington: Indiana University Linguistics Club.

Woodward, James. 1981. "Signs of Marking: 'Stage' Three Handshapes." *Studies in Honor of Robert J. DiPietro*, ed. Marcel Danesi, pp. 47–59. Lake Bluff, Ill.: Jupiter.

Wurzel, Wolfgang. 1987. "System-dependent Morphological Naturalness in Inflection." In *Leitmotifs in Natural Morphology,*, ed. W. Dressler, et. al., pp. 59–96. Amsterdam: John Benjamins.

Zipf, George K. 1949. *Human Behavior and the Principle of Least Effort*. Cambridge, Mass.: Addison-Wesley Press.

Zwicky, Arnold. 1978. "On Markedness in Morphology." *Der Sprache*. 24:129–43.

Name Index

Anaxagorias, 190
Andersen, Henning, 213n, 218n; on phonology, 119, 124, 213n, 219n, 220n, 222n, 224n; on language change, 156, 186, 227n, 229n; on markedness, 70–1, 95, 202n
Anderson, Stephen R., 202n, 204n
Andrews, Edna, 73, 202n, 207n, 208n, 209n, 213n
Aristotle, 190
Aronoff, Mark, 141, 225n

Bailey, Charles-James N., 56, 123, 186, 224n, 228n
Baker, C. L., 214n
Bally, Charles, 40
Baltaxe, Christiane A. M., 46
Bardovi-Harlig, Kathleen, 232n
Barthes, Roland, 234n
Bates, E., 44, 59, 211n
Bateson, Gregory, 200
Bateson, Mary, 200
Battistella, Edwin L., 167, 211n, 215n, 231n
Baudouin de Courtenay, Jan, 8, 12
Beidelman, T. O., 190–1
Belletti, Adriana, 213n
Benson, Bronsen, 230n, 232n
Bickerton, Derek, 213n
Bloomfield, Leonard, 133
Bodine, Ann, 85
Bolinger, Dwight, 72, 213n
Brakel, Arthur, 47, 52, 56, 202n
Braque, Georges, 13
Brasington, R. W. P., 224n
Brøndal, Viggo, 27, 40, 88, 116, 120, 163

Brown, Cecil, 58–9
Brown, Roger, 174–5, 178–9
Burke, Victoria, 213n
Bybee, Joan, 72, 210n, 211n, 213n, 217n

Cairns, Charles, 49, 56, 131, 135–7, 202n, 211n, 212n, 224n, 230n
Chomsky, Noam, 7, 73, 80–2, 92, 106, 214n, 214n, 233n; on phonology, 50, 52, 56, 147, 158, 203n, 207n, 224n, 226n, 227n, 228n; on Universal Grammar, 62–5, 148–9, 159, 183, 213n; on change, 155–6
Chvany, Catherine, 186, 202n, 204n, 208n, 213n, 217n
Clark, Eve, 211n
Clark, Herbert, 211n
Comrie, Bernard, 34, 94, 96, 98, 100, 107, 148, 160–1, 202n, 208n, 210n, 213n, 216n

Dennison, D., 231n
Denny, Rita, 186
Derrida, Jacques, 186
Dixon, R. M. W., 232n
Dokulil, M., 208n
Donegan, Patricia Jane, 52, 212n
Dressler, Wolfgang, 210n, 225n, 226n, 232n
Durych, Jaroslav, 9

Eckman, Fred, 62, 186, 232n
Ellegård, Alvar, 169, 231n
Evans, William, 232n

Evans-Pritchard, E. E., 187, 189

Farwell, Carol, 206–7n
Feinstein, Mark, 56, 160–1, 224n
Fellbaum, Marie, 232n
Ferguson, Charles, 206–7n
Fletcher, Charles, 79
Flier, Michael, 216n
Foley, William, 213n
Fortunatov, F., 12
Fox, Barbara, 186
Fox, James, 187, 189
Frank, Francine, 231n
Frank, Joseph, 202n
French, P., 234n
Frishberg, Nancy, 213n
Fritsch, Vilma, 188

Gamkrelidze, T. V., 56, 207n, 212n, 221n
Gilman, Albert, 174–5, 178–9
Givòn, Talmy, 72
Greenbaum, Sidney, 38–9, 73–5, 96, 99, 104, 210n
Greenberg, Joseph, 6, 7, 33–5, 37, 65, 201n, 207n, 208–9n, 210n, 211n, 216n; on phonology, 48, 50, 135, 224n; on grammar, 62, 84, 214n, 215n, 217n; on language change, 154–5, 227n, 229n; on universals, 147–9, 183
Gundel, Jeanette, 47

Haiman, John, 36, 71–2, 213n, 218n
Halle, Morris, 7, 10, 63, 204n, 207n; on phonology, 51–4, 56, 118, 124, 158, 203n, 204n, 206n, 224n, 226n, 227n, 228n; on language change, 155–6, 228n; on universals, 50–1, 147–8
Harris, R. J., 234n
Harsh, Wayne, 104
Haupt, Edward, 186

Hausmann, Robert, 169, 231n
Hawkins, John W., 218n, 227n
Hertz, Robert, 188–9, 193
Hjelmslev, Louis, 208n
Hock, Hans Heinrich, 230n
Holenstein, Elmar, 202n, 204n, 207n
Hopper, Paul, 44, 109, 211n, 217n, 227n, 228n
Houlihan, Kathleen, 47
Hyams, Nina, 63–4, 213n
Hyltenstam, Kenneth, 232n

Ingram, David, 207n

Jaeger, Jeri, 212n
Jackendoff, Ray, 214n
Jakobson, Roman, 7, 62, 71–2, 82, 184–6, 188, 193, 202n, 213n, 214n, 218n, 232n; biography, 8–10; on change, 85, 152–4, 227n, 227–8n; on markedness, 1–2, 5–6, 25, 27, 34–5, 44–5, 65–6, 163, 187, 201n, 208–9n, 211n, 215n; on phonology, 11–16, 49, 51–4, 56, 118–19, 123–4, 156, 204n, 206n, 207n; on grammar, 28–33, 40, 73–4, 77–8, 84, 111–12, 208n, 210n, 213n, 217n, 218n; on linguistic theory, 17–22, 202n, 203n, 204n, 207n, 208n; on universals, 50–1, 147–8, 221n
Johnson, Mark, 232n
Joseph, Brian, 222n

Kalmár, Ivan, 217n
Karcevskij, Serge, 30
Kaye, Jonathan, 130, 230n
Kean, Mary-Louise, 56, 124, 130, 147–8, 155, 157, 220–1n, 224n, 226n
Kennedy, Arthur G., 175
Khlebnikov, Velimir, 8
Khlebnikova, Irina, 95–6
Kiparsky, Paul, 213n, 230n

Kučera, Henry, 101–2, 202n, 208n, 210n, 216n
Kuhn, Thomas, 234n
Kuipers, Aert, 4–5, 119
Kuno, Susumu, 213n

Ladefoged, Peter, 52
Lakoff, George, 27, 41, 63, 211n, 232n
Langacker, Ronald, 202n
Lapointe, Steven, 213n
Lasnik, Howard, 63–5
Lass, Roger, 13, 56, 207n, 212n, 219n, 227n
Leach, Edmund, 187
Lehrer, Adrienne, 36
Lepschy, Giulio C., 202n, 219n
Lévi-Strauss, Claude, 10, 187–8, 203n, 232n, 223n
Lightfoot, David, 158–9, 169, 213n, 227n, 229n
Liszka, James Jakób, 233n
Lloyd, Geoffrey, 189–90
Longman, Tremper III, 186
Lowenstamm, Jean, 130, 230n
Lyons, John, 16–17, 34–6, 204n, 208n

MacWhinney, Brian, 44, 59, 211n, 225n
Majakovskij, Vladimir (see Mayakovsky)
Mannheim, Bruce 213n
Manzini, M. Rita, 81
Matthews, Peter, 210n
Mayakovsky, Vladimir, 5, 8, 187
Mayerthaler, Willi, 27, 34, 42–3, 84, 209n, 210n, 211n, 213n, 214n, 215n, 218n, 225n, 226–7n, 227n, 229–30n, 232n
McCardle, Peggy, 186
McCawley, James, 234n
McConnell-Ginet, Sally, 231n, 234n
McDaniel, Dana, 215n
Mead, Margaret, 200

Meillet, Antoine, 193
Melikishvili, Irina, 212n
Menn, Lise, 207n, 225n
Modor, Carol, 211n
Moravcsik, Edith, 26, 43–4, 202n, 211n

Nathan, Geoffrey, 212n, 225n
Needham, Rodney, 187–9, 191, 194–7
Newfield, Madeleine, 213n

Odlin, Terence, 225n
Orr, Eleanor Wilson, 234n

Parmenides, 190
Peirce, Charles S., 10, 71–2, 118, 213n, 218n
Peškovskij, A. M., 30
Postal, Paul, 133
Pustejovsky, James, 213n

Quirk, Randolph, 73–5, 96, 99, 104, 213n

Reichenbach, Hans, 96
Roberts, Ian, 169, 173
Robertson, John, 213n
Robins, R. H., 213n
Rosch, Eleanor, 27, 41
Ross, John R., 41, 109, 211n
Rouveret, Alain, 63

Salus, Mary W., 207n
Salus, Peter H., 207n
Sanders, Gerald K., 47
Sangster, Rodney, 207n, 208n
Saussure, Ferdinand de, 8, 12
Savan, David, 213n
Ščerba, L. V., 12
Schleifer, Ronald, 186
Schwartz, Linda, 38, 48, 209n, 216n

Scotton, Carol Myers, 186
Selkirk, Elizabeth, 227n
Shapiro, Michael, 82, 213n, 218n; on
    markedness, 71, 111, 113–14, 186,
    218n; on phonology, 56, 118–19,
    124, 126, 127, 130, 211n, 213n,
    220n, 224n; on grammar, 217n;
    225n, 225–6n; on language change,
    167
Silverstein, Michael, 44, 59, 214n
Solomon, M., 234n
Sommerstein, Alan, 134, 219n
Stampe, David, 212n
Steele, Susan, 158, 169, 218n
Stemberger, Joseph, 225n
Stidston, Russell O., 175
Szemerényi, O., 212n

Tai, James, 72
Tannen, Deborah, 200
Thom, R., 159
Thompson, Sandra, 44, 109, 211n,
    217n
Tiersma, Peter, 59–60
Timberlake, Alan, 216n
Tolstoy, Leo, 187
Tomíc, Olga M., 207n
Tomlin, Russell, 218n
Traugott, Elizabeth Closs, 158–9,
    227n, 229n
Treichler, Paula, 231n
Trnka, Bohumil, 208n
Trombetti, A., 153
Trubetzkoy, Nikolai, 5, 7, 9, 187,
    202n; phonological theories, 11–12;
    on the nature of oppositions, 14–16,

204n; on markedness, 1, 28, 46–7,
    49–50, 56–7, 208n, 212n, 213n; on
    neutralization, 46, 210n

Utaker, Arild, 232n

van Ginneken, J., 153
van Langendonck, W., 42, 44, 59,
    202n, 214n
van Oosten, Jeanne, 44
van Riemsdijk, Henk, 148, 213n
van Schooneveld, C. H., 10, 208n
van Valin, Robert, 213n
Vendler, Zeno, 101
Vennemann, Theo, 123, 137, 224n,
    227n, 228n, 228–9n, 230n
Vergnaud, Jean-Roger, 63
Visser, F. Th., 169, 231n

Waugh, Linda, on cultural oppositions,
    192, 198, 232–3n, 233n; on phonol-
    ogy, 48, 55–6, 124, 126, 163, 224n;
    on markedness, 201n, 204n, 207n,
    210n, 213n, 215n
White, Lydia, 64–5, 231n
Williams, Edwin, 63
Williams, Joseph, 231n
Winters, Margaret, 41–2, 203n, 210n,
    211n, 214n, 225n, 230n, 232n
Wirth, Jessica, 26, 43–4, 202n, 211n
Witkowski, Stanley R., 58–9
Wurzel, Wolfgang, 227n, 230n

Zipf, George K., 210n
Zwicky, Arnold, 207n

Subject Index

abrupt/nonabrupt, 15, 48, 52–3, 55,
120–3, 128, 130, 132–3, 143–5,
161–2
active/passive (*see* voice)
acute/grave, 16, 26, 49, 53–4, 56, 121,
123–8, 132, 142–5, 220n, 205–6n,
221n, 222n, 224n
adaptive rules, 156
Adyghe, 222n
analogy, 59, 70, 230n
animacy/inanimacy, 59, 109, 75–6,
86–8, 214n
antonyms, 3, 36–7
applied linguistics, 188
Arabic, 222n
aspect (*see* perfective aspect, progressive aspect, simple aspect)
auspicious/nonauspicious, 189–92

Basque, 213n
binarism, 14–17, 204n, 223n

case in English, 21, 72–82, 88, 112–
13, 139–40, 148–51; in Russian,
30–2, 73, 208n, 226n
Cayapa, 13–14
centrifugal (*see* compact)
checked/unchecked, 52, 54
Chinese, 215n
clause types, English, 105–111
clefting, 109
clothing, 5, 149, 200, 234n
compactness, 15, 48, 52–3, 119, 121,
124, 127–9, 130–4, 160, 162, 204n,
205–7n, 219–20n, 221n, 222n
complement convention, 220n

complexity (*see* simplicity)
consonant clusters, 159–63, 230n (*see
also* syllable codas, syllable onsets)
consonantal/nonconsonantal, 52–3,
119–20, 122–3, 128–9, 134, 143–5,
161–2, 205–7n
continuant (*see* abrupt/nonabrupt)
core grammar, 62–5, 159, 214n (*see
also* Universal Grammar)
criticism, literary, 114, 186
cultural dominance, 24, 42–4, 58–62,
67, 165–7
cultural oppositions, 5, 189–200, 214n,
232n, 233n, 234n
Czech, 78, 215n

deferential/nondeferential, 174–9
determinative aspect, 208n
diagrammaticity (*see* iconism)
diffuseness, 52–3, 55, 119, 124, 128,
130, 132, 134, 205–7n, 221n, 222n,
229n
distinctive features, 1, 9, 12–13, 51–7,
117–19, 147–9
distribution, breadth of, 26–7, 37–40,
45, 47–8, 65–7, 76–7, 80–1, 99,
104–5, 135, 141, 171
do, auxiliary, 167–74, 231n
double marking (multiple marking),
87, 120, 124, 132, 144, 160, 174–
80, 196, 224n
duality of patterning, 18–19
Dyirbal, 232n

early Modern English, 169–70
ellipsis, 77–80

evaluation metric, 63–4, 226n

female, sex role (*see* sex roles)
feminine gender (*see* gender, grammatical)
feminist/nonfeminist, 166–7, 231n
finiteness, 29, 32, 90–6, 105–7
flat/nonflat, 49–50, 52–4, 56, 123–9, 224n
formal marking, 33–7, 58–9, 61–2, 76–8, 88–92, 112–13, 138–40, 171–4, 215–6n
foundation principle, 153–5, 159, 164–7
French, 11, 15–16, 175, 203n
frequency, 26, 37–8, 41–2, 48, 50, 58–9, 62, 208n, 210n, 212n
Frisian, 60–1

gender, grammatical, 2, 24, 29, 33, 36, 38, 40, 44, 124, 165–7, 209n
generative grammar, 62–5, 149–150, 155–9, 213n, 226n, 227n, 228n, 229n
genitive case, in English, 74–80, 112–13, 142; in Russian, 31–2, 74
gravity (*see* acute/grave)
Greek borrowings, 131
Greek culture, 189–90
Grimm's Law, 154, 228–9n

handedness (*see* right and left)
Hawaiian, 221n
hierarchy (ranking), concept of, 18–22, 99, 117–19, 126–7, 152–3, 157, 163, 183–4, 204n, 219n, 229n
human/nonhuman, 87

iconism (diagrammaticity), 7, 10, 71–2, 108–11, 113–16, 137–46, 149, 167–74, 184, 213n, 217n, 225n
imperative, 81–2, 89–90, 92, 103–5, 111, 216n

implementation rules, 156
implicational laws (*see* typology)
indeterminate aspect, 29
indeterminateness, 26–8, 30–3, 37–8, 44–5, 51, 65–7
indicative mood, 29–30, 81–2, 90–5, 103–5
IndoEuropean, 193, 227–8n
infinitives (*see* nonfiniteness)
interpretant, Peircean, 186
invariant, 30, 52, 208n
inversion, of symbol values (*see* markedness reversal)
-*ion* suffix, 141–7
iterative verbs, 29, 95, 208n

Japanese, 126, 225n

Kaguru culture, 190–1
Korean, 47–8, 215n

language acquisition, 50, 63–4, 153, 186, 204–7n, 213n
language change, 151–2, 185, 229–30n, 230–1n; lexical 58–9, 62, 164–7, 174–80, 230n; phonological, 153–7, 159–63, 227n, 229n; syntactic, 59–61, 158–9, 167–74
language universals (*see* typology)
Latin, 231n
lax (*see* tense/lax)
life/death, 5, 187, 193–7, 232–3n

male sex role (*see* sex roles)
markedness: definition of, 1–5, 21–2, 25, 28, 65–7, 69, 147–9, 201n, 202n; function of, 88, 114–16, 146, 149–50, 186, 186–200; general, 59–61, 100–3; 217n; globality of, 6, 46, 66, 72, 115, 183–4, 216n; local, 59–61, 100–3, 106; phonological, 46–51, 54–8, 60–1, 118–129, 137–46, 152–7, 211n, 227n; semantic and

conceptual, 1–4, 28–33, 35–7, 44–
6, 51, 58–62, 137–46, 170–4, 204n,
208n, 211n; syntactic, 61–5, 158–9;
typological, 62
markedness assimilation, 7, 69–71,
74, 75, 78–80, 82–4, 88, 95,
98–9, 109–11, 114–16, 136–40,
166–7, 172–4, 192–4, 198, 202n,
220–1n
markedness complementarity, 69, 82,
111–16, 135, 137–46, 147–9, 172–4,
194–8, 218n, 219–20n, 225–6n
markedness conventions, 147–8, 155–
7, 226n, 228n
markedness reversal, 24–5, 56, 58–62,
106–7, 129–37, 140, 145, 147, 161–
2, 118–21, 177–8, 132–3, 194–200,
213n, 219n, 224n, 229–30n
markedness values: composite, 112,
122–3, 125–6, 128, 171; contextualization of, 4–5, 24–5, 39–40, 54–8,
66–7, 119–137, 148–9, 198–200,
217n, 224n; determination of, 6, 23,
25–8, 44–6, 183, 207n, 208n, 208–
9n; language particularity of, 6–7,
25, 56–67, 148–50, 152, 157, 180–
1, 185–6, 207n, 226n; language universality of, 6, 23–5, 55–8, 61–7,
147–50, 155–9, 180–1, 186–8,
208n, 213n, 226n
masculine (see gender, grammatical)
Middle English, 153, 159, 169–70,
173–4, 177–9
modal verbs, 92, 170–1
mood, verbal, 29, 70, 94, 103–5
multiple marking (see double marking)

nasality, 15, 48, 53–5, 120, 122–3,
128, 131, 161–3, 203n, 221n
natural phonology, 212n
naturalness, 213n; biological, 42–4,
49–50, 60–1; cultural, (see cultural
dominance); morphological, 225n,
229–30n; phonological, 48–50, 60–
1, 155–7, 228n; syntactic, 158–9

neutralization, 26, 37–40, 45–8, 51,
62, 65–7, 69–70, 75–7, 86, 112,
134, 147, 154, 156, 186, 208–9n,
210n, 214n, 224n, 231n
neutralization changes, 156
nominative case, 148, 213–4n; in English, 73–4, 82–3; in Russian, 31–2,
215n; (see also case)
nondistinctive features, 14, 117–19,
121, 126, 157, 203–4n, 220n,
222n
nonfiniteness, 29, 32, 80–1, 89, 91–2,
105–7
North Caucasian languages, 213n
number, grammatical, 4, 24, 28–9, 35,
38, 40, 42, 59–61, 70, 84–6, 88,
111–13, 138–40, 163, 215n
Nyoro culture, 191, 194–7

objective case, in English, 81–3, 73–6,
148 (see also case)
Old English, 133, 159, 169, 175–6,
227n, 230n, 231n
opposition, 1–5, 11–18, 91–2, 204n;
equipollent, 2, 14–15, 33, 45; privative, 2, 14–18, 33, 45, 66–7, 203n
optimality, 26, 46, 50–1, 55–7, 66–7,
124–5, 147, 152–5, 207n

participles, 90–2, 107, 216n, (see also
nonfiniteness)
passivization (see voice)
perfect aspect, 29, in English, 96–8,
104, 216n, 217n
perfectness, 97–8
person, grammatical, 28–9, 34–5, 40,
86–9, 111–13, 210n, 215n
personal/nonpersonal, 87
phonology, theory of, 8–9, 11–16,
117–19, 219n
phonotactics (see syllable onsets, syllables codas, consonant clusters)
Portuguese, 47
positive/negative, 33, 42, 44, 169–70

Prague School, 1, 5–8, 11, 18, 28, 38, 49, 65–6, 72, 115, 183, 185, 187, 201n, 202n, 218–19n
preposition stranding, 148
prestige usage, 74, 85, 98, 104, 109–10, 166, 199
principle of compensation, 40–1, 48, 88–9, 120, 122, 163–7, 165–9, 177, 230n
PRO, 80–3
progressive aspect, in English, 98–104, 216n, 217n
progressive/nonprogressive, 99–103
pronouns, English, 20–1, 72–84, 88, 112, 148, 165–7, 214n, 215n
prototypes, 26–8, 41–5, 49–50, 76, 79, 108–9, 210n, 211n, 212n
pseudoclefting, 110

ranking (see hierarchy)
reflexive pronouns, 77, 83–4, 88–9, 214n, 215n
right and left, 157, 188–97
Rotinese culture, 197
Russian, 1–2, 24, 28–32, 75, 78, 113–14, 126, 163, 213n, 215n, 225n

second person pronouns, loss of, 85–6, 174–80, 231–2n, 232n
secondary marking (unmarking), 141–6
sex roles, 16, 58, 189–92, 195–7, 232n, 234n
sharp/nonsharp, 53–4
signs, Peircean classification of, 71–2
simple aspect, in English, 93, 97–103
simplicity, 26–8, 45–6, 49–51, 66–7, 212n, 228n, 229n; of grammars, 158–9
stativity, 99–103
strident/nonstrident, 52–4, 121–3, 139
structuralism, 11, 13, 18, 187–8 (see also Prague School)
style, 74, 81–2, 84, 98, 104, 108–10, 148, 151, 166, 186, 214n, 215n, 216n, 231n

subjunctive mood, 70, 89–90, 92, 95, 103–5, 111, 158, 216n
syllable codas, in English, 134–6
syllable onsets, in English, 129–33, 224n, 230n
syllable structure, 54–5, 129–37
syncretization, 26–8, 40–1, 45–6, 48, 51, 62, 65–7, 105, 171, 196–7, 209n, 212n

tendency not to accumulate marks (see principle of compensation)
tense, 3–4, 24, 29, 40, 70, 89–90, 92, 93–6, 98, 100–7, 111, 216n
tense/lax, 47–8, 52–4, 121–3, 127–9, 203–4n, 223n, 224n, 227n
TH-forms (see second person pronouns, loss of)
that, 39
topic continuity, 79
topicalization, 110
Turkish, 12–14
typology (implicational laws), 9, 23, 26, 50–1, 62–3, 107, 135–6, 147–9, 152–5, 158–60, 184–5, 186–7, 208n, 221n, 222n, 226n
Tzeltel, 58–9

Universal Grammar, 62–5, 147–50, 159, 183, 213n, 226n, 227n, 233n
universals (see typology)

variation changes, 156
verb fronting, 109, 173
verbs, English, 35, 88–105, 167–74; Russian, 28–30, 111–3
vocalic/nonvocalic, 52–3, 119–20, 122–3, 129–30
voice, 107–10, 217n
voicing, 24, 47–8, 52–5, 57, 120–2, 128–32, 134, 138–9, 143–5, 153, 157, 203–4n, 212n, 221–2n, 222–3n

WH fronting, 109

word order, 217n; in English, 108–10

zero: 39, 137, 139; zero affix, 34–5, 80–3, 88–91, 111–3, 140–2, 210n, 216n; zero derivation, 225n; zero interpretation, 6, 33, 37, 40, 51; zero nouns and pronouns, 77–9, 80–3, 88; zero sign, 6, 29–30, 34–5, 40, 77–9, 201n, 208–9n